FIRST
KILL YOUR FAMILY

Child Soldiers of Uganda
and the Lord's Resistance Army

Peter Eichstaedt

Lawrence Hill Books

ISBN 978-1-61374-809-1

Library of Congress Cataloging-in-Publication Data
Eichstaedt, Peter H., 1947-
  First kill your family : child soldiers of Uganda and the Lord's Resistance
Army / Peter Eichstaedt. — 1st pbk. ed.
     p. cm.
  "First hardcover edition published 2009"—T.p. verso.
  Includes bibliographical references and index.
  Summary: Describes the experiences of children kidnapped into service for
the Lord's Resistance Army in Uganda, in which boys are required to complete
brutal initiations—murdering their parents, friends, and relatives—and girls
are forced into sexual slavery and labor.
  ISBN 978-1-61374-809-1 (pbk.)
  1. Children and war—Uganda. 2. Child soldiers—Uganda. 3. Lord's Resistance Army. 4. Human rights—Uganda. I. Title.
  HQ784.W3E33 2013
  303.6'4083096761—dc23
                                                              2012038098

Interior design: Jonathan Hahn
Cover design: Monica Baziuk
Cover photo: Villagers on the border between South Sudan and the Demo-
cratic Republic on the Congo, photo by Peter Eichstaedt
Map design: Chris Erichsen

All photos courtesy of the author

Printed in the United States of America
5 4 3 2 1

This book is dedicated to the people of northern Uganda who lost their lives or suffered at the hands of the Lord's Resistance Army.

May they find peace and justice.

Man's inhumanity to man is not only perpetrated by the vitriolic actions of those who are bad, it is also perpetrated by the vitiating inaction of those who are good.

—Martin Luther King Jr.

Contents

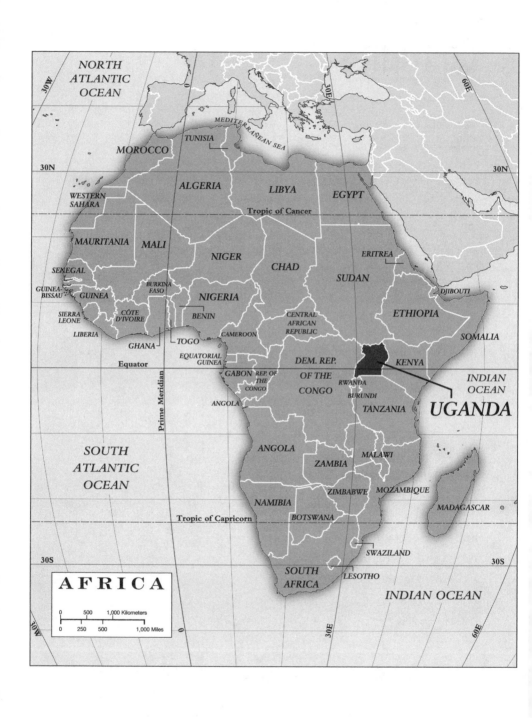

UGANDA

- □ Kony's camp
- LRA area of operations: 1986–2006
- XXX LRA area of operations: 2006–2008
- ✪ National capital
- ⊙ Cities
- --·--·-- International boundary
- ═══ Highways
- ───── Main roads
- ------- Minor roads

0   40   80 Kilometers
0 20 40   80 Miles

CENTRAL
AFRICAN
REPUBLIC

SUDAN

Obo

Yambio

Garamba Nat.
Park (DRC)

Kony's Camp

DEMOCRATIC
REPUBLIC
OF THE
CONGO

Kitgum

Atiak

Arua

Pader

Gulu

Moroto

Nebbi

Pakwach

Lira

Katakwi

Nakapiripirit

Apac

Soroti

Masindi

Lake
Albert

Hoima

Lake
Kyoga

Mbale

Luwero

Tororo

Fort Portal

Jinja

Moroto

Kampala

Entebbe

Equator

Lake
Edward

Mbarara

Masaka

KENYA

Kanungu

Kisoro

Lake Victoria

Kabale

RWANDA

TANZANIA

Preface

THE CALL FROM JOHANNESBURG came at 4:00 A.M. I struggled awake and fumbled for the phone.

"Did I wake you?" the voice said on the other end.

"Ah, yeah."

"It's Duncan."

"Duncan, what's up?"

"How'd you like to go to Africa?"

"Ah, well, I don't know. Where are you?"

"I'll take that as a yes," he said. "Look. I'll send you an e-mail. None of this is firm, OK? Cheers."

The line went dead.

"Who was that?" my wife asked.

"Duncan."

She sighed.

I stared into the darkness.

"Where was he?" she asked.

"South Africa."

"I always wanted to go to Africa."

So began my involvement with the East African country of Uganda that resulted in this book.

Duncan Furey is of the rare breed known as a rainmaker in the world of nonprofits. He finds grants. This requires going into some of the most unsavory places in the world, where all appears lost, then coming back and saying "We can fix this." He worked for the Institute for War and Peace Reporting (IWPR), a nonprofit organization based in London that develops journalists around the globe. The IWPR isn't the only organization doing this, of course, but what sets IWPR apart is that the local journalists' reports are published and posted on the Internet, making these original and unique stories available to the world.

I had known Furey when I worked with IWPR in Afghanistan in 2004 as part of a team of journalists who created Afghanistan's first independent news agency. It was a project the Afghan reporters named Pajhwok Afghan News (www.pajhwok.com). The name means "echo," and the agency continues.

In August 2005, nearly nine months after Furey's call, I finally set foot on Ugandan soil. I went there with IWPR to do much the same thing as we had done in Afghanistan; our task was to create Uganda's first independent news agency.

Uganda was an African success story and had become one of the "donor darlings" of the West, due largely to the progressive presidency of Yoweri Museveni. But when he tightened his grip on the country by orchestrating the removal of presidential term limits less than a year before he was due to step down, he rankled many of his foreign supporters. With no more term limits, Museveni was expected to win re-election in February 2006.

Although the news media in Uganda is well developed, it is generally divided into two camps: government-sponsored print, radio, and television; and virulent opposition.

A collection of European countries had agreed to sponsor IWPR's creation of a radio news agency that would provide impartial news and information surrounding the election. Most Ugandans got their news from the radio, and Furey asked me to get involved.

My first points of contact were Sam Gummah and Paul Kavuma, two talented Ugandans who knew the radio scene inside and out.

Gummah had been an originator of the wildly popular news talk radio in Uganda, and Kavuma was a skilled reporter and producer.

I soon moved into an upper room of a large house we had rented for our offices and news operation, which was in one of the better neighborhoods of the capital, Kampala.

As we began securing a satellite dish and office furniture and hiring staff, I became increasingly aware of the ongoing war in northern Uganda. It had received very little notoriety outside Uganda and East Africa, and getting a clear idea of what was going on there was not particularly easy, even with the Internet. Weary of twenty years of war, people in Uganda preferred to ignore it.

But the enormity of the tragedy was very apparent, and I was perplexed as to why the world didn't know more about it. This war had been going on for twenty years, had claimed nearly one hundred thousand lives, and had displaced nearly two million people in the north.

When Gummah suggested that we take a trip north to Gulu, the epicenter of the conflict, I jumped at the chance. We needed to make contact with reporters there and pitch our new agency to radio stations in the area, he said. And it would be a good chance for me to see firsthand what was going on.

Gummah provided plenty of background on the drive there. The next day we visited a couple of centers that took in the many abducted child soldiers and so-called child brides (a sanitized term for kidnapped girls and women used as sex slaves) who had managed to escape the rebel Lord's Resistance Army (LRA), or who had been captured by the Ugandan military and released for reintegration into society. We spoke with both child soldiers and the returning girls and women, many of whom were now mothers, and one of whom had been a wife of LRA leader Joseph Kony.

There was no turning back. I took any and all opportunities to meet with people who could help explain this tragedy and why it had continued for so long. I didn't have to go far, because the war had deeply affected all of Uganda. One of the men who guarded our house at night had been abducted and had fought with the rebel army for nearly six years. In the cool of the Ugandan evenings, he told me a lot about rebel life. The more I learned, the more I wanted to know.

I made frequent trips to Gulu and other areas in the north, and talked with many former soldiers and child "brides." Finally, just before I was to end my contract in Uganda, I traveled to Juba, South Sudan, where peace talks between the rebels and the government of Uganda began in late July 2006.

Now, as I write this nearly two years later, I had thought that I could say that this war and the Lord's Resistance Army were over. But I can't. I am back with IWPR, this time as Africa Editor, and I'm still as deeply involved in the story as ever. After nearly two years of peace talks in Juba, a peace agreement remains unsigned. The LRA has regrouped, rearmed, and may be preparing to fight again.

—Peter Eichstaedt
Denver, Colorado

Chronology

Uganda and the Lord's Resistance Army

Precolonial era — Southern Uganda is dominated by Bantu tribal empires, the north by various Nilotic tribes, with frequent contacts with Arabic tribes of Saharan Africa trading ivory and slaves for weapons.

1862 — Explorer John Hanning Speke wanders Uganda, discovers the source of the Nile River at the north shore of Lake Victoria.

1875 — Explorer and journalist Henry Morton Stanley visits Uganda.

1894 — Uganda becomes a British protectorate.

1960 — Political organizer Milton Obote forms the Uganda People's Congress.

1962 — Uganda gains independence; Obote becomes prime minister, eventually taking complete control of the government.

1971 — Ugandan military commander Idi Amin Dada launches a military coup, overthrowing Obote; he begins a reign of terror killing an estimated 300,000 people.

1979 — Amin overthrown by an alliance between Tanzania and the Ugandan National Liberation Army, which includes young commander Yoweri Museveni. Amin flees to Lybia, then Saudi Arabia; he dies in 2003.

1980 — Obote returns from exile and again becomes president following a disputed election.

1981 — Museveni forms the National Resistance Army and begins civil war against Obote's government. The war claims an estimated 100,000 lives.

1985 — Alice Auma of Opit village in northern Uganda claims to be possessed by a spirit called Lakwena ("messenger"), a name she takes, and forms the quasi-Christian religious group the Holy Spirit Movement.

1985 — Obote overthrown by his own generals and again goes into exile, dying in 2005. Tito Okello becomes military ruler.

1985 — Joseph Kony, a former witch doctor and cousin to Auma, becomes spiritual adviser to northern rebels, eventually forming his own militia.

1986 — Museveni's army enters Kampala, and he becomes president in January. His army chases Okello's forces, including those formerly loyal to Amin, to the north, some crossing into Sudan. Museveni occupies northern Uganda.

1986 — Alice Lakwena converts her followers into the Holy Spirit Mobile Forces and, bolstered by retreating army units, launches war against Museveni's army.

1987 — Kony refuses to join Lakwena's army under her command, remains in the north.

1987 — Lakwena's army is defeated east of Kampala. She flees to Kenya (and dies in a refugee camp in 2007).

1988 — Kony's army incorporates remnants of Lakwena's forces; he becomes the sole rebel leader in northern Uganda. His group becomes known as the Lord's Resistance Army, adopting many of Lakwena's quasi-Christian practices.

1994 — Peace talks between Kony and the Ugandan government fail. Kony finds support from the Sudan government, which is fighting a war with rebels in South Sudan, the Sudanese People's Liberation Army.

2002 — Uganda launches Operation Iron Fist after Sudan, under intense international pressure, agrees to let Uganda cross into South Sudan to attack Kony's bases.

2002–04 — Kony launches vicious counterattacks, and the war intensifies across the north.

2003 — Museveni approaches the International Criminal Court (ICC) in The Hague to investigate war crimes and crimes against humanity committed by the LRA.

2004 —— Renewed efforts to reach a peace agreement between Kony and Uganda fail at the end of the year.

2005 —— Kony and his top commanders are indicted by the ICC. Kony retreats, eventually taking refuge in Garamba National Park in the far northeastern corner of the Democratic Republic of the Congo.

2006 —— Peace talks begin in Juba, South Sudan, between Uganda and the LRA.

2008 —— Peace agreement reached between the LRA and Uganda, including a permanent cease-fire. Kony refuses to sign the agreement in April and again in May.

Prologue
Richard's Story

RICHARD OPIO HAS NEITHER the look of a cold-blooded killer nor the heart of one. Yet as his mother and father lay on the ground with their hands tied, Richard used the blunt end of an ax to crush their skulls. He was ordered to do this by a unit commander of the Lord's Resistance Army, a rebel group that has terrorized northern Uganda for twenty years. The memory racks Richard's slender body as he wipes away tears.

"The rebels said there would be no going home," he says with a weak and faltering voice. "The rebels told me that by killing my parents, it would be a sign of courage."

Richard was seventeen at the time, and it was June 2000, just after the rainy season, when the farmers in the north rise early to cultivate their gardens of cassava, corn, beans, and sweet potatoes. He was the oldest child and lived with his parents, a brother, and two sisters in a cluster of round mud huts with thatched roofs. His little village lay in the heart of rebel country, about thirty miles east of the northern Ugandan town of Gulu. They cooked their meals inside the hut over an open fire and slept on flat straw mats.

On the day he was captured, he was cultivating the family's field of sweet potatoes with his cousin, using a thick-handled, broad-bladed hoe to loosen the soil around the leafy plants. He froze with fear when the rebels suddenly appeared from the bush. He immediately recognized them as members of the Lord's Resistance Army, the ragtag militia of men and boys, many younger than himself, that have kidnapped and killed thousands in northern Uganda. He knew all too well what could happen to him. Many others his age and younger had been abducted and forced to become child soldiers for this so-called army. Those who resisted were mutilated, losing limbs, lips, and ears. Others were killed brutally, usually clubbed to death.

The rebels warned Richard not to run. He and his cousin complied, and the rebels grabbed and beat them. The rebels then forced Richard to take them to the family's granary, where they helped themselves to dried maize and cassava. Richard's younger brother and sisters were gone, so the rebels took him, his cousin, and Richard's parents.

"I was forced to tie their hands," he recalls.

After they had walked for several hours, the commander turned to Richard and told him, "It's no use keeping these old people around." The commander called for an ax, handed it to Richard, and ordered him to kill them. He refused.

Knowing that their death was inevitable, as well as Richard's if he refused, his parents pleaded for him do as the commander said. Richard had little choice if he wanted to survive.

"Both my parents told me to follow the rebels' instructions," he says. So Richard delivered the blows. "I killed them." He turns his face away as he cries.

For two decades the Lord's Resistance Army has ravaged much of northern Uganda, southern Sudan, and parts of the eastern Congo, making this region in eastern Africa one of the most dangerous on earth. As one of the longest-running conflicts on the planet, the war has pitted the LRA against the Ugandan national army and has killed tens of thousands, left many mutilated and permanently traumatized, and driven more than one and a half million people from a pastoral existence into the crowded squalor of two hundred internal refugee camps. For more than twenty years, the LRA has been led by the mysterious and rarely seen Joseph Kony, who claims to be a prophet and to possess powers that enable him to see the future and control the minds of his fighters. Kony's conscripts are children, easily convinced that his powers are real. Kony's mixture of charismatic spiritualism and brute force make his army a cult as much as a lawless militia that cloaks itself in Christian rhetoric and mysticism.

Richard Opio is just one of the thousands of young Ugandan boys who have been kidnapped, beaten, tortured, and forced to fight in the Lord's Resistance Army. It is a miracle he survived at all. No one knows exactly how many people have died in this chaotic civil war because no one has been keeping track. Estimates as of 2006 are that one hundred thousand men, women, and children have died, including death due to war-related side effects such as violence and disease in the refugee camps. One reliable report claims that as many as thirty-eight thousand children have been abducted since 1986, about 25 percent of them young girls who become porters, cooks, and sex slaves for Kony's soldiers. And as many as thirty-seven thousand adult men and women have been kidnapped, also becoming soldiers, cooks, porters, and of course sex slaves.[1]

After being abducted, Richard continued his nightmarish servitude to the LRA for two years, participating in attacks on towns, villages, and hapless travelers, pillaging what he could as the fighters conducted their hit-and-run guerrilla war with the Ugandan army. He was part of a unit that included about one hundred people, primarily abductees used as porters, camp cooks, and new recruits to support the fifty or so fighters and the commander. Since Richard was young and strong, he was immediately trained and taught how to handle a gun. Discipline was brutally enforced. The slightest infraction resulted in blows from the flat side of a machete, known as a *panga*. Once, he recalls, he was beaten for allowing smoke from a cooking fire to drift into the air, a severe violation because it could alert the Ugandan army to the rebel unit's presence. After a raid, "we were not allowed to go back empty-handed," he says, otherwise, "we would end up being beaten. It happened so many times. The only way to avoid punishment was to raid civilians."

The unit captured ammunition by attacking the Ugandan army and local defense militia outposts. It was a deadly and violent existence. "The most part of my life in the bush was killing people." Richard admits to killing seven people personally. "The killing was not by a gun. We would batter the civilians to death using any available tool," he says. He killed others in skirmishes and ambushes with the Ugandan army, but he didn't know the exact number. "It's a matter of life and death," he says, when confronting the national forces.

Finally, Richard had had enough. "Most of the time I was in the bush, I was thinking of home," he states. So he told the unit commander he was leaving. The commander laughed and taunted him. But, tormented by what he had done, Richard no longer feared death. He picked up his gun and walked away. The other soldiers turned to the commander and waited for the order to kill Richard. But the commander balked, thinking Richard would succumb to his fear and turn around. But Richard didn't.

"If they followed, I was ready to kill," he says. He walked for two days before coming to a national army unit where he thought he might find his uncle. Finally, his ordeal was over. He applied for and received amnesty. After a month of debriefing with the military, he was moved to a reintegration center in Gulu for former child soldiers.

The LRA war in northern Uganda has been going on for so long that most have forgotten why. The younger soldiers have no clear idea why they are fighting, only that they are. Yet this war has ground on for decades, virtually unnoticed by the international community at large, overshadowed by conflicts in the neighboring Darfur region of western Sudan, the Rwandan genocide, and fighting in the Congo and Somalia. It rivals Darfur for the death and destruction that has resulted, as well as the brutality, yet far exceeds Darfur with its longevity and lack of any clear ideology or purpose. Ironically, it has taken place in a country heralded all the while as an African success story.

Beyond the endless trauma inflicted on children, families, and whole communities, the LRA has disrupted centuries of traditional lifestyles and values among the Acholi, the primary ethnic people of northern Uganda. The war has destroyed the Acholi people's ability to feed or sustain themselves. They have been herded into internal refugee camps for their own protection, but the camps are over-crowded and poorly guarded, making them cesspools of disease and depravity and vulnerable to frequent attacks. The camp dwellers depend on the United Nations' World Food Program to survive.

"In the past, they were growing everything and they had plenty," explains Sam Gummah, a Ugandan journalist. "They never would ask for anything. It was the same as begging. They would rather starve to death than beg. Now we have a whole generation that only knows they must ask in order to survive."

Northern Uganda is a world out of control, where right is wrong and wrong is right, where carnage and chaos are the normal state of affairs. An army of brutal killers has been committing atrocities day after day, month after month, year after year, with no end in sight. In Sierra Leone people have been killed and mutilated by militias wanting to dig raw diamonds. The decades-long war in Sudan is based on tribalism and religion. The genocide in Rwanda was fomented by ethnic suppression and hatred. But this war in northern Uganda defies logic.

The years since Richard Opio's escape in 2002 have been a living hell for him. During the day he faces rejection and insults for his past. "They call us killers," he says of those both inside and outside the refugee camp. He is tortured by nightmares. "I see the people I've killed and they are crying for mercy. When the nightmares come, I end up with the feeling I should go back to the bush because there is nothing left [for me]." He has tried to make friends with others his age, but their parents objected, saying "Don't bring your bush life to my children." Richard finds solace only in the company of other former child soldiers. But even there he finds little comfort. "Many say they feel like going back to the bush," he says, because they face a future of alienation and distrust. Few received the resettlement packages promised by the Ugandan government. The package is supposed to include a foam sleeping pad, pans for cooking, grain, salt, and the equivalent of $130 in cash. "Many of us have not gotten anything," Richard says.

After living with a relative in one of the refugee camps, Richard and a couple of others secured a small place to live in Gulu, hoping for a new start. But when the landlord learned that he was a former rebel, "he told us we were bad people," and he threw them out. So Richard lives with an uncle in the nearby refugee camp, but the two rarely talk. When he shares his stories, the memories are painful. "What happens is . . . the bush comes back to my mind." Although his younger brother and two younger sisters also live in the camp, they rarely talk because of what he did to his parents. "Most of the time, I stay alone," he says. "I keep to myself."

The one bright spot in Richard's future is the opening of a training center and school funded by the Belgian government, just down the road from the camp. He would like to attend, he says, and perhaps learn a trade. If not that, "my wish would be to open a small business, like running a shop."

Richard is just one of the thousands of former child soldiers, child brides, and other victims of this living nightmare who face the difficult task of coming to grips with the horrors of their past. Beyond the individuals, entire communities have the daunting task of rebuilding and reclaiming their lost land, lives, and culture. But for the recovery to begin, there must be peace, and peace has eluded the region for decades.

1

Faded Luster of the Pearl

WINSTON CHURCHILL VISITED UGANDA in 1907 and was so taken by the country that in his memoirs of the trip, *My African Journey*, he wrote, "Uganda is the pearl."[1] A relatively small country, Uganda is one of three nations, along with Kenya and Tanzania, composing the heart of East Africa. About the size of Oregon, it sits west of Kenya and on the northern shores of Africa's largest body of freshwater, Lake Victoria, thought to be the headwaters of the Nile River. The country straddles the equator and is bordered on the south by Tanzania, on the southwest by Rwanda, and on the west by the Democratic Republic of the Congo. To the north is Sudan. Like the other East African countries, Uganda boasts a dramatic terrain. The snow-capped Rwenzori Mountains, also known as the Mountains of the Moon, form the western boundary. In northwestern Uganda, Murchison Falls National Park offers visitors lions, antelopes and gazelles, elephants, giraffes, hippos, and troops of baboons and monkeys. Among the park's famous visitors were writer Ernest Hemingway and his wife Mary, who were injured there in January 1954 when their single-engine plane crashed on the crocodile-infested banks of the Nile River after it swooped low over the torrent of white water and snagged a telegraph wire. Uganda also has the Bwindi Impenetrable Forest, which contains several hundred of the endangered mountain gorillas, the country's biggest tourist draw.

A British protectorate for the first half of the twentieth century, by all appearances Uganda is an African success story. The weather is moderate, the terrain green and varied, the soil rich, and the people educated and eager to reap the benefits of globalization. English is the official language of this country of twenty-eight million, and it has a 66 percent literacy rate. It is predominately Christian, with the Catholic, Protestant, and Pentecostal churches sharing about 60 percent of the population. The remainder are divided between Islam and animistic beliefs. Unlike some other parts of Africa, Uganda has controlled the AIDS epidemic and has lowered the infection rate to single digits.[2] The economy has thrived, due in part to a steady flow of foreign aid, which has made up about half of the Ugandan annual national budget. It is also bolstered by the presence of an enterprising Indian business community.

Despite the appearance of stability and prosperity, Uganda has rarely experienced a sustained peace within its borders. The atrocities committed by the seemingly undefeatable Lord's Resistance Army only underscore Uganda's inability to free itself from a brutal and bloody past.

Two months after I arrived in Uganda in August 2005, the LRA was international news. On October 14, 2005, the International Criminal Court (ICC) in The Hague, Netherlands, unsealed indictments against the army's leader, Joseph Kony, and his top four commanders. They were charged with a total of eighty-six counts of war crimes and crimes against humanity, largely based on evidence collected by the court investigators during the previous couple of years from LRA defectors, escapees, and legions of victims. It caused a surge of excitement in Uganda that finally, just maybe, the international community might do what no one has been able to do: put an end to the LRA. The initial excitement was quickly replaced by the sober realization that it was not up to the court, but the court's member countries, to arrest Kony. Uganda's president, Yoweri Museveni, had appealed for ICC action in late 2003, just two years earlier, and now that the indictments had been handed down, it would be up to Uganda to deliver the LRA commanders for trial. Despite decades of war, however, the Ugandan army had been unable to kill or capture Kony, who at the time was in South Sudan. Sudan had not signed the accord that created the ICC and was under no legal obligation to lift a hand against Kony. And Sudan was unlikely to act because it had found Kony very useful in the past; they had used him as one of their proxy militias to fight rebels in South Sudan. And further, the bulk of the LRA was in the jungles of northeastern Congo, led by Kony's second in command, Vincent Otti, and beyond the reach of the Sudanese army. Though the Democratic Republic of the Congo was a member of the international court, it had been unable to control or contain the myriad rampaging militias already inside its borders and depended on a massive UN force of some seventeen thousand peacekeepers for a modicum of stability. Many wondered what would change with the issuance of these indictments. In short, nothing changed.

But the court action was a step in the right direction. The indictments said the LRA "has established a pattern of brutalization of civilians by acts including murder, abduction, sexual enslavement, mutilation, as well as mass burnings of houses and looting of camp settlements; that abducted civilians, including children, are said to have been forcibly recruited as fighters, porters and sex slaves and to take part in attacks against the Ugandan army [UPDF] and civilian communities." Kony topped the list with thirty-three counts, including "enslavement, sexual enslavement, inhumane acts of inflicting serious bodily injury and suffering, murder, cruel treatment of civilians, intentionally directing an attack against a civilian population, pillaging, inducing rape, and forced enlisting of children." Otti had thirty-two counts of similar crimes; Okot Odhiambo had ten counts; Dominic Ongwen had seven; and Raska Lukwiya had four.[3]

This was not the first time that Uganda had been thrust onto the international stage by bizarre and bloodthirsty characters. During the 1970s, the notorious Idi Amin blazed onto the scene and quickly developed a reputation for living large and conducting a loathsome campaign inside Uganda to purge it of his perceived enemies.

Before Amin, there was Milton Obote, a schoolteacher who rose to prominence in the 1950s as one of Africa's early progressive leaders. While much of the African continent was mired in civil wars—the inevitable and bloody process of shaking off decades of European colonial rule—Obote forged a coalition called the Uganda People's Congress. Attempting to incorporate the traditional tribal system spurned by the colonialists, he formed the country's first government after Uganda achieved independence in 1962. The king of the dominant Buganda tribe, the country's largest ethnic group, was given the office of president, and Obote became the prime minister. But this attempt to merge Uganda's tribal past with its present was doomed. Uganda's traditional ethnic and tribal rivalries sabotaged Obote's plans. Bugandans believed they had been tricked when they realized that their president had very little power and that Obote ran the government as prime minister. When the Bugandan king attempted to assert himself, Obote's military chief, Idi Amin, stormed the king's palace. The Bugandan king fled to London, where he died in exile.

Tribal and ethnic rivalries bubble just below the surface of everyday life in Uganda. Most Ugandans identify themselves first by their tribe and then by their country. The distrust and historical animosities among the major tribes in Uganda have been the source of most of Uganda's tortured past and help explain the longevity of the Lord's Resistance Army. In the simplest terms, the country is divided into north and south by the Nile River, which flows out of Lake Victoria and angles northwesterly until it reaches Lake Edward, and then flows northward into Sudan. The north and east of Uganda are inhabited by the Nilotic tribes originally from regions of the upper Nile River in northern Africa. The south is inhabited by various Bantu tribes whose language and origin come from western and central Africa. Within these two broad categories, Uganda has several major ethnic groups and many minor ones, all of which were lumped together under the artificial construct that the colonialists called Uganda. The country is a veritable Tower of Babel, with dozens of languages and dialects. Long before the colonial era, these various tribes engaged in endless jockeying for power, which continues today. The northern region is dominated by the Acholi tribe and the closely related Langi, of whom Obote was a part. The east is dominated by the Teso and Karamajong people, who are primarily cattle herders. The south and central regions are dominated by the Buganda tribe, and the western mountains by the Bunyoro. The southwest has a mix, including the Anchole, of which President Museveni is a part.

As the country's first president, Obote realized that any successful government in Uganda had to include representation of the many ethic groups, some of whom had been enemies for centuries. This was why he selected Idi Amin as his army commander. Amin belonged to the Kakwa, a diverse group living in Uganda's northwestern region of West Nile. The Kakwa also populate southern Sudan and the eastern regions of the Democratic Republic of the Congo and are generally referred to by Ugandans as "Sudanese." Although ethnically from the north, Amin grew up in the south. Because of his size and strength, he shunned an education in favor of the British regiment known as the King's African Rifles. He was a vicious boxer and bullying leader, and quickly rose through the ranks to become a general. When Obote took power, Amin was a logical candidate for military commander. Obote believed that he would be protected from an overthrow because the majority of his army came from his trusted fellow Langi and Acholi tribesman.

Amin, however, had other ideas. He used his position to amass wealth and power and, distrustful of Obote's Langi and Acholi generals, replaced much of the army's command structure with his own and other ethnic groups from northwestern Uganda. A scandal eventually erupted when Amin was accused of corruption and his prime accuser was killed. Obote ordered Amin to prepare an explanation but in early 1971 left the country to attend a meeting of British Commonwealth heads of state in Singapore. Suspecting that Obote would return and arrest him, Amin staged a military coup. So began his brutal regime in which an estimated three hundred thousand Ugandans were killed in obscenely violent ways, their bodies tortured and mutilated. He methodically purged the professional classes, intimidated the intelligentsia, and then banished the Asian commercial community, seizing their properties and businesses and giving them ninety days to leave the country. Amin and his cronies took all they could steal. The economy eventually collapsed, schools and hospitals closed, roads deteriorated, and soldiers, loyal to Amin, roamed the countryside, slaughtering humans and wildlife with abandon.

In the process, Amin established himself as one of the world's most demented dictators by launching an outlandish lifestyle that included driving a bright red Italian sports car at breakneck speeds through the dirt-poor backcountry, hosting lavish feasts, and bragging that he and his men ate human flesh. While the world condemned Amin from a safe distance, he found a friend in Libya's Muammar Gadhafi, a fellow Muslim, who helped prop up the failing Ugandan economy. With his country in shambles, Amin did what bad leaders do to divert attention from their failures: he went to war. In late 1978, he invaded neighboring Tanzania over a minor border disagreement.

Any sense of victory was short-lived, however. In 1979, Amin's army crumbled in the face of a counterinvasion by the Tanzanian army and the Uganda National Liberation Army, a force of exiled

Ugandans who despised Amin and what he had done to their country. It included a young commander named Yoweri Museveni. Amin fled to Libya, eventually settling in Saudi Arabia, where he died in 2003. With Museveni as defense minister, a new Ugandan government called for democratic elections. Obote returned from exile and in 1980 was reelected president in a highly disputed election. Among the losing candidates was Museveni.

Never having been a fan of Obote and fearing a return to the past, Museveni formed the National Resistance Army and led them into the bush, intent on toppling Obote's government. Unlike Obote's and Amin's armies of drunken thugs, the NRA was disciplined, motivated, and included several thousand Rwandan fighters. Confronted with this serious challenge from Museveni, Obote struggled to maintain control of the country by imposing yet another repressive regime. Relieved of one despot, Uganda found itself saddled with another as Obote sent his army against civilians he accused of supporting Museveni. An estimated one hundred thousand died in this conflict. In 1985, after years of losses at the hands of Museveni's army, Obote was overthrown by a military coup of his own disenchanted generals. The coup was led by an Acholi general named Bazilio Okello, who marched on Kampala in July 1985 and installed another general, Tito Okello (unrelated), as the new president. Obote again fled, this time for good, and died in exile twenty years later.

The Okello regime was short-lived. Although the Acholi generals negotiated a peace deal with Museveni in December 1985, it failed because Museveni distrusted the coup's lingering ties to Obote and refused to let the northern Acholi hold on to power in either the government or the military. Museveni rolled into Kampala in late January 1986 and took over the government. His army then marched north and within two months had captured the key northern towns of Gulu, Pader, and Kitgum. The Acholi resistance was demolished; the Acholi fighters scattered and returned to their villages.

Museveni immediately set about rebuilding and reuniting Uganda. He offered amnesty to former soldiers and urged expatriate Ugandans to return. To impose unity on the disparate tribes and consolidate his power, he did away with partisan politics, which were more tribal than ideological, and created a one-party system called the National Resistance Movement. To appease traditionalists, he restored the tribal monarchies, but granted them only ceremonial authority. He invited the Asian commercial community back and returned their property. Still, not everyone was happy.

Acholi resentment smoldered in the wake of their humiliating defeat. Despite their common language of Luo, the Acholi were never a unified tribe under a single leader but rather a collection of related but independent chiefdoms. By the time Uganda became a British protectorate in 1894, the Acholi were armed and adept at raiding their neighbors, kidnapping women, and stealing cattle. When the British began their pacification of the Acholi in the early 1900s, they convinced the Acholi to surrender thousands of weapons with the promise that if they were peaceful, they could keep their rifles, but only if the rifles were registered. Once the rifles were collected, instead of registering them, the British destroyed them in public burnings.[4] This deceit generated lingering hostility and resentment. However, because the Acholi were traditional warriors, they were enlisted by the British in the army and used to help control the rest of the country. Some were even incorporated into British military units during World War II. The British mistreatment of the Acholi was later duplicated by Idi Amin, who killed thousands as he disarmed them, solidifying Acholi distrust of any occupying force in their homeland.

As Museveni attempted to consolidate his control over the country in 1986, his army in the north often resorted to brutal tactics as they disarmed the Acholi. Fearing that their fate could only worsen under Museveni, a new Acholi rebel group formed across the border in southern Sudan. Composed of former members of Amin's and

Obote's armies, the Uganda People's Democratic Army (UPDA) descended into northern Uganda and launched a guerrilla war.[5] Like any paramilitary force, the units operated independently and relied on the support of villagers. If that support was lacking, they took what they wanted. This established a necessary tactical pattern that Kony's army adopted.

In the midst of this seemingly endless turmoil in the north, a woman named Alice Auma appeared from the village of Opit, about twenty miles east of Gulu. Auma is remembered by some as a tomato seller who entertained her customers with tricks such as making rocks pop, as if they exploded. She claimed to have been visited by a spirit named Lakwena, a word that means "messenger" in the Acholi language, in early January 1985. Eventually taking the name of Lakwena as her own, she founded a religious sect called the Holy Spirit Movement.

But in August 1986, as war continued in Acholiland, the spirit Lakwena reportedly revisited Alice and told her to convert her movement into an army that she called the Holy Spirit Mobile Forces. This charismatic woman gathered about eighty disenfranchised Acholi soldiers who retrieved their weapons from hiding in their villages and in mid-October attacked the government army barracks in Gulu. Though Alice Lakwena's forces were repulsed, she attracted the attention of the rebel UPDA units fighting in the area, and soon about 150 UPDA soldiers joined her, forming the core of her army.[6]

Over the next year Lakwena conducted an amazingly successful war against Museveni's government. Her army practiced a bizarre form of warfare. Her soldiers smeared themselves with shea butter, sang hymns as they marched upright into battle, sprinkled the battlefield with holy water meant to deflect bullets, and hurled rocks that the soldiers were told would explode like bombs.[7] Lakwena's forces marched steadily toward Kampala until their horrifying defeat in November 1987, just fifty miles from the capital. Lakwena fled to northwestern Kenya, where she died in January 2007 in the Ito refugee camp surrounded by about fifty of her devoted followers.

While Lakwena's forces marched on Kampala, a young Acholi man named Joseph Kony also formed his own armed group in the north. Kony was born in the village of Odek, not far from Gulu, was raised a Catholic, and was reputed to have served as an altar boy. He was Lakwena's cousin, though the two had little contact. As a teenager, he apprenticed as a witch doctor under the tutelage of an older brother and took over that position in the village when his brother died. Villagers recall that he was skilled at the practice and respected for his knowledge of local herbs despite his young age.

Lakwena and Kony both claimed to have had profound spiritual experiences. Kony was possessed for three days by a spirit named Juma Oris. The real Juma Oris, a minister under Idi Amin and one of the founders of the rebel UPDA, was alive and well at the time. But this didn't prevent the identically named "spirit" from becoming Kony's supposed guide. The spirit told Kony to wage a war against evil, to rid the world of witchcraft, and to teach people to follow God. By early 1987, some six months before Lakwena was defeated, Kony had established ties with the UPDA rebels, serving as a spiritual adviser to the rebel army's fiercest fighters.[8] Kony convinced others of his amazing spiritual abilities and persuaded them to join him. Kony's group later attacked the UPDA, defeated them, and integrated them into his militia. He began to call this growing force simply the Lord's Army.

By the early spring of 1988, Lakwena was in Kenya, and by default Kony had established himself as the new rebel leader of northern Uganda. He began attacking hospitals and schools, stealing medical supplies, and kidnapping young girls for cooks, porters, and brides (sex slaves) for his fighters. Although the Museveni government was able to convince many of the remaining fighters in the north to disarm and return to farming, those who refused joined Kony, including the stragglers of Lakwena's army. By May 1988 Kony was at the head of the Lord's Resistance Army, a force of a thousand seasoned fighters.[9]

After Lakwena's defeat, her father, Severino Lukoya, attempted to keep her movement alive, but Kony would not tolerate the competition. In August 1988 he captured Lukoya, reportedly tying his uncle to a tree, and beat him severely with a cane pole, shouting that he would not tolerate any more Lakwenas. Kony kept Lukoya a prisoner for nearly six months until he escaped, only to be arrested by the Museveni government and imprisoned in Kampala. Lukoya was released in the early 1990s and returned to Gulu, where he now lives and operates a small church.

Kony's troops employed many of the tactics of Lakwena's Holy Spirit Mobile Forces, such as sprinkling themselves with holy water and refusing to take cover in the midst of battle, convinced that magic would protect them. Eventually, Kony realized he had to adopt more conventional guerrilla practices, such as taking cover when necessary, if his forces were to survive.

By the early 1990s Kony's Lord's Resistance Army fought throughout northern Uganda. When the Ugandan military moved aggressively against him, he took the LRA north to Sudan, where the Ugandan army could not follow. The significance of this cannot be underestimated. Kony found refuge there because the Islamic Sudanese government in Khartoum adhered to the Machiavellian maxim that "the enemy of my enemy is my friend." Before its war in the western Darfur region with the Sudanese Liberation Army, the Khartoum government fought a long and bitter civil war in the south with another Christian rebel group, the similarly named Sudanese People's Liberation Army, led by John Garang. Museveni and Garang had been friends and comrades going back to their university days in Dar es Salaam, Tanzania. Both were passionate about pan-Africanism and self-determination, and their politics were initially colored with Marxism, which had an organic appeal to the communal nature of African society. After taking power in 1986, Museveni supported Garang's fight against the Khartoum government, and Garang was often seen in Kampala. In retaliation, the Khartoum government granted safe haven to Kony in southern Sudan and supported and supplied the LRA. Kony's army spent months on end each year in Sudan, and this allowed the LRA, unlike its predecessors, to survive for decades.

As Kony waged his war of kidnapping, killing, and maiming his fellow Acholi, the Ugandan government responded by herding the Acholi into internal refugee camps. By the time I arrived in Uganda in August 2005, more than 1.5 million people, or nearly 95 percent of the population, had been living in the camps for at least a decade.

———

Like much of the African continent, Uganda has endured successive civil wars, military coups, and delusional maniacs. Yet this country seemed beyond all that. Kampala was a thriving capital city of towering office buildings, sparkling hotels, and teeming streets, with a lush countryside. By all appearances, Museveni had brought peace and prosperity to his country. But when I traveled north and crossed the Nile River, I entered a different country. Refugee camps flanked villages and small commercial centers. Armed soldiers patrolled the highways and dirt roads. The glitter was gone, and the faces were grim. It was obvious that the war with the LRA had taken a terrific toll. How and why had this war gone on for so long in the backyard of an Africa success story? President Museveni had led a rebel army that had defeated the nation's most seasoned and best-trained fighters. So why hadn't his disciplined force been able to defeat Kony's renegade militia in the north in twenty years' time?

Lieutenant Chris Magezi did not wear a uniform the day I talked with him, despite the fact that he was the spokesman for the northern regional command of the Ugandan army. We met at the army's military headquarters in Gulu. He was an affable man and not intimidated by the press, unlike most military personnel I have met.

The year 2002 had been a turning point in the war, Magezi explained. As in the past, the LRA was based in South Sudan and conducted its raids into northern Uganda at will. "They were given everything: weapons, medicine, and food," he said of the Sudan's support to the LRA. "They were farming in southern Sudan and growing crops of cassava, millet, maize, and sorghum." After farming for a season in Sudan, the LRA would sweep into Uganda "when the grass is tall, the forests are thick, and there is food in the gardens." This provided the rebels with not only a ready food supply but also thick cover of new vegetation, which allowed them to move undetected and hide when necessary. The Ugandan army had been severely hampered because it legally could not chase Kony and the LRA fighters across the border into Sudan.

But in 2002, after years of mounting diplomatic pressure, an agreement was forged. Because of peace negotiations between the Khartoum government and Garang's tenacious rebel army, Khartoum granted permission for the Ugandan military to chase the LRA across the border. But the Ugandan military could only go into Sudan to what was known as "the red line," a demarcation across South Sudan agreed upon by Khartoum. It was sufficient, however, for Uganda's army to attack LRA strongholds, but quickly made for a dangerous dynamic in southern Sudan. As Kony's renegades engaged in running gun battles with the Ugandan army, Kony's forces also skirmished with Garang's forces, the Sudanese People's Liberation Army. The SPLA also continued to confront the Sudan government's army, known as the Sudanese Armed Forces (SAF), which were garrisoned across southern Sudan and served as a conduit of arms and supplies for Kony.

The Ugandan army's invasion into Sudan was called Operation Iron Fist and resulted in the army's semipermanent bases there. The

Ugandans dislodged the LRA by destroying its crops and gardens and capturing equipment and weapons. "We rescued many children," Magezi said, claiming that about fifteen thousand Ugandan youngsters were freed over the next few years. The operation also captured soldiers and commanders who surrendered to take advantage of the amnesty program established by the Ugandan Parliament. Some of the returning commanders were enticed by a reward system in which they were given substantial amounts of money to start farms or businesses and return to civilian life.

If Operation Iron Fist was a success and the Ugandan army had had free movement in southern Sudan for the past three years, why was Kony still at large? "Southern Sudan is a big area," Magezi said. "It has not been easy to pin him down." Kony's second in command, Vincent Otti, had taken a large number of LRA fighters into the jungles of northeastern Congo in late 2005, and the Ugandan army wanted to go there as well, Magezi said. The Congo has refused permission for Uganda to enter the DRC, in part because the United Nations already has a massive force there, some seventeen thousand soldiers who were attempting to control a mind-boggling array of rampaging militias. The last thing the Congo wanted was another invading army. There was another reason the Congo was reluctant to help Uganda. The last time the Ugandan army had entered the country, it had overstayed its welcome by several years and helped itself to the Congo's timber and mineral wealth, including gold and diamonds. The Congo subsequently sued and won, and the UN's International Court of Justice had ordered Uganda to pay unspecified damages and reparations to the Congo. Magezi said that the Sudan government had promised to "take action" against Kony, who was still in Sudan at the time. "They say officially that they have cut off all support, but there are elements in the Sudanese military who still support him."

Though Kony eluded capture, Magezi insisted the Ugandan army had succeeded in containing the damage Kony could do by limiting the LRA's capacity to fight. "We have stopped their ability to reorganize. They are not an organized force." The last large-scale incident had taken place two years earlier, in February 2004 in the town of Lira, about fifty miles south of Gulu, when nearly three hundred people died in a vicious attack by the LRA on the Barlonyo refugee camp. Since then, "they only operate in small groups. There is no command structure. They now only operate independently." But the LRA operating in small, independent units created a new problem for the military to solve. The LRA fighters were seasoned and dedicated, and most of the commanders and subcommanders had known nothing except life in the bush with the LRA.

"Almost all of the fighters were abducted," Magezi said. "They have been indoctrinated. They think Kony is a prophet." The Ugandan military had adapted by deploying smaller, more mobile units, he said. The LRA units were being flushed out during the day, then pursued at night. It would take a long time to fully eradicate the remnants of the LRA, and future operations would consist of quick reactions to LRA attacks. "We will have to deal with the small pockets that remain" as long as they're around, he said.

A basic principle of guerrilla warfare is that it cannot survive without support from the local populace. The truth of this has been proved time and time again in Vietnam, Central America, Afghanistan, where Taliban units operate at will, and finally Iraq, where insurgents linger. Despite the atrocities, the government feared that the Acholi had managed to support Kony's rebels in subtle, obscure ways. With the Acholi forced into internal refugee camps, the government assumed that they could be controlled and prevented from joining or supporting the rebels. Yet Acholi support for the LRA was a grim reality, Magezi agreed. The explanation was simple. Most of the LRA fighters had been abducted and were forced to commit the atrocities against their will. "They still love their sons, even if they are rebels," he said of the villagers. "They want to keep their children alive. It has been a problem."

To the extent possible, the Ugandan army attempted to capture the rebels and encourage them to surrender, rather than kill them. "It is not in our interest to kill them. But many do not surrender. Many cannot think of a life outside the bush." The rebel fighters who remain are very dangerous, he said, because "they still want to fulfill what Kony expects of them," which is to wreak havoc. But if the LRA had disintegrated, wasn't the time ripe for peace talks and fulfillment of the amnesty program that some leading Acholis said was the best solution? Magezi dismissed the suggestion. "The people here are fed up. Even the ordinary man says no, peace talks are not possible. The only opportunity [for peace] is maintaining the military option."

The loss of life in northern Uganda and southern Sudan over the course of this twenty-year war was comparable to that in Darfur, Sudan. Yet it had been generally ignored by the international community. Stemming the tide of this humanitarian catastrophe were the workers of the UN food and other programs and dozens of under-funded religious and humanitarian aid groups. The war in northern Uganda was barely acknowledged, even by most Ugandans. That this war had persisted for so long and had done so much damage was staggering, even to the most hardened observers. But the more I looked, the more a shocking reality emerged.

2

The Lips Are Not There

SINCE 1994 MORE THAN seven thousand formerly kidnapped young boys and girls have passed through the gates of the Save the Children "welcome center" in Gulu. It was just one of many reintegration centers for returning child soldiers and child brides taken by the Lord's Resistance Army. Most of these survivors had risked their lives to flee the clutches of the LRA, but it was a risk they were willing to take. The crimes and atrocities they had been forced to commit, and the lack of any clear reason for them, had displaced any sense of meaning to their lives. They had risked death because it was preferable to life with the rebels. Some had been captured by the Ugandan military, and others, such as the women with children, had been allowed by the rebels to escape since they had become a burden to these highly mobile fighters.

Louis Okello, a tall and soft-spoken man, was one of the center managers. "Many are still very young and want to continue their schooling," he said during our interview in September 2005. Others preferred to learn practical job skills, "so that when the child returns [to his or her village] there will be a soft landing."

Landings here were anything but soft. The thousands of former abductees were plagued by physical, psychological, and social problems. Many were rejected by their families, villages, and the community at large because of what they had done and been forced to become. They were tainted, damaged, and many feared they brought an evil with them out of the bush that would infect the community. Sadly, these same victims of the LRA abductions again became victims of their home communities. They were labeled and rejected, as if they had contracted a disease for which there was no cure.

Young girls had been handed out to the soldiers as rewards. Because of the threat of AIDS, the commanders preferred young girls, Okello said, fearing that older kidnapped girls may have been "promiscuous." Some kidnapped girls never returned because they were shot if the children they carried were noisy or slowed the escape of the fighters. Okello said a two-month-old child had recently been found alive, still bound to its dead mother's back. When a child bride in the LRA returned from the bush, she was branded and rejected by her family and friends. If she had children, they were viewed as a burden, simply more mouths to feed in an already impoverished village. But food was not the only problem, Okello explained. One incident that typified the complexities of reintegration involved an orphaned child of a rebel soldier who was returned to its mother's family. The mother had been abducted, then impregnated by an LRA soldier, but she had died. The child's father had escaped the LRA and lived in a neighboring village. The dead mother's family refused to accept the child or forgive the former fighter until he married the dead woman in a mock wedding ceremony. He also had to pay the family the equivalent of four hundred dollars. As macabre as it was, it worked, Okello said, and the child and father were reunited and accepted by the woman's family.

I met Lily Adong at this same center. She was twenty-five and had recently been captured by the Ugandan army along with her three children. But she was no ordinary bride. She was the former number-one wife of the LRA's leader himself, Joseph Kony, who was reputed to have had at least fifty wives and fathered more than one hundred children. Her oldest child was a boy, aged seven, the middle child was a girl, aged three, and her youngest was a boy, just eleven months old. Abducted at the age of ten, Lily had spent fifteen years with the rebels. She was soft-spoken and shy as we sat in the shade of a tree within the protective walls of the center. She told of her first years of captivity when she and the other kidnapped girls were taught to prepare crude herbs and medicines to treat wounds and injuries. She held her youngest child on her lap and spoke through an interpreter, occasionally smoothing the wrinkles in her blue denim skirt.

"He is not a bad man," she said of Kony, revealing her love for the man, a feeling that few others could understand. She spent many of her years with the LRA in southern Sudan at one of its bases there, performing the routine chores of life in the bush: fetching water, cooking food, caring for her children, and growing a garden. She had last seen Kony in March 2005, six months before this interview. She had been captured by the Ugandan military in July. She readily admitted that she was "very happy to be out of there" and hoped to get on with her life. But she was worried. At her age, she said, "going back to school would be difficult." As we talked, she gazed longingly across the compound to one of the classrooms where others were learning how to become tailors and seamstresses. She wanted to go back to her village, she said, even though her parents were dead. She had been in contact with her thirty-year-old brother but didn't want to discuss it. I gathered that the reunion had not gone well. Because she'd been in the bush for fifteen years, she confessed, "I'm afraid of what will be said about me" in her village. She tried not to think about Kony, she said, preferring to focus on the future. Unfortunately, for thousands like Lily, that future looked cloudy at best.

In the nearby kitchen for the center, former child soldiers helped cooks prepare a midday meal by stirring a giant vat of soup simmering over a wood fire. Kitchen work was also part of the reintegration process. Among other deceits, the LRA had told the child soldiers that if they returned to the towns, angry residents would poison their food. By working in the kitchen and helping to prepare food, the former child soldiers saw for themselves how the food was made, dispelling their fears. Despite the extensive efforts by the center to assure the returnees that they were now safe, it was common for a child to flee the compound when rumors occasionally circulated of an impending LRA attack.

I looked in on the tailoring class and was greeted by two dozen smiling faces, each hard at work cutting cloth from patterns. Crude drawings and sketches on paper had been taped to the walls: men shooting automatic weapons, bodies strewn on the ground beside burning huts as helicopter gunships circled above. This generation had known nothing but war.

In January 2006 I went to the Unyama refugee camp, home to more than twenty thousand people just five miles outside of Gulu. The camp was typical of the two hundred across northern Uganda and was down a dusty road at the edge of rebel country. It was the dry season. The fields were brown and clouds of white smoke drifted across the land as farmers and cattle herders burned the dead grass, clearing the way for green shoots that grow with the advent of rains in March. Bundles of dried grass were sold along the roadsides and balanced atop the heads of women who walked carefully erect from the fields to their homes. The conical roofs would be patched and replaced before the coming rains.

I met Thomas Oneka, head of the village council, at the local trading center, which flanked the road out of town and consisted of windowless brick shops with heavy steel doors and bars. Here camp residents bought their clothes, food, washtubs, and an occasional beer if they could afford it. A wiry man with a friendly smile and an energetic manner, Oneka wore a polo shirt emblazoned with the logo of a U.S. university. This kind of clothing is usually obtained from local markets where the tons of used clothes donated and shipped out of the United States by charity groups end up for sale. The trading center was noisy and chaotic as bicycles, motorcycles, and the gleaming SUVs of the UN and aid organizations roared by, scattering the hundreds of people walking on the road. Oneka and I found a little solace on the concrete benches outside a small restaurant. "We have suffered a lot," he said of the ongoing conditions in the north. "The government has promised that we will go back [to the villages]," he said, dismissing the thought with a wave of his hand. "The LRA are still doing abductions. So, how can we go back to the villages?"

Dismantling the camps for the internally displaced people, called IDP camps, had been discussed frequently during the recent political campaign. The LRA attacks were in decline, and with each passing day the hope grew that maybe the war would be over. But Oneka knew the reality only too well. There had been periods of quiet before, but the LRA had always come back. The war had to end, he said, to really end, before anyone could return home.

Because of the war and the camps, traditional life for the Acholi people was all but a memory, he lamented. Most had raised large gardens of corn, vegetables, sweet potatoes, and cassava and had kept animals. But now, "there is no way to go and dig," he said, referring to their gardens. The LRA was still too much of a danger. Instead of vegetable gardens, they had the UN's World Food Program. "You wake up in the morning and you wait for the WFP food," which consisted of regular allotments of staples such as grain, sugar, and cooking oil. "It's not enough," he said. Despite their fears of the LRA and restrictions placed on camp residents by the military, many camp residents were able to cultivate small plots to supplement their meager diets. The army limited the amount of farming the camp residents could do by forcing them to wait until 9:00 A.M. to leave, which was after the roads to the fields supposedly had been patrolled and cleared of lurking LRA combatants. Their gardens could be no more than a couple miles from the camp, however, and the refugees were required to return by 5:00 P.M. or risk being shot as suspected rebel fighters.

The longevity of the refugee camps had damaged family structures as well as social and cultural traditions, Oneka said. "Our children are spoiled," meaning they had gone bad. The closeness of the camps bred promiscuity, and with babies to feed and raise, many young people tried to eke out an existence rather than attend school. "A young girl drops out of school and attends to her family," he said. In the past, boy-girl relations were more regulated, and marriages were arranged according to agreements between families and clans within a tribe. "Traditional ways are totally spoiled. Our traditional culture has vanished because of this situation. Now people are mixed up. That is why people are crying to go home. People are crying for peace to come. They want their children to grow up in a better environment."

Many Ugandans considered Kony and the LRA to be a problem confined to the north and to the region's Acholi and Langi tribes. Kony was an Acholi. He operated in Acholi territory, and those he abducted were Acholi children. But Oneka said it was larger than that: "When Kony went to Teso, this problem became national." The Teso region is to the south and east, and Kony rampaged through the region for a couple of years until a local militia called the Arrow Boys drove his forces out. But the LRA was also an international issue, he said, because Kony operated in Sudan and most of the LRA fighters had fled to the Congo. The solution to the LRA problem was to bring in an international force of peacekeepers, he said. "We tried peace talks and they failed. Do what you're doing in Congo," he said, referring to the UN soldiers there. "Then peace talks can start."

I suggested that such a massive operation was unnecessary because the situation was getting calmer by the day. He shook his head no.

Less than a week earlier, he said, camp residents who had risen early with the idea of sneaking away to their gardens had been surprised by a unit of LRA soldiers at dawn loping across the road about two hundred yards away.

We were interrupted by Ray Odoki, the refugee camp leader I had initially been searching for. He wore jeans and a nicely ironed shirt and had an intense, sincere face, looking very much like a camp leader. He preferred to talk to me in the camp, so we climbed back into my car and drove there. The camp was a dense sea of round mud huts with conical thatched roofs. It was quiet, and I felt like an intruder as we made our way among the crowded structures. They were remarkably simple yet efficiently cool in the searing heat, with just enough room for a small family to sleep and cook. Our presence did not disturb the unhurried rhythm of life here. As in most of Africa, life took place out in the open. The huts were just places to cook and sleep, not a place to spend a lot of time unless you were sick or had nowhere else to go. Smoke from cooking fires drifted in the air and children emerged from the dark interiors, some with smaller ones on their hips. Women bent over brightly colored plastic washtubs, sloshing clothes in soapy water. Odoki produced a couple of low-slung cane chairs from a nearby hut, and we sat in the shade of a towering mango tree on a patch of swept dirt. It was midday, and most of the men were gone, some to work in town, Odoki said, others to tend to their gardens and goats.

"The government gave us only twenty-four hours to leave our land," he said of the origins of the camp, which had opened in September 1996, almost ten years earlier. "We have lost our wealth, our animals," he said. He launched into a litany of problems in the camp. Not all families were getting their fair share of the UN food supplies, in part because camp officials didn't acknowledge the true number of people living in it. Children were missing out on education. "Because of a lack of classrooms and teachers, many children are left at home," he said. Sanitation was poor, and cholera was ever present. In the sprawling camp, "there is no space for new pit latrines." Health care was minimal. The camp had one emergency health care center and little or no support for a growing number of malnourished children. The crowded refugee camp was a breeding ground for tuberculosis and malaria. "Children are dying because we don't have enough medical staff," he said. And if a child or anyone else became sick in the middle of the night, they could not be taken to the hospital in Gulu because travel at night was prohibited by the military. Because of the restrictions, "we cannot afford to feed our children and we can't dig [a garden]."

Odoki suggested that the army's restrictions were prompted by reasons other than the refugees' safety. Tension between the soldiers and the camp residents was high and a source of constant trouble, he said, creating an atmosphere of distrust. Many in the military were not Acholi and not from the north. The military required the gardens to be close to the camp because it suspected that camp residents grew them to support the rebels. "The army says we are feeding them," Odoki said. If refugees were allowed to cultivate gardens far from camp, the army reasoned, the LRA rebels could harvest them unnoticed. Sometimes the army raided the gardens and took the produce for themselves, he said.

"Let's bring the war to an end," he pleaded. "With the war, we have lost our culture, our wealth, our education. Most of our children do not know how to read and write well." Instead of school, which many miss because jobs don't exist and parents can't pay the small school fees, "some kids just go to the [trading] centers and see videos. It does not teach children in a good way." He hoped a return to more traditional life would resurrect the culture and life that many young people had never known. "We have many schools in the villages," but they had been abandoned because of the war. "We pray to God for this war to end," he said. "We are tired of the war. We are suffering. In the future, when we leave the camps, we will be free."

Many in the camp had personal reasons for wanting the war to end. A year before this interview, rebels had attacked the camp, Odoki said. The army fought back, and a camp resident was killed in the crossfire. But the rebels managed to kidnap two children. Not long after, an army patrol found the children's bodies, Odoki said, about twelve miles away. But the army refused to let the parents and relatives, all camp residents, retrieve and bury the children. "The skeletons are still out there," he said.

Odoki also had a personal reason to hate the war. A few months after the last rebel attack on the camp, his daughter, an educated woman who was working for the local government, was on her way to a village about twenty-five miles north of Gulu. In broad daylight, five rebels ambushed the vehicle, yanked her out, and cut off her lips and ears. "[They] told her to go back to the UPDF [army] and say that the LRA is waiting." Silence hung in the air as he looked at me with watery eyes. "The lips are not there," he said. "She has difficulty eating and drinking."

The offices of James A. A. Otto, the director of Human Rights Focus, an organization that investigated and prosecuted the abuses committed by the Ugandan army, were just a ten-minute walk from the army's Gulu headquarters. Otto had an infectious smile and, with his white hair, was an image of knowledge and wisdom. I jokingly told him that, because the war was supposedly winding down, he would soon be out of a job.

He frowned at the thought. "The human rights situation here is still bad," he said. Armed conflicts are environments in which human rights abuses proliferate, he explained. Because of years of atrocities committed by the LRA, such abuses "are more the norm than the exception," he said. But when it comes to the Ugandan military, such abuses have become institutionalized. Despite the denials by the military, he said, "in the [refugee] camps torture exists and it is rampant." A study by his organization showed that 70 percent of all incidents of torture against camp residents were committed by the LRA, but the remaining 30 percent were committed "by the very army that is supposed to protect them." During a hearing on this problem by the Ugandan Human Rights Commission, the UPDF said it had recorded 501 cases of human rights abuses in 2005 committed by its soldiers. The figure was revealed as the military defended itself against accusations of abuse, claiming it was dealing with the problem.

Otto said no one knew how many cases went unreported and were never investigated. Regardless, his group kept busy with what it had. At the time of our interview, he had taken eighteen cases to court, but it had not been easy. Although the Ugandan constitution stated that torture was a crime, torture was not defined. "What is not defined does not exist," he said. But under international law, he said, torture was an abuse committed by an authority, in the course of duty, to extract information or a confession. Each of the cases he had investigated met that definition.

In one case, LRA rebels had abducted a handful of people including a sixty-two-year-old man from a refugee camp guarded by an army unit. The man escaped, however, along with the other abductees and returned to the camp. Instead of being welcomed back, the abductees were ordered by the army into the middle of the camp and forced to explain what had happened. The old man was largely silent, so the unit commander accused him of being a rebel sympathizer. The man was beaten and kicked, then thrown into what was considered a jail but was no more than a pit occasionally used as a latrine. In another case, a woman was returning from her garden plot with a group of children when they came across a cloth bag hidden in the bush. Knowing that it did not belong to any of them and could contain weapons, she told the children not to touch it. But back at the camp, the children told their friends about what they had found, and within hours soldiers arrested the woman and accused her of hiding a bag full of money meant for the LRA. She was beaten. Otto showed me pictures of her wounds on his computer screen. She took the soldiers to find the bag, which contained only clothes and some personal items of a camp resident who had hidden the bag so it would not be stolen. "When [the army] becomes worse than the LRA, this is unacceptable," he said.

But it had been relatively quiet for months, I said, compared with the peak of LRA activity just a year ago.

"The LRA has been weakened," he admitted. For the war to return to what it was once was improbable, he agreed. But he was not optimistic the war was over because too many people were profiting from it. "It was for monetary gain for the top brass," he said. If the war ended, so would the flow of foreign aid money to Uganda. "The conduit of money into their pockets would be cut by the cessation of the conflict."

On that account, he was correct. President Yoweri Museveni had been forced to replace the army's top commanders over blatant abuses of the military budget, most of which was designated for the war in the north. The abuses included inflated numbers of soldiers fighting in the north, which allowed commanders to pad payrolls and pocket the money intended for their "ghost soldiers." Deals had been made for the purchase of uniforms from China that did not fit the long and lean bodies of most of the soldiers. Huge commissions were reportedly paid to commanders who purchased broken-down helicopters from former Soviet countries. Otto could only shake his head at the insanity.

But there was the problem at hand. If peace was to come and the 1.5 million camp residents were to return to their farms, security had to be assured. "The soldiers need to be sensitized," he said. "They need to relax their grip on the civilians." As long as the camp residents couldn't travel at night, could only tend their gardens during daylight hours, were herded into and out of camps, and were generally treated like cattle, "the conflict is not over."

President Museveni's lack of popularity in the north was a severe problem for the entire country, Otto said. Museveni needed to do much more to reach out to the residents of the north who have been suffering for the past twenty years of war. If he didn't, "we will have two countries divided by the Nile River," which pretty much described the country as it had existed for decades. Otto said the split between the south and the north was serious and that many social and psychological bridges had to be built for peace to take hold in the north. "Winning an election is one thing," he said of Museveni's re-election, "but having the legitimacy to rule is another. The two can't be separated." If more was not done to end the war and distribute the so-called peace dividends to the north, Otto issued a dire warning: "Our children will be fighting about something else."

———

It was pitch black in Gulu that night. There was no electricity, and the few lights in the distance, other than an occasional set of headlights, were powered by generators. A sliver of a moon appeared from behind puffy clouds and offered little light. I stumbled across a broad enclosure, drawn by the sound of energetic young voices. I could see only the faint outlines of dancing, clapping children assembled on a concrete slab. This was Noah's Ark and these were the "night commuters," the hundreds and occasionally thousands of children who fled the refugee camps surrounding Gulu every evening for the safety of this fortified enclosure. The children were singing their "devotionals," giving thanks to be alive another day, just as they did every night before slipping off to find a place on the plastic tarps strewn over concrete floors of the dormitories and tents here. The harsh glare of a video camera spotlight wielded by a documentary film crew cast the children into ghostly surreal figures that moved in and out of the dark night.

Only about fifty children participated in the evening songs of late, said director Annet Kurui, because the number of night commuters had dropped dramatically down to just about three or four hundred nightly due to the lull in fighting. But no one expected the peace to last, despite the Ugandan army insisting that it would. "Are they sure it is really, really finished?" Kurui asked skeptically. "We are trying to resettle [the villages]," she said of the camp residents, "but we are also trying to think of what happens if things turn bad." Returning to the villages was premature because the LRA units still roamed the countryside. "What do you say to a villager who was attacked? You can't recover a life that has been lost."

Noah's Ark was started in 2002 by a couple of Dutch missionaries, Kurui said, because "there was a need to get [children] out of the street" at night. Fearing rebel attacks on the poorly guarded refugee camps, thousands of children had once lived in the streets of Gulu and the other northern towns of Kitgum and Pader. They had taken to sleeping in doorways and on street corners. Exposed and vulnerable, they were abused, beaten, and raped by roaming drunks. She said, "We thought we had to do something."

Noah's Ark opened with room for about three hundred children, she recalled, but within two weeks, fifteen hundred children flocked into the compound as word of its existence spread. The shelter opened just in time, she said, because the LRA attacks around Gulu escalated until finally, in May 2003, fighting came literally to their doorstep. That month about forty-five hundred children crammed into the center each night. And as the fighting raged around Gulu through 2004, they took in more than seven thousand nightly. With meager resources, the organization could do little but provide them shelter. The starving were given bowls of oatmeal. Blankets were scarce, and only several counselors were on hand to supervise.

Though regional security had improved, Noah's Ark continued to house hundreds of children nightly because conditions in the refugee camps were wretched, she said. Some of the mud huts had fifteen people sleeping in them, forcing children to flee the camps, not because of the LRA but because of the sexual abuse. Some desperate children had returned to their villages, despite the dangers of the LRA attacks, just to escape the camps.

It was at Noah's Ark where I met Koncy Akot, a thirteen-year-old girl who had been abducted just six months earlier from the Amuru camp outside Gulu. Rebels broke into the hut where she slept with several other children. One child was killed, another shot and wounded, and she alone was taken. She spent four months in the bush with the LRA before she escaped. In a weak and timid voice, she explained how she accompanied soldiers on their raids to steal food and supplies and was told that if she dropped anything, she'd be killed. Akot was never more than twenty-five or thirty miles away from Gulu, but she didn't try to escape because she didn't know which direction to go in the sameness of the scrub and brush. Her unit consisted of about one hundred fighters, largely kidnapped child soldiers. Most of the rebels wore uniforms and were rarely chased by the Ugandan army.

"They did not follow us regularly," she said. She was not sexually abused, because she was considered too young. She was treated "as a child."

Was she ever afraid?

"You do not have to fear if you stay close and obey," she said. Her opportunity to escape came during an army ambush, but her return from the bush was bittersweet.

Once she found her way to one of Gulu's reintegration centers, she learned that her parents had been killed in an LRA raid. After food distribution by the World Food Program, the rebels had raided the camp, abducted her parents, and killed them both. Akot was handed over to her uncle, who was willing to let her live with his family in a camp. But Akot preferred Noah's Ark, fearing that if she were abducted again, the LRA would kill her for having escaped.

Dennis Ojok, age eleven, then a habitué of Noah's Ark, had been abducted by the LRA from his home north of Gulu in the spring of 2003. He had moved with the rebels on foot to southern Sudan where he had survived an ambush by the Sudanese People's Liberation Army, the allies of the Ugandan army. He had been taught how to handle an AK-47 and had roamed with a group of twenty-one armed rebels, ten women, and eight smaller children. In one attack on the Ajulu refugee camp north of Gulu, he stole sacks of food, three cows, and some goats. The LRA ranged freely and struck at will, he said, and it was not unusual for them to attack an army detachment, their source of weapons and ammunition, in broad daylight. Often the Ugandan soldiers and militia would flee, leaving the refugee camps vulnerable to plunder and kidnapping at will. He saw many of his fellow child soldiers killed.

His chance to escape came during an attack by a helicopter gunship. He was an escort to the unit's commander, who had been targeted by the gunship. The commander told Ojok to run, otherwise he'd surely be killed. So he did, running for hours until he came to Gulu. He knew of Noah's Ark and went there directly. When he tried to find his parents, he learned that they were dead. His closest relative, his grandmother, lived in one of the refugee camps north of Gulu and cultivated a small garden. The garden did not produce enough to feed them both, he said, so he lived on the streets in Gulu. He, like Akot, feared returning to the camp because he did not want to be abducted again. He attended school on most days and scavenged for food. Often his only meal was a bowl of oatmeal at Noah's Ark, where he spent his nights. When he could, he ran errands and picked up a tip here and there, trying to earn enough money to visit his grandmother once in a while. It was a life with prospects that were few and far between.

The scope of the tragedy in northern Uganda was hard to grasp, but spending time with children such as Akot and Ojok made it very real. It was not just them but each and every one of the children who had been jubilantly singing and dancing in the darkness of the Gulu night. There were thousands of others, some better off, but many worse off. This felt like the end of civilization. That humans were capable of doing such things for years on end was hard to fathom. This deplorable state had become normal, and as difficult as it was to imagine, I was only beginning to comprehend.

3

Anatomy of an Attack

FEAR CLOUDED THE EYES of Tom Okeng and strained his voice as he described the early March 2006 attack on his village by ten rebels of the Lord's Resistance Army. As his small children cried and his horrified wife screamed, the rebels dragged him out of his thatch-roofed mud hut in the dark of night and forced him to the ground. They bound his hands and jabbed him repeatedly with a bayonet. The rebels had wanted money, he recalled nervously, watching the waning light of day. Soon it would be evening and too late for him and his family to return to the refugee camp five miles away. It meant another night in the bush and another night of vulnerability to yet another rebel attack. Yet Okeng remained, and, as he touched the scabs and bandages on his head and body, he continued to tell me about that night. He readily lifted his shirt to show me all the puncture wounds.

His memories of the attack were still raw, and his words came slowly. Okeng had protested and told the rebels he had no money, but they refused to believe him. The ordeal continued for twenty or thirty minutes until the rebel leader called for a pistol and said he was going to kill Okeng. Hearing something being handed around, Okeng knew his death was at hand. He struggled free, leaped to his feet, and swung fiercely at the nearest rebel, but he only struck the man's rifle. He darted into the darkness as bullets whizzed near his head, shouting a warning to his neighbors, "Run, the rebels are coming."

The Uganda military later said these attacks were an increasingly rare occurrence and soon would be a thing of the past. But for the residents of Orem village, just twenty miles from the town of Lira, it felt all too real. Lira was on the periphery of rebel territory, and this attack took place very close to a detachment of the Amuka, or Rhino militia, one of the paramilitary units placed beside refugee camps that supplemented regular army forces. The detachments consisted of dozens of crudely made mud huts erected over dugout pits.

Earlier that day I had visited the Lira hospital, a depressingly crowded building where I was told Okeng was still recovering. In the courtyard, people sat in the dirt or leaned against trees, watching me with eerie intensity. I scaled concrete steps and skirted several dozen people sprawled on the porch, mostly relatives of patients, who knew there was little they could do for those inside but wish them well. I stopped at the nurse's station, a grimy cubicle of an office. There was no power, so it was dark. The nurses shook their heads and insisted that Okeng was not there, saying I was free to check. The ward was a pathetic display of human misery. Creaky metal-framed beds crowded a large, open room where the wizened and the wounded lay motionless on mattresses of thin, spongy foam, wrapped with their own dirty blankets. They were in various states of demise, some bandaged, some gasping for breath. This was the detritus of the apocalypse. My companion, Ugandan journalist Joe Wacha, asked one patient after another if anyone had seen a man named Okeng. Each wearily shook his head until one motioned to another bed. In it lay a young man with blood-soaked bandages around his chest and shoulders. He had been shot a couple of days earlier by a gang of armed men. But he was not Tom Okeng, and they were not rebels.

Forty-five minutes and twenty miles of bone-jarring roads later, we reached the Bar refugee camp. Rats scurried in and out of a debris-clogged culvert as we got directions. We were assured the village was "not far." I distrusted the term because in Africa it can mean five blocks, five miles, or a day's drive. I also didn't gauge distance by asking if one could walk to a place. The answer was always yes, because if one can't afford any other way, one can walk anywhere: to Kenya, to Ethiopia, even to Europe.

Moments later we headed into a no-man's-land of scrub brush and grassy savannah occupied by villagers tending garden plots sprouting with tall and leafy cassava plants. The farmers hacked at the ground with their heavy hoes, turning the soil in preparation for planting. My driver, Eddie, knew this territory well. He had fought here as a soldier in the Ugandan army some twenty years earlier against Alice Lakwena's rebels. Age had padded his middle and filled his cheeks. I called him Sergeant Eddie. He also knew that the setting sun signaled coming danger.

We braked after a couple of miles beside a gangly young man whose limbs had outgrown his pants and shirt. The young man nodded when we asked about Orem village. Okeng was his neighbor, and he would take us to him. The young man was Joshua Ongany, age nineteen, and he had a permanent look somewhere between bewilderment and fear. He climbed in and proceeded to tell us what he knew of the rebels' attack that night, meanwhile directing Eddie off the road and onto a footpath, which our vehicle straddled as we plowed through the brush.

We stopped at a clearing of mud huts when we could drive no farther. Eddie crossed his arms and leaned against the chrome bars that protected the grille, then squinted warily as he surveyed the landscape. It looked pastoral and harmless to me: hand-hoed fields, clusters of trees, occasional towering palms, bushy mangoes, and acacias dotted the nearby hills. Another hundred yards on, the peaks of yet more thatched roofs poked above the bush. A couple of small kids wandered over to us from the nearby huts, so Eddie decided to stay with the vehicle to prevent any mischief. Wacha and I followed Ongany into the bush.

We walked through a cluster of huts, more bush, up a small incline, and after another hundred yards we arrived at Okeng's hut. The place was empty. Okeng was coming, Ongany assured me. We hunkered down on the hard-packed dirt to wait. How did Ongany feel now, knowing that the rebels could come back any time?

"We are afraid," he said. "They told people they will come back. They have seen many things [here], like chickens and food." The attack had disrupted the natural rhythm of village life. "For us at night, we sleep in the bush, not in the house." They did this to stay close to their animals, food, and meager belongings yet avoid detection and capture. It was a rugged, mean life, and now it was cold and damp, since the rains had begun. Sometimes, he confessed, "at evening we . . . go to the [Bar refugee] camp."

A woman appeared from behind the hut with two small children in tow. This was Lucy Akullo, Okeng's twenty-nine-year-old wife, who confirmed that Tom was on his way. She had just returned from cultivating her millet, beans, and cassava, and she wanted to return to the refugee camp.

"I am afraid," she said, because the rebels had vowed to return. Lucy remembered the night of the attack well. She was awakened by one of her children crying for some water. As she sat up, she noticed the beam of a flashlight through the cracks in the small wooden door to their hut. "A man was trying to kick the door down," she said. She opened the door and several men barged in, each armed and wearing camouflaged military clothing. She recognized them as rebels because they spoke heavily accented Luo, not the dialect from her region. They quickly grabbed whatever they could: beans, dried cassava, clothes.

Our attention was drawn away when Okeng walked out of the bush with a somber, forlorn look. He wasted no time recounting the story as other villagers quickly gathered around, undoubtedly having heard the tale many times. After escaping that night, Okeng hid in the darkness until morning when he could get medical attention at the refugee camp clinic. If he had attempted to enter the camp before sunrise, the militia would have assumed he was a rebel and shot him. After receiving some basic care, he had in fact been taken to the Lira hospital where I had looked for him. But Okeng left because the hospital had no medication. His brothers pooled their money so that he could obtain treatment at a small and better-equipped private clinic. After a couple of days, he had returned home.

I thought that he would be angry, want revenge, and perhaps join the militia. No, he said, because the militia didn't pay well. Besides, neither the militia nor the army had been able to stop the attacks. A few weeks earlier, the LRA had hit another village less than a mile away and kidnapped eight children. The militia had pursued the rebels and rescued all of the children, but this obviously had not stopped the rebels. It was an endless game of hide-and-seek, hit-and-run, attack and counterattack that had gone on for years. The villagers were used to it. Why expose yourself to more danger by picking up a gun? The LRA would strike again, he said, and probably kidnap others.

Nearly twenty villagers had now gathered around us. One of them was Lily Aburu, a forty-year-old woman with closely cropped hair who wore a blue dress with a gold sash around her hips, surprisingly formal for the bush. She was among those who had been kidnapped that night. I had walked past her hut, she said, which was just down the hill from where we were standing.

She woke in the night when rebel soldiers pulled her half naked from her sleeping mat and pushed her outside.

"There were ten soldiers in my house with flashlights," she said. "I thought it was the end."

They forced her to carry the stolen food. But as the rebels and their captives headed into the night, the band split into two groups for tactical reasons. A gunshot rang out, throwing the rebels into a panic, thinking they had walked into a trap set by the militia.

"They thought soldiers had surrounded them," she said, and they began firing at each other. In the chaos, "we all ran off in different directions," Lucy said.

She hid herself in the bush for the remainder of the night and at first light made her way back to her hut. She knew she was lucky.

"I thought I had reached the last," she said. "I am happy because God decided to save my life." Okeng was lucky, too, she said. "If Tom had not taken his chance to run, he would not have survived."

Did she feel safer since her escape?

"We worry when the sun begins to set," she said. They were in a precarious position: too far from the direct protection of the soldiers and, as such, easy prey for the rebels. Yet they remained.

The hopeless resignation of these villagers brought to mind the Japanese film classic *The Seven Samurai,* which is about impoverished farmers who convince wandering samurai, fighters for hire, to help them defend and ultimately defeat raiding brigands. It is an inspiring story of humble farmers who find courage they never thought they had, and of cynical samurai swordsmen, weary of killing only for hire, who join forces and find new meaning to their lives. In 1960 the story was remade as a highly successful western, *The Magnificent Seven,* about seven gunslingers who help a Mexican village fight off rampaging banditos. What is the African version of this story? Okeng was not interested in joining the local militia, and no one else seemed outraged enough to pick up a gun and fight back. Rather, at night they ran to the squalor of the refugee camps and hoped the militia would do something about the rebels. But even Okeng knew that would never happen. Hope was all they had, and it was all but gone.

Okeng told me the rebels had sliced the head off a chicken and sprinkled the blood on the doorway of his hut that night. The purpose was to prevent the spirits from the village, Okeng's long-dead ancestors, from following them into the bush to get revenge.

Was that what stopped him from fighting back?

Okeng shrugged again.

The scattering of chicken blood underscores the deeply rooted animistic beliefs that permeate the countryside. The LRA fighters not only believe in such practices but use them to their advantage. The LRA often proclaimed that theirs was a spiritual movement as much as it was a military force. Was Okeng afraid of the rebels because of their perceived mystical powers, or the fact that they were brutal killers?

Unwilling to answer the question directly, he only said softly, "I am afraid," then glanced again at the orange-red sun poised on the horizon. "They frequent the place," he said with a casual wave of his hand, as if the rebels were as much a part of the landscape as his ancestors' spirits. "I think they will be back once the moon is full. They will come back."

How long would they tolerate this? Again, Okeng could only shrug at the question.

Then Ongany explained that because "the soldiers have failed to stop this war," the villagers felt resigned to the fact that fighting was useless.

Did he ever expect the war to end, or did he think this was a permanent condition?

"Me, I don't have an idea about that one," Ongany said. "Maybe God will do something."

Another villager, Robert Akona, thirty-three, had been squatting in the dirt nearby, listening attentively to the conversation. He, too, was convinced the rebels would return soon and that an end to the war was hard to predict.

"I am leaving it all to God and prayers," Akona said with a shrug. "If God can help," he said, the war will end soon.

But why does it persist? I asked.

"It's a punishment," he replied.

Punishment for what? I asked.

He shook his head sadly and said he could not explain.

———————

The Acholi Inn in Gulu was home to a handful of former LRA commanders who had been granted amnesty, as well as some ranking Ugandan army officers. Among these officers was Colonel Charles Otema, chief of intelligence for the Ugandan army in the north, who held court under a large tree in the corner of the inn's sprawling flagstone patio. A burly man, he was well spoken and confident. Otema joked about his girth as he ordered a breakfast that included soup, fruit, eggs, meat, and bread. Otema chortled that a thin waist was for a young man, not him. If he didn't maintain a big belly, "no one will take me seriously," he said, and dug into his food.

I told him that just a day earlier a village near Lira had been attacked by the LRA. And before that, the LRA had attacked a military convoy north of Gulu, and a Ugandan army major had been seriously wounded and a civilian killed. How could the Ugandan army claim that the LRA was all but dead?

He dismissed my question with a wave of his hand. These were disparate bands of the LRA that roamed the north doing the only thing they knew: conducting raids. "They are not in contact with Kony," he said. "If Kony surrendered today, they would still be there. They've gone berserk. They're just thieves." He called them "a few remnants . . . who have turned to thuggery."

But they were still a dangerous armed force.

He nodded in agreement and said the army was doing what it could to ferret them out. For example, the army pursued the rebels who had attacked the military convoy north of Gulu, killing four of them and capturing their weapons. In all, he thought there were about twenty soldiers in the band. "It was a mop-up [operation] we're trying to do. If there's an attack, we pursue, we chase them, and crush them."

It sounded so simple, so final, but then Kony had been down before. The LRA was trying to regroup in the Congo, he said, which was why the Ugandan government was seeking permission to reenter the country. "Once we attack that group, then end of story. We are talking months. These people cannot hold."

Yet most people in the north, such as those I'd met in Orem village, were still afraid.

"In the villages, people are feeling safe, gradually," Otema said. The army was slowly expanding the amount of land that the villagers could cultivate so that they could begin to leave the refugee camps and return to their communities and farms. But in order for villagers to feel safe, the LRA had to be eradicated. Though the rebel bands were small, they were still deadly.

"A dying horse kicks harder," he explained. These bands were probably among the toughest the army had ever faced in the north, he admitted, because they were the most hard-core. Almost all had been kidnapped as children and taught to fight. "They don't think there is any other life than that of the bush."

In all, he suspected that at that point the LRA consisted of no more than several hundred fighters. "Northern Uganda is generally peaceful," he said; in southern Sudan, there were only about fifty fighters left, in the Congo, a couple hundred. His numbers proved to be extremely low, although it was impossible to know because the LRA operated in such scattered groups. He reiterated that Uganda should be allowed into the Congo to finish the LRA. "We are pressuring the international community to allow us to deal with them," he said. "They should not be there."

Something else had given Ugandans hope that the LRA might be captured. On March 19, 2006, Congolese militia commander Thomas Lubanga was sent to the International Criminal Court in The Hague.

The pending prosecution of Lubanga renewed talk that Kony and Otti might also eventually face the same court. Lubanga, alleged to have killed two thousand civilians during recent regional Congo conflicts, had been jailed and faced charges of kidnapping children and forcing them to become child soldiers in his militia—one of the many crimes that Kony could be tried for.

Another reason for hope was that, as publicity escalated around the conflict in the Darfur region of western Sudan, calls had increased for UN intervention there. And if the UN was going to go into Sudan, then why not northern Uganda? A UN Security Council resolution that asked then–secretary general Kofi Annan to develop a plan for the Sudan mission logically also directed him to develop plans for the UN to help end the conflict in northern Uganda.[1] But a plan was just a plan.

Likewise, the conflict in the north had drawn the attention of the U.S. Congress. Both houses considered measures to encourage a speedy resolution to the war being waged by the LRA in 2004, 2005, and 2006.[2] In March 2007, Congress adopted a resolution calling on the government of Uganda and the Lord's Resistance Army to recommit to a political solution to the conflict in northern Uganda and to restart the stalled talks. Throughout late 2007 and early 2008, the United States became more actively engaged in the talks than it had in the past by placing a state department observer at the talks. In reality, the end of the war was no closer than it had ever been.

Shortly after my meeting with Otema, a consortium of aid groups called the Civil Society Organizations for Peace in Northern Uganda issued a report that revealed the horrific cost of the war in the north in terms of life and health. Titled "Counting the Cost: Twenty Years of War in Northern Uganda," it affixed numbers to the terrible toll the war had taken. It opened with the following statement: "Since 1986 northern Uganda has been trapped in a deadly cycle of violence and suffering. After twenty years the war shows no real signs of abating, and every day it goes on, it exacts a greater toll from the women, men and children affected by the crisis." The report contained an avalanche of appalling statistics. Most alarming was that thirty-five hundred people in the north die each month not from direct killing in the conflict but from "easily preventable diseases, extreme violence, and torture." Nearly two million people had been herded into the 202 refugee camps scattered across the north and "forced to live in squalid and life-threatening conditions, dependent on relief and denied access to incomes and education." Some of the camps had more than sixty thousand residents, and more than 50 percent of those in the camps were under the age of fifteen. The rate of violent death in the north was three times higher than the mortality rate in Iraq in the months that followed the invasion in 2003, the report said. The death rate in northern Uganda was three times higher than the death rate recorded in Darfur, Sudan, in October 2005, yet Darfur received much more attention. The breakdown was that more than nine hundred people died each week and nearly 146 died each day as a result of the war and its consequences. Most of the deaths were labeled as "excess" deaths, meaning that they would not have occurred if the war were not taking place. This translated into fifty-eight children under the age of five dying each day.

The report was among the first to point out the extent of the situation that had been devolving for twenty years in northern Uganda: more than twenty-five thousand children had been abducted during the course of the war, a number that would be later increased by other studies. During the periods of highest rebel activity, from about 2002 to early 2005, as many as forty-five thousand children, known as "night commuters," had left their homes in the so-called protected refugee camps in the evening to spend the nights on the streets in the regions' towns. Most of the north's public schools had long been closed, and an estimated 250,000 children in the north had received no education at all. The twenty years of war had cost the government of Uganda an estimated $1.7 billion, or about $85 million a year.[3] It was a staggering cost in lives and dollars but, most of all, lost opportunities.

———

Bernard Nyang was a typical eleven-year-old in many ways. His dark eyes sparkled, his smile came quickly, and he had a shy, soft-spoken manner. We sat on a bench at a broad wooden table. He was slight for a boy of his age and shifted nervously beside me as we talked, not quite knowing what to do with his hands. One difference between Bernard and most other eleven-year-olds was that he could handle an AK-47 quite well. He had a lot of practice during three years in the bush as a child soldier, a typical abductee of the LRA rebels. We talked in one of the cavernous rooms of the Rachele Rehabilitation Center in Lira, named after the courageous nun Sister Rachele, who more than a decade before had chased down a band of LRA fighters who had abducted 130 young girls from a Catholic school in the village of Aboke, not far away. It was an incredible display of determination and outrage at the senseless killing, maiming, and abduction that had continued in northern Uganda.

With me was Joan Aja, a social worker at the center. On the wall hung a large board with numbers. Since the center opened in October 2003, less than three years earlier, 2,368 child soldiers and child brides had passed through it. The center only took returning child fighters eighteen years or younger. Like the other centers throughout the north, it provided personal and group therapy. Drawings by abductees of men with guns, burning villages, and dead and dying villagers adorned the walls. Toy guns and other weapons were piled in the corner and used for role-playing exercises in which the returnees acted out some of their experiences.

"We try to get out of them what they've gone through," Aja explained. The killing was the hardest to discuss, she said, but it was easy for them to talk of their escapes. "They tell us that with a smile." Most of the returning soldiers went back to the refugee camps, she said. "We give them hope that this [war] will come to an end and they will go back home."

The center also focused on personal hygiene, which was minimal or nonexistent in the bush. Testing for AIDS infection was voluntary. But many agreed to be tested, she said, because the kidnapped girls were told by LRA commanders that everyone in the "outside world" is infected with the AIDS virus as a way to keep them from leaving. The incidence of AIDS among the returnees, however, was low.

Nyang was fresh from the bush, having escaped from the LRA just a few days earlier. It must have been as bizarre for him to be sitting there talking to me, a *muzungu* many times his age, as it was for me to be talking to a boy who had more war experience and had seen more death than many regular army soldiers in other countries.

"I had gone to my sister's place in Aloi," he said about the day he was captured in August 2003. "[LRA] soldiers had just looted the trading center." Aloi was a small town east of Lira, one of the areas where the disparate bands of the LRA continued to operate. After his capture, he was taken southeast of the Lira district to the Teso region during the LRA's 2004 offensive, then later to Pader in the north. He was kidnapped with two other children, a brother and sister, and their first task was to be beasts of burden. The unit survived much as they all do, by stealing whatever it could. He carried about thirty pounds of salt.

The unit was on the run and there was little time to rest. "We were constantly being pursued by the Ugandan army," he said, and often the unit walked the whole night, rarely taking time to sleep. When they rested during the day, they cooked using charcoal for smokeless fires. At such times he was given a gun and told to climb a tree and guard the camp. It was a position they called OP, for "outpost," but dozing could be deadly. "If they found you asleep, they would kill you." When his guard duty was over, he gave the gun to the next person. When the unit was on the move, he stayed among the most forward. If he spotted Ugandan forces, he reported back to the commanders, who would then divert the unit.

Did he ever use the gun?

"I shot it twice," he said. Did he kill anyone? He said he didn't know because he fired it blindly and couldn't see. Bernard admitted that he had seen his friends killed, but did not elaborate. Then he quietly said, "The newly abducted were killed. They liked killing older people . . . people with gray hair."

Aja told me that most of the child soldiers were not as affected as one might think by the killing they were forced to commit because they could psychologically distance themselves from it. "The trauma may not be in killing someone, because they don't feel responsible for the death. They were forced to kill." It was a self-defense mechanism. "It comes to be a normal thing." The children suffered more trauma from seeing someone hacked to death, Aja explained, because they were witnesses, not the executioners.

Nyang was lucky because he usually had food, he said, but most of all he was thankful he had been able to escape. "From the time he was abducted, he had plans to escape," Aja said. His chance came during a night raid. He had been assigned to watch for an attack by the Ugandan army, then became separated from the unit. He walked in the darkness toward where he suspected the Ugandan forces were patrolling and hid himself in the bush until morning. At dawn, he ambled down the road until he found some civilians, who took him to the military barracks where he turned himself in. Bernard missed his mother, who had already come to visit him, and his father, who had died while he was in captivity. Bernard was not sure of the future, except that he wanted to go back to school like others his age. Now free of the LRA, he would have that chance.

4

God, Grace, and the Aboke Girls

FATHER JOHN FRASER IS a Catholic priest who knows the Acholi people as well as any outsider can. Canadian by birth, Fraser has worked in Lira since 1960, two years before Uganda gained independence. He and most of the other priests in northern Uganda are members of the Italian Comboni missionaries, named after Daniel Comboni, who first set foot in Africa in 1857 and died twenty-four years later as the Bishop of Khartoum. Comboni had been charged with saving souls in central Africa and had worked a full fifteen years there before the infamous journalist and explorer Henry Morton Stanley found Dr. David Livingstone. Comboni arrived in Sudan amid an influx from the Western world who came not only to Christianize the continent but also to battle the flourishing slave trade. By the time Fraser arrived in Uganda, mission work in the region had a century of precedent.

A fluent speaker of the Acholi language of Luo, Fraser has an office in Radio Wa, one of several high-powered radio stations in Uganda supported by the Catholic Church. It sets a high standard for entertainment and news, promoting objective reporting, balanced and lively call-in talk shows, and airtime for local musicians, entertainers, and politicians. Like most radio stations in Uganda, one of its major money streams comes from personal on-air advertisements: birth and death announcements, professions of love, messages of condolence, and outright solicitations. Radio Wa broadcasts from the shade of several towering trees, and its covered concrete porch serves as a fresh-air waiting room and gathering point where listeners wait to pay for their two dollars' worth of airtime.

Fraser's office is an enclave of serenity; on the busy street just beyond his barred windows, walkers, bike riders, and smoke-belching vehicles bounce over and around the gaping potholes. It is furnished with a big desk and a comfortable couch and is enclosed by wood and glass panels.

I met with Father Fraser in early 2006, just two weeks after the Christmas holidays. A small plastic Christmas tree still sat atop a corner shelf, its lights twinkling and Christmas carols emanating. On his desk a plaque proclaimed WITH GOD ALL THINGS ARE POSSIBLE, a note of hope in a corner of the world that has known little of it in recent years. Despite a lifetime of work in this remote and often desperate region, he had a friendly, youthful air and a lively wit accented with an impish grin.

"It was the end of an era," he recalled of Uganda forty-six years earlier. "I got my driver's license from a British policeman." As a British protectorate from 1894 to 1962, Uganda had been another world, a world before notorious dictators and vicious militias ravaged the land. "Bribery and corruption did not exist. Who can you trust if you begin bribing the police? Now they're the second most corrupt people in the country."

The second? Who was the first?

He had to think about his answer, but offered that it was the national power company. "The revenue authority used to be the worst," he said, because it controlled customs. Among other things, the revenue officials imported cars, claiming they were old but selling them as new. Today, that culture of corruption permeated the world of humanitarian aid, he said, noting that the vast majority of humanitarian aid never reaches the people for whom it is intended. A shipment of mosquito nets donated by the Red Cross for the hospital in Lira to protect patients from the malaria-carrying insects never arrived. Instead, the nets were hawked in the local bars. Likewise, bales of used clothing from the United States meant for distribution to the inhabitants of the country's poverty-stricken refugee camps usually ended up for sale in the local markets. "People can and do make money out of suffering," he said with a note of resignation.

For the last twenty years, life in northern Uganda had been radically altered by the Lord's Resistance Army, Fraser explained, habitually licking his lips as if he relished this rare opportunity to tell what he knew. At the core of this ongoing and vicious conflict were ethnic animosities baffling to casual observers and difficult to explain, even by experienced counselors such as himself. Northern Uganda would always be the land of the warlike Acholi and the Langi tribes, he explained. The larger Buganda tribe of the south and the Bunyoro of the west were cattle herders and farmers. In the precolonial era, the Bunyoro and Buganda had often hired the Acholi to fight for them and paid them in cattle and women, he said. And below the surface were the Acholi's ancient clan conflicts, territorial rivalries, and language variations.

Before Kony's ascendancy, Fraser knew all about the ill-fated mystic Alice Lakwena, who was born just forty miles to the north. Fraser marveled that Lakwena's movement, which she led with otherworldly authority and conviction, was so successful. She developed a surprisingly strong following by telling the Acholi, "We can get together again. I will anoint you with oil and the bullets won't be able to hurt you." It was a message the Acholi fighters wanted to hear, he conceded, because it allowed them to resume their warrior lifestyle. "They were quite good at it," he said of the victories of the Holy Spirit Mobile

Forces. Most puzzling, however, was that "the Acholi are not particularly religious," Fraser said. "We were amazed that all these people could be recruited and told to die for the Holy Spirit." Fraser paused, dipping into his reservoir of recollection, then added, "These were desperate people looking for a leader. She gave them hope because they would have God on their side [and be] immune from the bullets of their enemy."

When Lakwena fled Uganda with her forces in disarray, the door opened for Kony. His name meant "help" in Luo, Fraser explained, smiling at the sad irony. Kony had not helped the Acholi. Rather he had made them the pitiful victims of their own homegrown guerrilla movement. After years of counseling former captives of the LRA, including a few of Kony's ex-wives, Fraser developed his own notions of the man. Most of the time Kony was thoughtful and rational. "But when he prayed, you left him alone. He would go out by himself. They said he communed with spirits. He'd go talk with spirits. The witch doctors do the same thing. It sounds like madness."

Kony once called Fraser's radio station to complain that the station's disc jockeys had labeled the LRA a bunch of rebels. "We are not rebels," Kony had said. "We are an army." When the deejay on air asked Kony what his army was fighting for, Kony replied that they want a government ruled by the Ten Commandments. Fraser again licked his lips. "There is none that they have not broken." Radio Wa continued to broadcast frank and outspoken criticisms of the horrific brutality of the LRA's tactics, even though the LRA fighters were regular callers to late-night talk shows. The LRA eventually struck. On the night of September 27, 2002, the LRA attacked the radio station with rocket-propelled grenades. The station, housed in the back of a large church in Ngetta, on the outskirts of town, was not staffed at the time, so no one was injured. The morning deejay discovered the attack when he came across the smoldering ruins in the dim light of dawn. What intrigued Fraser was the LRA's fascination with soda. No money or equipment was stolen, only soda. The station's refrigerator had been smashed open and the soda bottles emptied, presumably into the common twenty-liter plastic canisters that the rebels used for easier transport. The attack was carried out by a unit of the LRA whose name in Luo means "swimming in blood," he said. Though it took several years, Fraser was able to solicit enough donations not only to restore his radio station, which moved to its present quarters, but to finance the region's first local television station in the renovated church space. For that, Fraser said, he had to thank Kony.

That year had been a particularly dangerous one for the Catholic priests in the area, marked with vicious encounters with Kony and the LRA as well as the national army. Priests were kidnapped regularly, along with the impoverished children they were trying to educate. On April 25, LRA rebels abducted Father Gabriel Durigon, an Italian parish priest, when they attacked Gulu Cathedral, the headquarters of the Catholic Church in northern Uganda. On May 11, LRA rebels abducted forty-four young seminarians from the Sacred Heart Minor Seminary in Lacor, also near Gulu. Four of the students were later rescued by the Ugandan army after a battle in Pader District to the north and east. Seven others were reportedly killed. On June 6, LRA rebels abducted Father Alex Ojera, a parish priest of Alito Catholic Mission in Apac District, south of Lira, along with sixteen children. Father Ojera was released shortly thereafter, but the children were not. On June 12, Kony reportedly ordered all his troops to destroy church missions and kill all priests in Northern Uganda. The *Daily Monitor* newspaper in Kampala quoted Kony on June 16 speaking on a local radio station as saying, "Catholic missions must be destroyed, priests and all missionaries killed in cold blood and nuns beaten black and blue." On September 14, just two weeks before the LRA rebels attacked Fraser's Radio Wa, they overran a military detachment in Lakwena's home village of Opit, attacking the Opit Catholic mission and abducting two more Comboni missionaries, Fathers Ponziano Velluto and

Alex Pizzi. The two priests were released after twelve hours. The rebels also stole communications equipment. But, most tragic of all, on March 21, 2002, Father Michael Declan O'Toole, an Irish priest, and two other persons were shot and killed at a Ugandan military road-block in Kotido District. The response came swiftly. Five days later two soldiers charged with the killings faced a court-martial tribunal and were later executed. Father O'Toole had been highly critical of security forces in the area and incurred the wrath of the army.[1]

The frequent contact Fraser's parishioners had with the LRA underscored his conviction that "if you have a guerrilla army with the support of the community, you will never defeat it." That support could be as subtle as a code of silence. No one would report the location of the LRA fighters and their units, even when spotted, he explained. This allowed the LRA to escape, hide, and set up camps in relative secrecy. Meanwhile the fighters survived on roasted cassava and corn collected from Acholi gardens because it staved off hunger and could be eaten on the run.

But the key to the longevity of the LRA had been the Islamic government in Sudan, Fraser insisted. One of the most persistent rumors of the 1990s was that before Osama bin Laden fled Sudan for Afghanistan, bin Laden had supplied Kony with weapons in a simple deal: one gun for every Ugandan child that Kony could deliver. The children were used as slave labor for bin Laden's poppy farms, Fraser said, admitting that he had no proof. Poppies, opium, and heroin sales are often rumored to be among the methods used to finance bin Laden's al-Qaeda organization. Thousands of children have been kidnapped from northern Uganda, and many have never been seen or heard from again. If true, the kidnappings are the vestiges of the slave trade that went on for a millennium as Arab slave traders reached deep into Africa for their human chattel. Fraser feared that this was how Kony had obtained substantial quantities of arms during the 1990s.

But support from Sudan alone was not enough to explain the persistence of the rebel movement. The Ugandan government shared some of the blame for the way it had handled the LRA problem, he said. Because it rightly suspected Acholi support of these homegrown rebels, the Ugandan government had herded more than 90 percent of the population into the internal refugee camps. They functioned as prison camps, despite being loosely guarded and wholly lacking in defense barriers such as barbed wire, chain-link fences, or enclosures. As the Ugandan army emptied the countryside, it deepened Acholi resentment against the government because it made them captives in their own land.

"Despite the atrocities, the LRA has the sympathy of some Acholi," Fraser said. This conviction was underscored during one of his infrequent home leaves when he met Acholis who were living in Toronto, Los Angeles, and London and who were secret donors and LRA fundraisers. Fraser said he was shocked, having witnessed murder and mutilation of the Acholi by the LRA rebels. In one particularly gruesome incident, he recalled, the LRA had kidnapped a group of young girls, then cut off their lips and breasts.

"[The fund-raisers] were in total denial that the Acholi [rebels] could do these atrocious things to their own people. They refused to accept it," he said, and they insisted the acts were committed by the government and attributed to the LRA for propaganda purposes. This denial had permeated all of northern Uganda, I suggested, and Fraser agreed.

"The Acholi have never admitted defeat," he said, despite the fact that Museveni had been in power for twenty years. The continued existence of the LRA "has crystallized the anti-Museveni feeling" and showed the world that the northern tribes had never succumbed to Museveni's army or the will of his government. Even if the LRA were destroyed, disbanded, and disappeared, Museveni and the government knew that "the Acholi will always be a threat. The people in the south all know that."

The Acholi were keenly aware that their culture and social structure were being destroyed by the camps, and this generated a resistance mentality in support of the LRA. Fraser once counseled a young girl who had been abducted by the LRA and forced to become a child bride of a commander. She escaped the LRA, but after spending time with her relatives in one of the Acholi refugee camps, she had returned to the LRA. In the bush she had status as the wife of a ranking commander. She had bragged that she drank soda every day. Life in the refugee camp, by comparison, was one of abject poverty, defeat, boredom, humiliation, and sexual abuse. "The life of the rebel [was] a little romantic. They were somewhat looked up to." Although Acholi children were kidnapped, it was tolerated because the LRA was recruiting soldiers to fight Museveni. "That's the overall [Acholi] strategy."

When I balked at the thought that the Acholi could rationalize the inexplicable brutality of Kony's fighters against his own people, Fraser pointed out that several top religious and cultural Acholi figureheads had refused to sign a statement condemning Kony for the atrocities committed by his LRA. Instead, these Acholi leaders had steadfastly supported an amnesty program for the LRA fighters approved by the Ugandan Parliament. Additionally, the Acholi leaders not only criticized the International Criminal Court's indictments of Kony and his top commanders but had fought to delay their issuance and implementation. They had argued that the indictments were a disincentive for LRA fighters to lay down their weapons and that they sabotaged the amnesty program. For example, they had argued, one former ranking LRA commander was said to have been dropped from the indictments list as a condition of accepting the amnesty program. He lived in Gulu at government expense. The Archbishop of Gulu, John Baptist Odama, so opposed the indictments that he offered himself up to the ICC for prosecution as a proxy for Kony, who had eluded capture. Fraser shook his head at the uselessness of the suggestion.

The reality of the LRA was never clearer than when it conducted one of the most notorious raids of LRA history. On the night of October 9, 1996, a band of heavily armed LRA soldiers forced their way into the dormitories of a large Catholic girls' school in the village of Aboke, twenty miles west of Lira. The band of some fifty young LRA soldiers forced 139 girls between the ages of twelve and fifteen into the bush under the threat of death. Remarkably, the nun in charge of the school, Sister Rachele, chased down the abductors, parleyed with the commander, and secured the release of 109 of the girls. The remaining thirty stayed in captivity. The story of the girls' struggle to survive, and the massive international rescue effort mounted by Sister Rachele and the girls' parents, are recounted in the book *Aboke Girls* by Dutch journalist and writer Els Tammerman.

The thirty captive girls never gave up hope, and some were able to stick together, eventually helping one another escape the clutches of the LRA. After more than eight years, all but six of the Aboke girls had returned. Four died at the hands of the LRA, and two remained in captivity. Some had children, the result of forced relations with the LRA's top commanders. The girls were highly prized "brides" because they were educated. Most were in their early twenties when they escaped, and with the help of supporters, the Aboke girls were reclaiming their lives. When I encountered them, most had enrolled in a Catholic school in Kampala, "where no Kony rebel can reach them," Fraser said.

Though the years of horror were behind the girls, Fraser struggled with questions that still surrounded the kidnapping. The Catholic school in Aboke, an imposing collection of buildings, included a towering church and stout structures of classrooms. Days before the fateful kidnapping in 1996, the LRA had conducted a number of raids in the area, and the Ugandan army was on alert. A unit of the army had been posted at the school in response to appeals for protection by Sister Rachele. But on the night of the attack, the soldiers were withdrawn when the local commander claimed his forces were stretched too thin and had other security assignments. Yet that was the night the LRA chose to attack. Also puzzling was the LRA's selection of that particular girls' school for the abduction, Fraser said. There were many other similar schools across the north, and most were closer and more easily accessed from the LRA's known bases in the north.

Fraser noted that the rebels had to pass several other schools to reach Aboke. "Why they picked Aboke, we don't know. We've never been told. It's just another girls' school run by the Catholic Church."

Fraser's musings raised a troubling question: Could the Ugandan army have been complicit in the kidnappings? It was not impossible, considering that some Acholis asserted that the government's dismal failure to subdue the LRA was intentional. The argument was that if the Ugandan army kept the north in chaos by allowing the LRA to wage a low-level war, it justified keeping the Acholi in camps and a massive military presence in the north.

Due to Sister Rachele's efforts, the Aboke girls became an international cause célèbre, and their captivity briefly caught the attention of the UN and the world news. Despite agreeing to negotiations for the girls' release, the LRA ultimately denied that the girls were among their ranks, and therefore they could not be released. Although she was unable to free the remaining girls, Sister Rachele's work in raising international awareness of LRA problem landed her a job at the Vatican.

Since her departure, Fraser has counseled the girls and worked closely with their supporters. Fraser arranged for me to meet eight of the Aboke girls just as they were completing a two-week retreat. It was early February 2006, and the girls were due to return to school in Kampala after an extended semester break with their families. We met in the outdoor courtyard of Radio Wa, a bare dirt and cracked concrete yard surrounded by a high plastered wall. A couple of small antelopes, commonly known as dik-dik, panted against the heat of the dry season. We sat awkwardly around a large shaded table, talking over the hum of an air conditioner and street sounds outside the walls. While most of the girls would divulge only a few details of the horrors they had endured, they readily spoke of their flights to freedom and their hopes for the future. Here are their stories.

Grace Acan

Grace, now twenty-four, had been the leader of the abducted girls and during the interview, nearly ten years after the abduction, still held an unspoken command over them. Grace escaped from the LRA on September 4, 2004, during the height of the LRA's war in the north.

"I just ran," she said, despite the tight security under which the girls were kept. "You were always being watched." The guards followed those who tried to escape, "and they would kill that person. I was afraid. If they could catch me, they would kill me. It was the very deep bush. I was alone for a week. I had nothing. I'm so happy to be back."

Grace recalled that, in the first couple of months after their kidnapping, the girls were taken to the LRA safe havens in southern Sudan. As months passed without any sign of rescue, they resigned themselves to their dismal fate, she said. But about a year later, their hopes suddenly lifted when they learned that Sister Rachele and several of the girls' parents had arrived in southern Sudan, accompanied by UN officials, the culmination of months of tricky negotiations via clandestine contacts with the LRA. Despite having earlier assured Sister Rachele and the others that the girls would be freed, the LRA balked at the last minute and denied that the girls were present in Sudan, claiming their whereabouts were unknown.

But Grace said the girls were present and were convinced their rescue was at hand. "They knew [the girls were there]," she said of the LRA commanders, "but they hid us. We were happy that [Sister Rachele] came. We knew she'd take us back. There was nothing we were doing there except undergoing torture."

Instead of handing them over to Sister Rachele, their LRA captors spirited the girls off to lives of servitude. "It was so hard. Sometimes there was no water," Grace recalled, and the girls were forced to dig in dry riverbeds to find it. "We had to begin digging gardens to plant crops to survive" such as beans, cabbages, and potatoes, she said. When the LRA was on the move, which was most of the time, "We had to walk long distances." But the girls never lost faith. "We knew that God was there and that we'd be back. We kept on praying."

Now that she was back, she continued to raise her child, one of two born during her years with the LRA and the only one to survive. Her most ardent desire was to obtain a graduation certificate, after which she would decide what to do with her life. "I feel that time [with the LRA] has been wasted. When I see my friends, they are now working."

Did she hate the LRA?

"Of course," she said bluntly.

Having been close to the LRA's command structure, could she explain the LRA's survival?

Grace struggled for an answer. "I don't know where their strength lies."

Was it Kony?

She shook her head no. "He's just a man, like any other man. The way he talks to [his men], he's just a normal man."

Did she blame the government for the existence of the LRA?

"He has tried, but he has failed," she said of President Museveni's efforts to defeat the LRA.

Did the community in the north support it?

She shook her head. "No one supports the LRA. They must take the food by force."

Grace was given as a "wife" to one of the ranking commanders who later received amnesty from the government. She had little to say about what for her was clearly an agonizing memory. She said only that he "was sometimes quarrelsome" and was often in the camps because he was "not always involved in the fighting."

How did she feel about her time in the bush?

"I can forgive, but to forget is too hard. I pray for God to remove the pain from my heart."

Charlotte Awino

Charlotte escaped from the LRA in July 2004 as guards watched her walk away. Though she was willing to be beaten to death rather than endure the LRA, the guards didn't suspect she was leaving because she had been with them for so long.

"They saw me, but they thought I was going to stop." At the time, the unit was camped near the northern town of Pader, and Charlotte was able to walk into one of the refugee camps. "They asked me who I was."

What was that like?

"I felt kind of free, but I was also afraid." The LRA commanders had told her she'd die if she reached the camp. "The UPDF will kill you, and the civilians will kill you," because the camp had recently been attacked.

Was her reception hostile?

She shook her head no. "There was nothing."

Charlotte had been in southern Sudan in 2002 when the Ugandan army launched Operation Iron Fist into southern Sudan to chase the rebels. It was a terrifying and difficult time, she said, because the LRA was under attack and on the run. What helped her and the others survive was the bond of friendship the Aboke girls shared. "We had to walk miles. We trusted one another. We prayed with each other whenever we'd see each other. We'd say, let's keep going."

What finally prompted her to flee?

"I prayed and said, God, tomorrow I'm going. If they kill me, so what?" She escaped with her two children born in the bush.

Did she or the other girls resent the children they had due to their forced relations?

Charlotte shrugged to answer the question, then admitted, "Maybe the love has grown."

Janet Akella

Janet escaped in August 2004. "It was during a fight" in southern Sudan, she said. In the midst of the chaos, "I found myself alone" and seized the moment to disappear into the darkness. "I walked [all] night. I was afraid. They told [me] that if I reached Juba, they'd make me a slave." But she decided to risk it. "I went to Juba," a rough garrison town of dilapidated buildings and makeshift shelters in the southern Sudan desert. But to get there, she had to pass through territory controlled by the Sudanese People's Liberation Army, the army of the provisional government, who, along with the Ugandan army, was fighting the LRA rebels. It was a bold move for the young girl. "[The SPLA] were our enemies." She went to a child returnee center and was soon airlifted out of Sudan and back to Uganda. Learning that she was flying to Gulu, "I was very happy."

Janet had two children from her years with the LRA, and the children, now five and seven, had survived many battles. Janet, twenty-four, said she wanted to become an evangelist. "I've experienced the love of God, so I have to serve him."

Susan Ejang

Susan escaped in November 2004 near the northern Ugandan town of Kitgum. "I was sick," she said. Her unit had just been ambushed, and "the others left me behind," not wanting her to slow them down and assuming she would soon die. Instead, she clung to life and wandered aimlessly, delusional with fever. "I walked for two days," she said. "I didn't know where to go. I wandered the bush." She survived on a small container of water and two pieces of cassava root. She eventually came to a main road and made her way into Kitgum. It was none too soon.

Sickness and death were common among the LRA, particularly malaria and scabies, she said. Because "there was no proper food" the soldiers were constantly sent on raids. "Getting food was difficult. They'd get mostly dried maize." The corn was then ground into meal on grinding stones. She spent six of her years with the LRA in southern Sudan, and only after the seventh did her unit return to Uganda, where she escaped.

The close bond between the Aboke girls helped keep her alive. "We were not allowed to talk to each other," she said, since the commanders suspected they plotted escapes. But sometimes "on the way to the well, we'd get a chance to talk." Any infractions of the rules, resistance, or acts of defiance resulted in incredible brutality. "They mostly used sticks to beat the others," often to death. "Sometimes they used *pangas* [machetes]. They'd do it to scare you." It worked. "It can discourage you. Even if you had a plan, it will stop you." Regardless, many chose to risk it. "Most people [tried] to escape with the hope they will survive," she said, and Susan was among them. "I thought of only getting away." That chance came when she fell ill.

Did she resent that the LRA unit had abandoned her to die?

No, she said. "I was very sick. They had to run. They were scared of the bullets."

Was she angry at the LRA?

She looked at me with a steady gaze. "Yes."

Carolyn Anyango

Carolyn, twenty-five, left the LRA near Kitgum, during a cease-fire, she said, and was released along with four others. She relished her return to a normal life, living again with her parents and going to school. She enjoyed math and science and hoped to become a scientist. But the memories haunted her. "Sometimes [I] can still recall" life in the bush, she said with a shudder.

Was she also angry about what happened?

"I was," she said. "I feel anger because my future was wasted."

Was it possible to forgive and forget?

"It is not easy," she said.

Was she forced to commit atrocities?

No, she says, but she witnessed the murder of one young boy. "He was cut and beaten to death."

Jacklyn Alabo

Jacklyn, twenty-four, escaped in August 2004 near the northern Ugandan town of Anaka. "They release[d] us because they had no food for the children," she said. Jacklyn was among a group of five women and six of their children. She had been separated from the other Aboke girls when she was made the "wife" of a forty-year-old commander named Livingston Opio. The man spoke Arabic and worked as a liaison between the LRA and its Arab-speaking supporters.

"He was educated, but not to be a doctor," she said, though "he knew something about medicine." Pregnant women were kept separate from the rest of the LRA units, she explained. She had spent most of her years with the LRA in southern Sudan and did not return to Uganda until 2002, the first year of Operation Iron Fist, when the LRA returned to Uganda.

"You carried a child on your back and food on your head, and other things as well. I was very hungry. The situation was so bad. You'd never think you'd get a chance of escaping. There was always tight security. I saw two killed who tried to escape. I was so scared." The commanders normally forced the newly abducted children to kill the escapees or be killed themselves, she said. "They told us the same would happen to us." The units were often on the move and at night would sleep for just a few hours, then move again. The diet was largely "some wild food in the bush," she said, and despite her desire to escape, "I never thought of running. I was so weak that walking was hard."

Her release came as a surprise. "I thought it was not going to happen." The women and children started to walk. "We met people on the way. At first I was so scared. I thought they were going to kill me." Like many other Aboke girls, she brought her child, a son, with her from the bush, who at the time of our interview was three years old. She was happy to have her life back and to be considering a future. "I didn't think I would be able to go back to school."

Sylvia Alabo

Sylvia, twenty-three, escaped in January 2005 along with twenty other women during an ambush of LRA units in southern Sudan by the Ugandan army. She put her hands up, she said, so the army knew she was surrendering along with her child, a two-year-old girl named Rebecca. "I was scared. I thought I would be killed." Instead she was identified and airlifted to Kitgum. "They told me my parents were waiting for me. I saw my parents that very day. I was very happy."

What kept her alive?

"I always prayed."

Jackie Wegesa

Jackie escaped in January 2005 after her LRA unit returned to Uganda from Sudan in August 2004. "I was very weak," she recalled, but she fled with others when the unit was attacked by a helicopter gunship. "People were running in all different directions. When it is shooting, you have to hide." She disappeared into the bush and kept quiet. "I thought I'd meet people. I didn't know the way. I stayed in one position." But when she realized the others had disappeared and she was alone, she knew she had to find help. "I walked for a day. That is when I reached the main road." She continued to walk until she found a detachment of Ugandan army soldiers near Kitgum, turned herself in, and eventually was returned to Lira.

What sustained her in the bush?

"I used to pray because I had nothing [else] to do. All those years, we never had time to be alone." She felt blessed to have escaped. "It was a privilege," she said, but she has not forgotten the girls who remained in captivity. "We have to pray for them that they can escape and come back."

"I'm not happy about it," she said of those years. Her former schoolmates have graduated and are working and living normal lives. "For us it was time wasted," she said. Her goal was to pass her exams and enter a university. "I want to become a political personality," she said.

5

Witch Doctors, Rattles, and Unholy Ghosts

"WE HAD CHILDREN IN the school who were attacked by spirits," said Amos Mugisa, a science teacher at the Kiisita Primary School, a typical public school some thirty minutes outside of Hoima, a modest town in the foothills of the Rwenzori Mountains on Uganda's western border. A large grassy sports field fronted the school's long, white one-story buildings with classrooms of concrete floors, open doors and windows, and corrugated metal roofs. The children "would run outside and fall down, then roll, and come back into the classroom," Mugisa said. They appeared to be possessed, he said. He sighed deeply, adding that "some would make sounds you couldn't understand." These were not pranks or attempts to cut class, he said. It was witch doctors at work.

I had been drawn to Hoima by a news story about demons attacking children in a school. I had scoffed at the claim, which drew the consternation of several Ugandan colleagues who insisted that it was quite possible. I was in the newsroom of Uganda Radio Network, the start-up news agency where I worked that was funded by a group of European countries. The purpose of the agency was to provide an alternative source of news for Ugandan radio stations in advance of the 2006 presidential and parliamentary elections. I went to Hoima with Sam Gummah, a veteran Ugandan radio journalist who headed the agency and who had first taken me to Gulu. The weather was comfortably warm and sunny, typical of these foothills where sugarcane and tea plantations thrive. At the school we drew curious stares from youthful eyes distracted from the lessons of the day. Mugisa ushered us into the closet-sized office of deputy headmaster Eston Kahwa.

I was incredulous, I said, that they could claim evil spirits were attacking their students and driving them away. They looked at me sympathetically.

Most of the residents in this area are illiterate and eke out a meager living by growing onions, Mugisa said. They are very superstitious and believe deeply in witchcraft. "They think they cannot survive without their [fetishes]," he said, handmade objects that most carry in their pockets for protection against evil spirits. The demon problem only worsened an already serious absentee problem caused by other social ills such as rape and incest, which are "very common."

After some investigating, Mugisa and Kahwa found that the ownership of the school's land was disputed. A couple of local families were fighting over it. "The people in the region have their differences," Kahwa said, and one family resented that its land had been used for a school. The family had hired a witch doctor to send demons into the school and torment the children, he said. This, the family believed, would drive the children away. Once the school was abandoned, they could reclaim it.

Mugisa and Kahwa visited the witch doctor and found drums, rattles, animal skins, carved figures, and fetishes—the standard paraphernalia used to summon demons and cast spells. They asked the man to stop. Their appeal fell on deaf ears, Mugisa lamented, and the demon problem persisted.

Of the 380 students who normally attended, more than half had been pulled out of the school by their parents. Daily attendance was down to about 180 in grades one through seven. "The parents are not comfortable" leaving their children in the school, he said, and the teachers could do little about it. Even the local police got involved, ordering the parents to send their children to school, but with little effect. The repeated strange events troubled the teachers. Those who formerly would spend the night at the school to protect it from theft had refused to do so, also fearing the spirits.

They decided to fight back in another way. "There's a charismatic group that prays here," Mugisa said. It was approached along with other Christian groups and asked to participate in all-night prayer sessions intended to drive away the demons. Prayer was only one tactic. The teachers were convinced that the spirits inhabited a tree behind the school as well as a nearby mound of termites, commonly called white ants. One weekend the teachers and their friends knocked down the termite mound, which was some six feet high and just as wide, doused it with gasoline, and burned it. The tree was cut down because the possessed students would run to it and throw themselves against it, Mugisa said, as if compelled by an unseen power. We went outside to look. The tree had been crudely hacked and lay on the ground, felled like an innocent victim of mysterious and cruel forces. The termite mound was exposed, its honeycombed cells and passageways charred.

As a teacher of science, how did Mugisa explain such things?

He shrugged and struggled for an answer. He had grown up in a society rooted in animistic beliefs handed down from one generation to the next since the dawn of time. Yet he was a rational man, educated according to a system that looked at empirical evidence to extract an explanation. Because he and others at the school had witnessed this phenomenon at least twenty times, the most recent occurring a week earlier, they all wrestled for answers.

"It is external," he offered. "An environmental disturbance. There must be an influence. It is like somebody having epilepsy." But the what and how of these events were elusive. "When a child is attacked by that thing, we pray for them," Mugisa confessed, being left with no alternative. "It takes a long time for them to recover." Mugisa and Kahwa feared that some child would eventually be badly injured or killed. If that happened, the already tense situation would deteriorate. "It will spark community violence," Kahwa said, as families would take matters into their own hands and exact revenge.

As we left the school, my skepticism was shaken. Had I encountered the inexplicable, witnessed evidence of the supernatural? As tempting as it was to dismiss all of this as the vestiges of primordial thinking, I reminded myself that, despite the Western world's reliance on science and technology, the spirit world lingers in the darkened attics of our consciousness. Shakespeare's plays are riddled with witches and ghosts. The French burned Joan of Arc for being a witch, and Salem, Massachusetts, had famously torched them. The award-winning film *The Exorcist*, based on a true story, one of the most successful movies ever, had gripped the country just a couple of decades earlier. The Catholic Church maintains its rites of exorcism. Mysticism, mediums, and the occult in film and literature remain as popular as ever. Gummah was similarly affected. At the small cantina near the school, he arranged for several cases of soda to be delivered to the teachers as small recompense.

I had arrived in Africa with an image of witch doctors as cartoon characters: scantily clad, bone-in-nose men, clutching spears as they jumped around a boiling cauldron containing some mustachioed adventurer wearing a pith helmet. About a month later, as I settled into Kampala, I read of a woman who had been stoned to death in the southern Ugandan town of Masaka. She had been labeled a witch. I asked about it and similar events that occurred with surprising regularity and was eventually able to piece together a picture of modern-day witch doctors.

The stigma of being deemed a witch is usually the work of a local witch doctor—the "doctor" who solves your witch problem. In reality witch doctors are those to whom one goes for counseling and advice or to be cured of ailments—disease, distress, infertility—or to catch a glimpse of the future. Typically a witch doctor consults with the client's ancestors, acting as a spirit medium. The spirits are not only dead relatives; they can be ancient spirits or even the spirits of foreigners who act much like missionaries or aid workers of the netherworld. Once consulted, normally at an exorbitant cost, the witch doctor, either a man or a woman, announces the solution. The source of the ailment or problem is most often a secret enemy or a local witch who has cast a spell on the victim-client. The cure for a physical ailment can be as simple as an herbal remedy or a magic potion. Or it might require removing an evil spell, conjuring another spirit to fight the evil, or even killing the alleged witch causing the problem. Of course nobody wants a working witch in their neighborhood. Being labeled a witch by a credible witch doctor means certain death. In cases where a witch is not the cause, a sacrifice has to be made to appease a spirit that has been angered because of something bad that the client has done. This sacrifice can be simple, such as a gift of food or money, or as extreme as a human sacrifice, even a young child. Occasionally stories surface of the arrest of people suspected of having killed a child at the behest of a witch doctor to appease spirits.

Christian theology incorporates aspects of the occult into its doctrines and relies on mysticism, miracles, and unquestioning faith. But this is something different. What I saw in Uganda were two seemingly contradictory belief systems, animism and Christianity, blended much like oil and water. The term *animism* comes from the Latin *anima*, meaning "soul." It is a broad label that includes the belief that the world is filled with spirits that exist in and of themselves, separate from bodies, just as the Western world describes ghosts. These spirits are entities of good and evil and are taken very seriously. Anyone who can manipulate these spirits is feared.

The ability to make use of these two belief systems is no more apparent than with Joseph Kony and his Lord's Resistance Army. The so-called spiritual beliefs of the LRA were derived largely from Alice Lakwena's Holy Spirit Movement, which was nearly a religion of itself. The practices and beliefs of Lakwena's group had originated, ironically, to counter the widespread practice of witchcraft, which she and others thought was the root cause of the Acholi problems. As Heike Behrend explained in *Alice Lakwena and the Holy Spirits,* the Acholi believe that when a person is killed violently, as in battle, the angry and wounded spirit lingers, seeking revenge. This is like the Western idea of ghosts, said to be spirits of people who die in unexpected and violent ways and likewise remain trapped in this world. In the Acholi language, these spirits are called *cen* (pronounced "tchen"). The Acholi have long been warriors and have created a lot of angry *cen* who are dangerous and can be used against the Acholi.

Much of Lakwena's bizarre practices were about cleansing the Acholi of their past and protecting them against the *cen*. Lakwena insisted that all of her fighters go through an elaborate purification ceremony that also protected them in battle. It began with an initiation. As Behrend says, "The [UPDA] were purified with consecrated water; if they refused to join the Holy Spirit Movement, they were chopped to pieces with a *panga* [machete]."[1] This was an eerie precursor to the practice of Kony's LRA fighters, who brutally killed anyone who refused to go along with them or tried to escape. It was also the human version of a symbolic practice that Behrend describes in which they smashed little clay figurines that represented the vicious *cen* that Lakwena wanted to destroy.

Lakwena developed bizarre rules of engagement largely based on spiritual and animistic beliefs. Soldiers could not take cover when attacked, nor could they hide behind termite mounds or trees. They had been told the Lord was their protection. Behrend states, "They had to face the enemy standing erect and with naked torso. Nor were they to remain silent, but [were] to sing hymns for ten, fifteen, thirty, or forty-five minutes, as directed by the spirit."[2]

Lakwena's soldiers also were not allowed to aim their rifles. Instead, they were told that spirits would guide the bullets and would decide who would die. This way the soldiers could not be blamed for killing or creating more *cen* and therefore could remain pure. The night before battles, Lakwena selected a certain number of soldiers for the battle, only some of whom would get rifles and a limited amount of ammunition. The soldiers then were "loaded" with the Holy Spirit before each battle by "technicians," or ritual experts. The rituals used model guns made of wire that were coated with powders and burned, then waved over the heads of the soldiers. This was done to make them immune to the enemy's weapons. The soldiers were then sprinkled with holy water. The morning of a battle, they were anointed with a mixture of shea butter and ocher to make them bulletproof. Once anointed, the soldiers were not allowed to cover their torsos or to sit or kneel. They were led to the battlefield and settled into position, and then they began to sing. A timekeeper would blow a whistle, and the soldiers would start marching forward, shouting "James Bond! James Bond!" This summoned the spirit of the movement's chief technician, who called himself James Bond after Ian Fleming's fictional and seemingly invincible British secret agent.

The soldiers were preceded by "stone commanders" who carried rocks wrapped in cloth, which were called "grenades" and were thrown toward the enemy. These stones represented the point beyond which the enemy bullets supposedly could not pass and beyond which the attacking soldiers were not allowed to go until the stones were moved forward again. Behind the stone commanders were "controllers" who carried about five liters of holy water that they sprinkled ahead of the troops, intended to confuse the enemy and protect the soldiers.[3]

Behrend pointed out that, as much as Lakwena had wanted to rid the Acholi of witchcraft, she only deepened the practice:

> And, although Alice fought against witchcraft and sorcery like the Christian missionaries, she introduced a process of remagnification, thus in the end entrenching what she combated. Her interpretation of Christian teaching clung to the magical, and her discourse did not effect any truly radical epistemological break that would have put an end to witchcraft. Even if she was able to purify the Holy Spirit Movement of witchcraft internally, she reapplied the idiom of witchcraft in her outward struggle against the [National Resistance Army].[4]

Traveling around Uganda, I relied on the knowledge and goodwill of several different drivers, including Sergeant Eddie, whom I mentioned previously. He is a veteran of dozens of battles with Lakwena's forces and other rebel groups and was wounded twice, prompting him to give up soldiering and take up driving. He said Lakwena sent letters to the army commanders via messengers that detailed when and where battles would take place. The government soldiers heard the forces singing long before they saw them. They charged by running straight up, disregarding the hail of bullets they faced, often overrunning the army's positions. Lakwena's forces inflicted heavy casualties. During each encounter, some twenty to thirty government soldiers were killed, he said, yet the army kept the casualty count secret. The dead were collected from the battlefield in the evening, loaded into trucks, then taken under the cover of darkness to mass graves.

Kony incorporated much of Lakwena's spiritualized battle techniques and also a belief system that, like Lakwena's, seemed to distance him from his Acholi and pre-Christian past, masking it under a Christian pretext. Kony adopted the Judeo-Christian codex of the Ten Commandments as the moral guide for his rebels and further attempted to Christianize his force by calling it the "Lord's" army. If the fighters believed strongly enough, the commandments would protect them from harm, as if the commandments worked like protective spirits. One former child soldier with the LRA, John Otto, told me in late 2005 about the protection he had been afforded by the Ten Commandments, which were printed on a card that he had been given by his unit commander.

In another case, a former LRA rebel, George Abedo, described to a Kampala court how he had been trained by the LRA. "They were training us how to fight and they told us that the kind of military training we underwent, we don't lie down, but just fire bullets while standing," Abedo said. "The leader who was training us was Kony himself."[5]

Although Lakwena's movement was overtly spiritual, it became political out of the necessity to fight the "evil" that had taken over Uganda, namely Museveni's National Resistance Army. Likewise, Kony's army had a dual political-spiritual purpose, as Abedo further explained. "They told us that we had to fight to overthrow the government. It is Kony himself who told us that."[6]

I spoke with Lakwena by phone on two successive days in mid-April 2006—nine months before she died—from the Ito refugee camp in northern Kenya, where she lived in exile with some fifty followers since the defeat of her army. She had been in periodic talks with the government about returning to northern Uganda. The government, apparently, no longer considered Lakwena a serious threat and saw her return as an opportunity to extend an olive branch of peace to the north. But Lakwena placed demands on her return that the government refused to grant, among them the replacement of three thousand head of cattle that she claimed Museveni's soldiers had killed and/or stolen from her. She also wanted an estimated $150,000 as compensation for her homes in Opit that had been destroyed. According to one report, the government had already given her $50,000 and refused to provide anything more.

During our conversations, Lakwena easily became excited and spoke in heavily accented, colloquial English, often shouting incomprehensibly. When I asked why she wanted to return, she became indignant. "It is my native land," she wailed. "I want to go home. I am so much worried that I must go home. If they will give me my money, I will come back tomorrow. I am coming together with them," she said of her followers. "We're going [back] together. I cannot live in this remote area." Ever the high priestess of her movement, she claimed her return to Uganda had been prophesied. "It is a word that God has confirmed," she said.

Lakwena claimed she had been working on behalf of good and had developed a cure for AIDS. She had given up her violent ways, vowing that she was no longer interested in "shooting people" as she had done in the past. She scoffed when I asked if she worried about being killed or kidnapped by Kony and his LRA. She had no idea where he was and didn't seem to care.

"If he comes to attack me at war [sic], I will know that he is there. But if he won't disturb me, I will not know. Who can bother me? Kony? No, no, no, no. I am a commander. I was there at the beginning. He will not disturb me." She refused to speculate why Kony had been able to fight his war for twenty years when she had been defeated in less than a year. "Don't ask me about Kony," she said. She ultimately did return, however, but in body only, with the help of the Ugandan government.

Kony is said to have been a very good witch doctor. Whatever one thinks of his army and its tactics, Kony obviously thoroughly understands and can effectively manipulate the Acholi's profound beliefs in mysticism, the spirit world, and witch doctors. I soon learned that I had only scratched the surface of this exceedingly frightening world.

Father Fraser told me of a colleague, Father Joseph Russo, another Comboni missionary, perhaps the world's leading expert on witch doctors. I tracked him down at the Comboni Fathers' House in Ngetta, just outside Lira. Russo had come to northern Uganda from his native Italy in 1947 after making an arduous trip up the Nile River. Arriving in Lira, he found meager facilities. If the area was to have a church, he had to build it, which he did from the ground up. Almost thirty years later, in 1974, he decided to focus on what he considered to be one of the greatest evils affecting the people in his parish. He began to convert witch doctors to Christianity. Largely successful, he claimed to have converted nearly five hundred practicing witch doctors throughout the north. At the time we met, Russo was eighty-seven years old, an energetic and enthusiastic priest with an infectious smile, a hearty laugh, and a thick white goatee.

"It is not easy to change the mind of someone trained to be a liar and a thief," he said, articulating his deep disdain for witch doctors. He opened a thick file of published reports of killings and deaths linked to witch doctors. It was gruesome stuff: beheadings, mutilations, even cannibalism of exhumed corpses.

His first convert was a woman whose children he had been teaching in his catechism class. He repeatedly confronted the woman about her witchcraft, telling her she had to give it up. Eventually she agreed.

"It was shocking," Russo said. "Every conversion is a miracle."

That conversion led to others, and soon Russo conducted public gatherings where the witch doctors burned their fetishes and spiritual objects "to show people these [were] not objects to be afraid of." One of the most feared concoctions was a *kifaro,* an assembly of goat horns—a truly ugly, demonic artifice. Over the years, Russo collected an amazing array of witch doctor accoutrements, including black-haired wigs, leopard skins, gourd rattles, spears, and dozens of other objects and fetishes that supposedly harbor spirits. Russo happily demonstrated the techniques he had learned from his converts by picking up a gourd rattle, shaking it, and groaning "*Ooo-maaarrr-aaah,*" the traditional chant to summon Omara, the animistic god of evil.

Witch doctors work hard to perpetuate belief in their spiritual powers and the powers of their objects, Russo said. It is vital to their economic survival. The potential loss of income is the main reason most witch doctors refuse to convert. Russo called witch doctoring a criminal enterprise because poor people are swindled and innocent people are killed after being labeled a witch, or *ajok,* in Luo.

"An *ajok* is a killer, in the minds of the people," he said. Many people spend an inordinate amount of time worrying about evil spirits, often to the point of obsession. Russo explained the thought process as "I must try to keep [the spirits] quiet, even give them my child." Every family has an *abila,* a small and sacred place that houses the ancestors' spirits. Families pay homage at the *abila* by leaving food and drink, including booze. It is a place to consult with deceased family members, grandparents, and revered relatives, but it can also be dangerous. The ancestors might be demanding or easily angered. If they are not properly appeased, they can bring trouble, even disease and death.

Russo described instances of human sacrifices to appease evil spirits or *cen,* including beheadings and mutilation of sexual organs. Often these acts are committed after a witch doctor convinces his or her client that he or she has no other choice. But a witch doctor is nothing more than a classic con artist, a conclusion Russo drew from the confessions of hundreds of converts. He showed me a photo of a naked man standing in front of a witch doctor's hut, waiting to be summoned inside. Is this man being rational? Russo asked. Anyone willing to pay money to strip naked, crawl inside a dark mud hut, and listen to a witch doctor pretend to be a spirit medium will be vulnerable to anything, mentally and physically.

"They are ready to be a slave," he said, to a witch doctor's demands. Though it is natural for people to seek counsel in times of trouble, at such moments people are distraught and susceptible and, as such, have to be handled carefully. "Your emotions are alive, you are not yourself," Russo said. "You are like a child." Witch doctors take advantage of this and put on a show. "It's up to the witch doctors to make things as fearful as possible so they can get what they want. They change their voices . . . and people believe it is that of the spirits." The witch doctors then "ask for money or whatever it is that they want." And people pay dearly. "People are afraid of showing they have no money," otherwise, "[the witch doctor] will kill you."

The enabling idea behind this highly successful enterprise, Russo noted, is that "when anything happens, people don't ask why it has happened, but 'Who has done this?'" Witch doctors eagerly provide answers. "When something bad happens, there is somebody responsible. If you get rid of him or her, then it will be OK." If the cause of the problem is a witch, "they will die terribly," and the prestige of the identifying witch doctor is enhanced. The fees increase. "All this business with witchcraft is covered up with secrecy," Russo said. "I haven't found a single one who says, 'I wanted to become a witch doctor.' They're all initiated," and must swear an oath not to reveal the techniques. "It's like a secret society. They'll never tell the truth." They play on the fact that among uneducated and emotional people it is easier to blame someone rather than something or an unknown or mysterious scientific process.

"The unknown is very attractive," Russo said, and if someone convinces another that he or she has penetrated the unknown and is able to use such unseen forces, such powers are worth something. Russo speculated that the belief in spirits and witchcraft is rooted in the communal nature of African society. On a continent of dense forests and jungles, of sprawling deserts and ferocious animals, reliance on one another is the key to survival. When good things happen, it is because of other people. Likewise, when bad things happen, it is because of other people. That much of Africa remained isolated from the rest of the world for so long kept the societies insulated from new ways of looking at and explaining the world. Russo was convinced that it would take generations for such deeply rooted beliefs to change.

Angella Polino was Father Russo's most important convert. Polino had been a witch doctor for twenty-two of his fifty-five years, and he had been the personal witch doctor to Tito Okello, the Acholi general who was the only Acholi ever to rule Uganda. After participating in the military coup that forced Milton Obote out of office in 1985, Okello was put at the helm of government. But his rule lasted less than a year, as he was forced out of office by Yoweri Museveni's National Resistance Army in January 1986.

In 1968, when still a teenager, Polino apprenticed to be a witch doctor after he fell ill. When he first became sick, his parents suggested he go to a hospital, but instead he visited a witch doctor named Rogolina Abongo.

Her diagnosis was that he "had spirits of his ancestors in him who were disturbing his brain," Polino said. The only way to be cured was to become a witch doctor himself, she told him. "I knew it was a lie," Polino told me as we talked under a shady tree in Lira. But nonetheless he agreed to study with the witch doctor, and so his work began. She showed him tricks to get money out of clients. Much of it was theatrics that included voice and facial feature changes, he said, and Polino demonstrated by groaning out the word *o-mar-a* just as Father Russo had. "It's like he [the god] talks to the client," he explained.

Polino detested his former profession. Even though witch doctors don't directly kill people, "they create a situation that results in death." When a person visits a witch doctor, the first question is "Do you have anyone in the family or a neighbor who hates you?" The answer tells the witch doctor what to recommend. "After a ceremony, he tells the client to kill another person." The cause of the trouble is always who, Polino affirmed, and never what. "When the answer of who comes in, it creates a lot of problems in a family."

Polino grew rich as a witch doctor. His fees started at only about three dollars, but after the first consultation, his fees went up dramatically. Depending on the services provided, the payment could be as small as a goat or as large as a bull, which was worth hundreds of dollars. This was nearly twenty years ago and was a hefty fee in a country where the current average income is only fifty dollars a month. At one point in his career, Polino proudly possessed 70 cows, 210 goats, 800 chickens, a car, a motorcycle, and a big house, and he had six wives. Somewhat wistfully, he said that he lost his car when rebels burned it, and that five of his six wives were killed. He married his current wife in a church after he converted.

Polino became President Okello's personal witch doctor quite by accident. In the early 1980s, Polino had moved to Kampala and plied his trade near an army barracks. The soldiers wanted protection from bullets, so he would put them through elaborate rituals. He had soldiers stand in the steaming water of a large cauldron placed over a fire for twenty or thirty minutes. As he gained the confidence of the soldiers, his clientele came from higher and higher ranks until he was eventually recommended to Okello. Though a general and the president, Okello knew he had a tenuous grasp on the reins of government.

"He thought someone from the outside would overthrow the government," Polino said.

So he provided Okello with magic powders to ward off evil spirits and protect him from assassination. Polino said he was one of six witch doctors employed by Okello. He didn't mind competition because most of the cabinet ministers and other generals also sought him out, purchasing herbal potions that he concocted "to strengthen their power and to increase their rank."

Polino became adept at manipulating a client's mental state by using a drug that he suspects was a mild poison that caused temporary disorientation. He would dab it on a person's forehead. "You don't know what is happening. It would confuse you for about ten minutes. When you regain your senses, everything seems different." There are several different names for the drug, depending on the country it comes from, but generally it consists of crushed and dried herbs, bark, and the pulverized ribs of a crocodile. It was his most popular potion.

Polino was at the height of his trade when Lakwena waged her war against the government. I asked him about the witch doctors whom she recruited as "technicians" to conduct the cleansing rituals and as "controllers" who sprinkled holy water ahead of the attacking soldiers. He shook his head at the thought. In reality, he said, these practices were "meant to give the followers courage." Polino doubted that Lakwena or Kony truly had anything spiritual in mind with their movements and were only interested in power and wealth. The rest was all for show. "They wanted things for survival," he said.

In 1990, several years after Lakwena left the country, Polino met Father Russo. It was not a pleasant encounter. Polino had been losing business because of Russo, and when Russo came around telling him to convert, Polino grabbed one of his ornate spears and threatened to kill him. But subsequent meetings were not so dramatic. Polino asked Russo, "What if I drop this business? How can I take care of my family?"

Russo responded simply, "God will take care of you." Despite a very successful career as a witch doctor, Polino gave it up. "One day I burned down my shrine," the *abila,* and he joined Russo's work.

Polino was adamant that Joseph Kony used witchcraft to maintain his power. "Witchcraft is all about death," he said. "You have to kill. [Witchcraft] is meant to kill, rob, tell lies, and get rich in ways that [are] not proper. If you want respect as a witch doctor, you have to be a killer. Otherwise no one fears you. Joseph Kony is a killer. That kind of culture is deeply rooted," he said. "[The Acholi] have a strong belief in it. If the LRA abducts people, they don't want them to escape," and so convince them of Kony's powers.

What should be done with Kony?

"Killing him would be an immediate solution," he said, but he didn't want that. Rather, nature should be allowed to take its course. "No one is above God," he said. "Sometime he [Kony] is going to die. That is what can stop him."

Doing nothing would allow the LRA to commit more atrocities, I suggested.

Polino shrugged and told me that Father Russo had talked with Kony by phone just a few months earlier, in late 2005. Russo had pleaded with Kony to stop. What did Kony reply? "He said his spirit will live on for one hundred years," even after his death.

Did Polino think Kony believed in his own immortality?

Polino shrugged again, and let Kony's response speak for itself.

After meeting with Russo and Polino, I felt as if they were winning their undeclared war against witchcraft. Yet the spirit world is as real in most people's minds as the rising and setting of the sun. It provides a strong subtext for life in Uganda, a psychological framework for a perplexing and changing world. When I joked about it with Ugandan friends, they assured me that everyone uses witch doctors, from the lowliest goat herder to the presidents and prime ministers throughout sub-Saharan Africa.

Not long after I met with Russo, he died tragically in a single-car accident. He was returning from Gulu where he had spent a week preparing for yet more encounters with the purveyors of witchcraft.

Had it been the work of witches or demons—the work of vengeful witch doctors? I did not ask because I already knew what the answer would be. Any lingering doubts I had about the pervasiveness of witchcraft were soon obliterated.

The spring of 2006 in central and northern Uganda was exceptionally dry. The annual dry season usually begins in December, and it most often ends by March or April. But it was already late May, and in some parts of the country, the rain had not come. People were on edge. And no wonder. Uganda depends on agriculture and domestic animals. Rain is vital. The area around Lira was particularly parched. I returned there after our news agency reported that a woman had barely escaped being buried alive. Villagers had accused her of being a witch who had stopped the rain.

By the time I got to Lira, however, we were splashing through puddles in the potholed roads, and pregnant gray and white clouds gathered most afternoons to dump furious downpours that materialized out of the crystalline blue skies of morning. The humidity verged on oppressive until the rains cooled and cleared the air with the crackle and flash of lightning, gusting winds, and the rumble of distant thunder.

It was midmorning, and the sun was high and hot as I arrived in the village of Acero, some ten miles west of Lira. The town is little more than a smattering of conical-roofed huts clustered in occasional clearings along muddy ruts that snake through the bush for about a quarter mile. There I found Alfonso Opio, a local teacher whose hair and mustache were speckled with white. Clad in a well-worn shirt, rolled-up trousers, and rubber sandals, he confirmed that the woman who had nearly been killed for stopping the rain had lived close by.

The situation got out of hand because of persistent rumors that the woman was a practicing witch, he said. For weeks the clouds amassed each day, and the skies darkened, but no rain fell. Finally, locals gathered to complain to the village leader. Suspicious villagers formed a delegation that went to the woman's hut, where they found herbs associated with witchcraft, Opio said. In addition, the woman had a knot of dried grass tied to her leg, yet another sign of witchcraft, and this sealed her fate.

Opio shook his head and said she was not a witch. The woman was often sick with diarrhea and kept herbs that she chewed for medicine. Her name was Albina Akai, and she was forty-eight years old. He escorted me down a path through the brush to a small cluster of mud-and-grass huts where she had lived beside her sister, Jenty Achola, age fifty-one, and her brother-in-law, Celestino Otyang, sixty-two. They had little to say, except to deny that the woman was a witch. They had clearly been frightened by the event.

The delegation members told a different story, which the local officials related as we sat on boards balanced on rocks in the dark and dust of the mud-and-brick structure that served as the village office. Among the investigators had been Patrick Oketch, the local police official. He claimed that Albina had often been seen naked, exposing her butt to the sky "whenever the clouds would gather." These reports upset the community, said local chairman Peter Aboi, and they hounded him with complaints that she was blocking the rain. Having just been elected, Aboi wanted to prove his worth and called a community meeting. Hundreds of people attended. He tried to manage the meeting with civility by allowing people to air their complaints and present evidence.

"I confirmed that whenever the clouds would gather, they would [soon] disperse," without dropping rain, he said, but there were more accusations. "She wanted to disturb people because she was barren" was the general consensus, he said. She was accused of making men impotent and making women sick. Some in the crowd, such as Bernard Omodi, age twenty-four, were already convinced and began digging her grave on the spot. Surrounded by an increasingly hostile crowd, Albina broke down. "She confessed she was doing it," Aboi said, and she agreed to leave the community. Aboi accepted her offer, but he warned her that "if she returned, I would order the people to have her killed." But the crowd demanded immediate satisfaction, and Aboi realized they would kill her. He snatched her from the crowd, grabbed a friend's bicycle, and rode her to the local police station for protection. "I saved her life." Albina had not been seen since.

I sat in silence as the story ended. Did Aboi *really* think that a woman like Albina could stop the rain from falling?

He shrugged.

Did he and the others really think that killing her would solve the problem?

He looked at me, then nodded, explaining that the community had demanded action.

Was he a Christian? I asked.

He laughed, as if the question were absurd. Of course.

Wasn't the weather, including the rain or lack of it, the work of God?

He nodded again. "God does bring the rain, but there are also people responsible for blocking the rain," he said. Rounding up Albina and banishing her from the village were justified because "on the day she was evicted from here, it started to rain. Many people are happy with me."

6

A Game of Blood and Spiritualism

THE VILLAGE OF KANUNGU is nestled in the hills of southwestern Uganda, a place of spectacular scenery. Graveled roads cut across slopes covered with thick tangles of jungle. Lake Edward shimmers in the distance, a silver platter against hazy emerald mountains. The lake is among several astride the Great Rift Valley, the colossal continental fracture that winds its way up the eastern third of Africa, from Mozambique to Egypt. To the south lie active volcanoes, now quiet, as if catching a breath before the next eruption. To the west is the restive Congo, to the north the scorching horrors of Sudan and the Sahara, and far beyond the obscure eastern horizon spread the grasslands of the Serengeti Plain and the melting snows of Mount Kilimanjaro. This is the crux of the world.

Once little more than a remote enclave carved out of the surrounding jungle, Kanungu is now a district capital. Uncluttered and proud of its few new buildings due to the recent government construction, the town profits from the trickle of tourists on their way to track the endangered mountain gorillas in the nearby Bwindi Impenetrable National Park.

But in 2000, a grim pallor hung over the village as investigators sifted through the charred debris at the site of one of the world's worst cult mass murders. Details remain vague as to the exact number who died, but best guesses are that it was about eight hundred, many of them children, and all members of a Christian cult called the Movement for the Restoration of the Ten Commandments of God.

Like Kony's marauding rebels, the movement professed strict adherence to the Ten Commandments. It had been created by Cledonia Mwerinde, a former Kanungu barmaid and reputed prostitute who, like Kony, announced she had had a vision. Mwerinde claimed she had been visited by the Virgin Mary and that it had brought a profound reversal in her life. She became a devout Christian. In the late 1980s, however, apparently chafing under the restrictions of the Catholic Church, she joined forces with a charismatic but defrocked Catholic priest named Joseph Kibwetere and the cult came into being. Like all churches, it survived on donations. But Mwerinde and Kibwetere demanded more than most. The pair required cult members to donate all of their earthly belongings to the movement.

By the early 1990s, the cult had established itself on Mwerinde's family property, a grassy and prominent knoll at the outskirts of Kanungu. Over the next decade the group constructed a secretive compound that included a church, a school, administrative offices, a private chapel, and living quarters for its hundreds of adherents. They lived an austere life of prayer and farm labor, but, most important, they prepared for the end of the world. Mwerinde had predicted it would come with the new millennium at the stroke of midnight, December 31, 1999. When the millennium passed uneventfully and the world continued just as it always had, church members began to grumble. They challenged the validity of the church and demanded their money and possessions back. Mwerinde conceded that she may have been mistaken on the precise date of the world's final demise and kept pushing the end deeper into the new year.

Finally, on March 17, 2000, she gathered some four to five hundred devotees in the church, which had been boarded shut and loaded with canisters of petroleum and acid. Candles were lighted as part of a final service in which her followers were to ascend into heaven, and the deadly explosive mixture was ignited. Everyone died.

At first investigators thought it was a mass suicide akin to the infamous 1978 incident in which 913 members of the California-based Peoples Temple community drank poison in the South American jungle enclave of Jonestown, Guyana. But as the investigation broadened and mass graves were unearthed at the homes of the movement's leaders in several other cities, the picture of a calculated cult murder came into focus. Among the cult leaders was Dominic Kataribabo, sixty-four years old, also a defrocked priest, under whose bedroom and garden some 150 bodies were found. Neither Mwerinde nor Kibwetere, who also was in his sixties at the time, was found. Some speculate they were both killed; others claim that Mwerinde fled to the Congo with Kataribabo and the congregation's money.

The day was gray and overcast when I visited the cult compound in Kanungu. An eerie silence hung over the lush green valley. Tall eucalyptus trees draped with vines climbed the steep hillsides. The silence was broken by the occasional clank of a cowbell, the cry of goats, and the shouts of children kicking a raggedy soccer ball. Residents of Kanungu were understandably reluctant to discuss the horrifying event that had brought a clamoring and questioning world to their doorstep.

But Charles Mukuru, thirty-five, remembered it. I met Mukuru at the local motorcycle taxi stand where I had asked for directions to the cult compound. He volunteered to guide me. After a short drive from the town center, we walked down an overgrown gravel road, balanced on the remains of a log bridge to cross a trickling stream, then climbed the curving road to the compound. Some of the buildings had collapsed, and sections of the metal roofing were gone. A small brick guardhouse strategically overlooked the drive and provided a clear view of any who would approach.

Mukuru took me around to the back of the main building and pointed to a dark pit under the floor. Investigators had discovered it shortly after the fateful fire. Reportedly called Noah's Ark, this was a dungeon where dozens of bodies had been found in various stages of decomposition. Mukuru explained that those who complained and insisted that their property be returned had been given a special "meeting" with the movement's prime executioner, said to have been a former soldier in Idi Amin's army. They were taken into one of several closet-sized rooms and given a can of poisoned soda. The dead bodies were thrown into the basement and doused with acid. These death chambers, one painted a dark red and another dark green, were conveniently within arm's reach of the pit. The bodies soon disappeared.

Our footsteps crackled eerily on the grit covering the floors. The agonizing memories of relatives lost in the deadly conflagration filled the hollow rooms whose walls were covered with searing graffiti scrawled with pieces of charcoal. One read "This is worse than the act[s] of Kony." Another read "Our father and our mother died in this place. Now we are orphans. May God the Lord bless the deceased and may their soul[s] rest in eternal peace."

In another part of the main building, we stepped into what had been Mwerinde's private chapel, the place where she prayed and sup-posedly communed with the Virgin Mary. It was here, Mukuru said, that she had been told when the world would end. I could almost hear her mumbled prayers and her droning voice as she knelt at the altar, which was remarkably undamaged despite six years of disuse.

Outside, we paused at the edge of a small grassy field. Now a place where goats and cows grazed, it was all that remained of the church site where hundreds of adherents had died. The field had been bull-dozed shortly after the incident, creating a mass grave of bone, ash, and dirt.

The road to town was close behind us, and I remarked that the burning church must have been quite visible from town. Like other villagers, Mukuru had heard the explosion that day and had run to the site.

"It was like a bomb," he recalled, as the canisters of petroleum and acid exploded and the church erupted in flames. They could do nothing but watch helplessly. "Even children were burned completely. Everybody [had been] forced to come." He suspected that Mwerinde killed her followers because she could not return their money and possessions. "The leaders didn't have anything to give back."

Most Kanungu residents had long been suspicious of the cult, he said, but had done nothing about it because the church members kept to themselves. They were forbidden to speak aloud on the church grounds or communicate with local townsfolk. Also forbidden was the use of modern medicines, and as a result many children died. Mukuru gestured to the forested hilltop beyond the compound and said it was a graveyard for the church. He recalled hearing the cult members singing funeral hymns at night when they buried their dead.

Very few of the cult members came from Kanungu because residents remembered Mwerinde from the days when she ran a bar selling locally made banana wine and beer, Mukuru said. Few took her visions of the Virgin Mary seriously. It was only after the disaster was revealed that residents began to ask questions. They blamed local government officials for letting the cult flourish. The district governor was accused of taking bribes and turning a blind eye to the cult's activities. The governor was removed from office and now drove a taxi in the next town, Mukunu said.

Although most in Kanungu were still uncomfortable with the stigma that the cult had put on the town, an effort was under way to turn the site into a tourist attraction. "This was the scene of a crime," but the Kanungu city council saw potential in that, said Elias Byamungu, the chief administrative officer for the district. The restoration project would help the community come to grips with the tragedy, he suggested. "It is part of our history. We are trying to incorporate the negative into the positive."

A religious man, he had adorned his office with a large crucifix. I waited as he reviewed his thick case file on the cult before answering any more of my questions. "The place has gone wild," he said, as if the lack of upkeep reflected the community's neglect of its obligations. The scavenged metal roofing from the site had been recovered, and the government planned to restore the compound so it was safe to visit. But nothing tangible had been done because the government was still seeking a clear title to the site, which remained in the hands of the national police as evidence in the case. Though the site was privately owned, he didn't expect trouble from Mwerinde's relatives, who apparently wanted to distance themselves from it all.

Byamungu blamed Mwerinde's cult on poverty and a general lack of education in Uganda but most of all on a fatal fascination with the occult. "The easiest thing to do to attract people is to use magic, spiritualism, and mysticism," he said, and Mwerinde used all of them. He speculated the cult was a cover for devil worship. "Fire is part of [its] business," he said, offering the cult's final inferno as proof. Lifting his hands and shrugging, Byamungu said people are drawn to characters like Mwerinde who claim to have visions. "They assume they can get answers to the unknown." People like Mwerinde and Kony simply convince others that they possess special powers. It's easier than one might think, he said. "It is a game of blood and spiritualism."

A game? I flinched at the thought. But I could not ignore the ring of truth in what Byamungu said. The truth grew like a thick tangle of vines that choked the life out of any naïve notions I had to the contrary. Like Mwerinde's church, Kony's army of the "Lord" was simply a pseudospiritual means to an earthly end: money and power. It certainly was not without precedent. Leaders of the world's organized religions wield wealth and influence, sparking wars. Most leaders of great religions have metastasized across the centuries from humble aspirants into field marshals in the corridors of power.

But if this is only a game of blood and spiritualism, it means that there are no boundaries or demarcations as to what is right or wrong in this corner of the world, only ascendancy and domination or total annihilation. Appeals to the Aristotelian notion of man's highest aspect, the soul, are little more than deceptive sales gimmicks, crude tricks on a street corner that rob the poor of what little they have, even life and limb. Everything and everyone is fair game. And it is all done for the aggrandizement of the hucksters and the silver-tongued preachers. There is no moral center of gravity here, no spiritual compass that one can hold against the horizon to escape the clamor and chaos. The heartfelt prayers, the soaring hymns, the frenzied sermons, mean nothing. Yet the trappings of Christianity are here, the Ten Commandments carved in stone that came crashing down from the mountain in the hands of Moses. By legend they had come directly from God. But here they are uttered, adored, then totally ignored.

Christianity was imported to the African continent by individuals like Dr. David Livingstone, Father Daniel Comboni, whose missionary order I had come to know, and dozens upon dozens of others in all corners of the continent. Their contemporaries inundated Uganda and much of East Africa. I had arrived in Kampala with a planeload of them: well scrubbed, chubby cheeked, sporting T-shirts with religious slogans and rolling out of the American heartland all too eager to dish out buckets of oatmeal and milk to thousands of hungry children.

But Christianity arrived here in the eleventh hour. It was hastily grafted onto the thick and gnarly African tree of life, onto a culture that had taken root as the antediluvian volcanic ash settled on the clefts and crevasses of the continent's Great Rift. Just as I had seen in the

displays at Tanzania's Olduvai Gorge, upright man had left his foot-
prints in the muddy ash millions of years ago as he and his mate
trudged into a dark and dangerous future. The species had thrived in
a world with only one rule: survival.

The Acholi Inn is on the north side of Gulu, just a few blocks from
the heart of town, which is marked by a circular, nonfunctioning
fountain. It is by far the best hotel in town. With slick, white tile floors
and a polished wood reception desk, it attracts the area's elite, visiting dignitaries, aid executives, and foreign correspondents. It was also
where several former officers of the LRA now lived in a gilded cage,
at government expense, monitored by men such as Colonel Charles
Otema, the Ugandan army intelligence chief for the north. It was here
also that I met with three former commanders in the Lord's Resistance
Army who had accepted the government's amnesty program. Each
had been with the LRA for most of the group's twenty bloody years.
Each had held critical positions in the rebel army and had been close
to Kony. They were members of the inner circle, if such a thing
existed. They carried out his directives and gave reality to the organization's ideology and purpose. If anyone knew the inner workings
of the LRA, it would be these men.

We spent an afternoon sitting in the shade sipping sodas and
wrestling with the core issue of the army's existence: Was Kony's
army a heavily armed religious cult caught in a political struggle, or
was it a militia with a political agenda carrying a religious banner? The
answers were more disturbing than I had feared.

Major Jackson Acama

Acama, age forty-four, abandoned the LRA in April 2004, almost two
years prior to the day that we quietly discussed his life among the

cultish rebel army. Jackson had been an elementary school English teacher in the town of Alero, north of Gulu, from 1983 to 1986. After losing his family in a rebel attack, he was taken by the LRA in 1987, seemingly with little resistance.

Acama was articulate and frank. He was also missing most of his right leg, the result of a gunshot he suffered in 1994. He had been with the LRA in southern Sudan at the time, and his leg became infected. He was taken to Juba, and from there the Sudanese government flew him to a hospital in Khartoum, where the leg was amputated. The Islamic Khartoum government provided medical treatment for the LRA routinely, he said. After one particularly difficult battle in Aru, he recalled that some forty-seven rebel soldiers were airlifted out for treatment. "In Sudan there is what they call 'democracy of the gun,'" he said, by way of explaining Sudan's concept of civil society.

"In the beginning, they screened people," he said of the LRA. Able-bodied men and women were kidnapped and assigned duties according to their talents. Acama spent much of his seventeen years with the LRA working closely with Kony. "Joseph Kony talked about two things. First, you should have faith in God. And two, we should overthrow the government."

What kind of a God did he believe in?

"He believes in the Christian God. He follows the Catholic procedures." But as Acama described those in detail, what emerged were practices and terminology borrowed directly from Lakwena's movement. "There is a place where the spirit is," called the "yard," and it is "where God exercises power."

What kind of power?

"When you pray . . . if you want rain to come, you sprinkle water."

I asked Acama if the LRA was a political or spiritual movement.

He unhesitatingly said, "It is a spiritual movement. That is why [Kony] does not accommodate any politicians. He's a pure fundamentalist."

If it was a religious movement, then why did Kony and the LRA commit such crimes?

"Joseph Kony says he's doing exactly what God tells him to do," Acama explained. "When a generation rejects a prophet, then any crime committed against them is not a crime." This was how the LRA justified raiding, stealing, mutilation, and killing. "When the crops are ready, you go and displace people because the food is not theirs." He proudly told me that one Sudanese government official had called the LRA "the true children of God. They were holy." Kony had told them that "those who commit the worst atrocities are the closest to God. The killing is not even a crime. God is passing judgment. God is punishing a generation." The "generation" was the Acholi people, who were being punished because they had rejected Kony, a prophet sent by God who would lead them to glory, establish a government under the rule of the Ten Commandments, and ultimately create a new world order. "He told us several times we should learn many languages" because a time would come when the world would be united under one new religion, presumably Kony's.

Acama drew a parallel to the Old Testament prophets who tried to steer the errant Israelites from their wicked ways. When they refused, they were severely punished. Kony was both prophet and punisher of the Acholi.

"It is just a punishment against them," he said of the rebel atrocities. "Even a newborn baby is part of the [evil] generation. Kony does not care how many people die. He is doing what God tells him to do."

When I pressed Acama about why the Acholi are evil and therefore need to be punished, he simply said, "The Acholi are a very bad tribe." They had been the bulk of Uganda's military forces since independence and were a warrior tribe long before that. "We shed a lot of innocent blood of other people. God is inflicting punishment."

Kony was convinced of his divine mission. "Kony will never give up until people accept him as a prophet, or he is killed."

Acama's claim suggested that efforts to find a peaceful end to the madness were futile.

"The possibility of people negotiating with a prophet is null and void. If Joseph Kony is a prophet as he says, he will never accept peace talks."

Did Acama believe that Kony was a prophet?

Unflinchingly, he said, "Yes."

Acama had been deeply caught up in and blinded by belief that the LRA was, in fact, doing good. But now, two years after being away from the LRA, he was beginning to see it differently.

"When you are with [Kony], you cannot see the bad that is being done. Now I feel bad about what was done." Kony may also be realizing that all is not well with his army, he said, and that was why he had fled to the Democratic Republic of the Congo. Yet those who remained with Kony were convinced of his holiness. "They believe that Kony is a prophet," Acama said. "To wipe out this belief is very difficult."

Lieutenant Colonel Okwango Alero

Alero, now forty-two, began his life as a fighter with the Uganda People's Democratic Army, one of the precursors to the LRA, in 1986. Before that he had been with the Uganda National Liberation Army, which had ousted Idi Amin. In 1996, while living the life of a farmer with his family in the village of Alero, he was abducted during an LRA attack. Because of his military experience, he was assigned to train the newly kidnapped children to become soldiers, and he did so well that he eventually became Kony's security director. As he put it, he was "very close to Kony" and had no doubts that, although the LRA had a political purpose, it was guided by spiritual precepts, not politics. Alero said the fighters were told "the major aim was to fight and overthrow the government, but at the same time, they fight under the Ten Commandments of God." Alero claimed that he did not participate in battles, and neither did Kony. "Kony is a human being. He wants to be alive, so when danger comes, he leaves." He said the LRA is very well organized into standard fighting units such as platoons, brigades, and divisions, but Kony remains in the rear guard because "he is also chairman of the movement." Alero said Kony was generally oblivious to the atrocities committed by his fighters. "Kony is not aware of all the actions, only that troops are deployed."

But at the same time, he explained, cutting off hands, lips, and ears was "a soldier's recognized duty." Such brutality was punishment for resisting or attempting to alert the Ugandan army to the presence of LRA units. "To show [that] making alarm is bad, they cut off arms and lips so that the next time, they will not make [an] alarm." Alero said it is an ancient practice. "Cutting off the hands comes from the use of bow and arrow and spears," he said, because without them, an enemy is rendered incapable of using such weapons. The practice is useful in an era of guns. "The hand is cut off when you do such a thing," he said, like shooting at the LRA.

Alero also doubted that Kony would ever give up. "As long as Joseph Kony is alive, the LRA will continue to exist."

I asked if he truly thought that Kony was possessed by a spirit and took his directions from God.

"It is difficult to know if he talks to God or not," Alero said, but added, "He's not crazy. He's a clever man."

Alero was with the LRA for nearly ten years, and I asked what made him leave.

He sighed and said, "I came out because I saw the suffering of the people."

It took ten years to see that?

When he joined, he said, "the LRA was strong. They are no longer. The movement has weakened" and "lost direction and focus."

Captain Raymond Apere

Also known as the Bishop, Apere was one of Kony's spiritual advisers. He was abducted from his village in 1988 and left behind his life as a farmer, his wife, and three children, who, he said, are now together and living in Kitgum.

"I was a drunkard once," he confessed, and he was dead drunk when the rebels took him. He was thankful to the LRA because he was forced to quit drinking, because they forbid alcohol and tobacco. He also claimed he never had to fight or kill. Rather, his job was managing the LRA's religious affairs and making something he called a "holy spirit drug," a concoction of herbs used for healing.

Apere was intimately aware of how Kony thought and viewed himself and was convinced that he and Kony were part of something cosmic, a movement much larger than the rebel war in northern Uganda. Like Acama, he compared Kony to the prophets of old.

He stated, "History repeats itself, but it cannot be repeated in the same manner. What is happening is the same thing as in the time of Moses. It is difficult for people to accept the presence of a prophet when he is still alive." Moses had wandered in the wilderness for forty years, he said, after he led the Israelites out of Egypt. Similarly, Kony had been wandering a wilderness for twenty years. John the Baptist, who forecast Jesus's coming, was also killed by the ruling powers. "When a prophet comes, they are at loggerheads with the government." Apere said Kony was more like Jesus than Moses because it was only "after Jesus's death [that] they realized his usefulness. He is like Jesus." Again suggesting that Kony was a modern-day messiah, "The movement will not end" after Kony is killed or dies. Instead, it will expand and evolve. The purpose of the army, he said, is to create a new world religion combining elements of Christianity, Islam, and animistic beliefs.

"Everything in the world has its time. [Kony's] time will come to an end. He is like Alice [Lakwena]. [The] time came for her to go. It is the same [with Kony]." Apere's time to leave the LRA had come, he said, because he saw that the "spirit" had left Kony. Like his fellow officers, he began to doubt the validity of the LRA. Apere questioned Kony about the kidnappings, killings, and mutilations, and when he was answered with silence, he feared he would be killed. "For me it was not right. That is why the LRA is being punished," had been losing battles with the Ugandan army, and was being abandoned by its fighters. Kony had warned his commanders that they would know the end was near when he killed some of his own fighters. "So why should I stay inside the punishment?" Apere asked. The tables had turned on the LRA, he said, because "God is inflicting punishment. You will reap what you sow."

Though convinced that punishment was being meted out by God, Apere believed that amnesty was the best way to settle the war because it was Acholi tradition to forgive and forget, no matter how heinous the crime. "You don't [re]pay death by death," he said. "It is the only way to make peace here in Uganda."

Now out of the LRA, Apere helped at one of the reintegration centers for returning child soldiers. "When they see me, they start laughing," because he was a familiar face and they realized they were not going to be summarily killed, as Kony had warned.

Not long after I talked with Acama, Alero, and Apere, they surfaced in an investigation by the *Daily Monitor*, Uganda's leading newspaper, into abuses at a World Bank–funded reintegration project called the Labora Farm. The allegations included slave labor, denial of medical treatment, and sexual abuse. The Labora Farm near Gulu was managed by the Northern Uganda Social Action Fund. The raison d'être was to help returning abductees reintegrate into society through farmwork. It had seemed a model project. Former child soldiers and child brides hand-tilled about fifty acres of government land, growing corn, cassava, beans, and *matooke,* the staple green banana. Heading the farm operation was Kony's notorious former number-three commander, Kenneth Banya. He had collected around him some of his former deputies, including Acama, Alero, and Apere, re-creating something akin to his LRA command. As many as 120 former abductees worked the farm "in slavery conditions," according to the report. Their pay was the promise of food from the harvest, a promise that never materialized.[1]

The investigative story focused on a young farmworker named Denis Okonya, who had lost an eye while fighting as a LRA soldier. "I [w]ould not be allowed to go for treatment even when I once told the commander that my eye was hurting. He shouted at me and told me that I'm giving excuses to dodge work," Okonya said. "I have worked there for months now [but] I have been given nothing. I have decided to leave and try something else."[2] But Okonya complained that he could not leave and was trapped at the farm because he lost both parents in the war. He had nowhere else to go.

Two young women complained of bad treatment and specifically mentioned Alero. "When I tried to take some food home, he [Alero] slashed my polythene bag open and my maize poured in the garden. Alero . . . hurls very obscene insults at us and threatens violence all the time," the woman claimed.

The farm was composed of seven gardens, each headed by an ex-LRA officer, including Acama, Alero, and Apere. Among other abuses uncovered by the report, Acama was said to be living on the farm with the same four wives he had had in the bush. Two were teenage mothers who also worked at Labora. "They want to be with me," Acama said. "Even when one was stolen by her family, she escaped back to me."[3]

Two weeks after the story appeared, the LRA commanders were fired from their roles as managers on Labora Farm, and government officials stated it had nothing to do with the claims of abuse.[4] Now under new management, the farm has been divided into individual plots, and each former LRA abductee grows and sells his or her own produce.

I walked away from Acama, Alero, and Apere that day aghast at what I had heard. I felt paralyzed, my mind wavering between abject horror and gut-wrenching disgust. I felt like I was standing at the edge of a great abyss, about to be sucked into a black hole. I despaired that these men could justify the years of atrocities, convinced that they were acting on the side of good, then insist that amnesty and forgiveness were the only way to have peace.

That evening I stepped across the street and took a table at a patio bar screened from the street. I ordered *waragi,* the Ugandan-made gin, and a warm beer (no electricity most days) with a dinner of roasted chicken and fried potatoes. I watched life pass on the street: schoolgirls in uniforms joking and teasing one another; women with babies bound to their backs and children by the hand, toting black plastic sacks of maize flour; groups of young men joking and jostling; aid workers striding to appointments; and an occasional truck loaded with soldiers. Life went on.

Lakwena, Mwerinde, and Kony professed to follow the Ten Commandments and believe in the Christian God, convinced they were part of a new world order, chosen people guaranteed a special place in heaven. It clearly echoed the rants of suicidal Islamic extremists, also convinced that wanton destruction of themselves and others brought blessings in an afterlife. What drove such deadly human desire to escape from the world? Was it insanity? It was perhaps understandable if one lived a dangerous, difficult, if not morbid, existence, as did much of the Third World. Any alternate reality was better than the real one. When someone came along with glowing eyes and a confident voice, it was easy to believe. Why not? Why not kill and die if you ultimately must anyway? What was there to lose? A world glutted with remorseless killers, maniacal warlords, craven politicians, delusional religious fanatics? In a world bereft of justice, kindness, or honor, any ray of hope was better than none, no matter how ridiculously morbid and demented.

But Kony was not a prophet, nor was his army cleansing the Acholi of their sins, nor was he about to or would he ever topple the Ugandan government. Rather, for twenty years this forlorn region had become a carnival of craven bloodshed with Kony madly working the levers of a merry-go-round of monstrosities. Yet Kony was a man, not a demigod, and he had led an army of boys and men who had carried guns and wielded machetes to work their will. Was Kony invincible?

The Acholi were unwilling and the Ugandan army unable to stop him. But the LRA had been stopped once, stopped dead in its tracks.

7

The Arrow Boys

LEAVING THE TROUBLES OF northern Uganda far behind, my driver
Aziz and I passed thick sugarcane and tea bushes covering the rolling
hills east of Kampala, reminiscent of colonial lifestyles long gone. It
was harvest season, and the chopped cane was piled at road's edge
while the browning foliage was burned, sending smoke skyward. We
came to Jinja, a city built by the British at the headwaters of the Nile.
The search for the Nile's headwaters had generated the term *muzungu,*
applied to most whites. It is a variation of the Swahili word meaning
"dizzy" and describes the early explorers who wandered somewhat
aimlessly around this part of Africa bent on discovering the source of
the Nile. Why that was so important, Africans could only guess.

Past Jinja, the corn stalks stood in the fallow gardens, posing like
bent and wizened stick soldiers. It was also mango season, and the
thick green fruit hung heavily from the robust, leafy trees. The fruit
would sustain the people until the rains arrived, restoring the land and
prompting the next planting season. We rolled past sporadic collec-
tions of buildings made of mortared bricks, some fresh and new, the
plaster emblazoned with bright advertisements for skin lotion, mobile

telephone service, and beer. The buildings here are partitioned into crowded little shops, most selling the same things: pots, pans, paper goods, beverages, or food. The heavy wood or metal doors were flung open, padlocks hanging from forged steel bolts, reminding me of the steel shipping containers converted into shops that line the roads in Afghanistan where I had spent much of 2004. But this was a far cry from the desperation I had seen in Afghanistan and was a testament to the simple prosperity that came with years of peace.

As we approached Mbale, the foothills of Mount Elgon along the eastern border of Uganda emerged from the haze like humped elephants shrouded in dark clouds. We turned through the town, angling along divided streets with median strips of dirt. Mbale was bustling, crowded with walkers and bike riders, the shops filled with dry goods, meats and vegetables, mobile telephones, rubber sandals, and black bags for laptop computers that most people would never own.

This was not my first trip to eastern Uganda. A couple of months earlier I'd ambled through the crusty town of Tororo, known for a stone butte that marked the landscape, its silhouette imprinted on every bag produced at the Tororo cement factory. The predominant tribe of the region, the Iteso, had been pressing President Museveni for their own administrative district and, to show that they were deserving, demonstrated that their culture had survived modernity by eating live rats.

We ate our lunch at one of the town's Indian restaurants, and it was some of the best Indian food I'd eaten anywhere, prepared by an Indian family that was part of Uganda's widespread and prosperous merchant class. At the foot of the concrete steps to the restaurant were about a dozen khat sellers. Khat is a bitter and mildly narcotic plant that grows wild and is among the area's underground exports. The sellers squatted on the sidewalks, hunched over clear plastic bags crammed with the fresh, green leaves that they chewed constantly, along with mint gum to kill the taste. A couple of dollars would buy

(ABOVE) Former child soldiers singing and playing handmade instruments at the World Vision reintegration center in Gulu, Uganda, September 2005.

(LEFT) Woman with child at the Unyama refugee camp outside Gulu.

Three children at Unyama camp near Gulu, Uganda.

Women selling fruit and vegetables by the roadside south of Gulu.

Residents of the Orem village about thirty miles from Lira, Uganda, which was attacked by the LRA. Tom Okeng, wearing Coca-Cola shirt, suffered multiple stab wounds.

The late Father Joseph Russo with staff and other witch doctor paraphernalia at his mission office at Ngetta, outside Lira, Uganda.

Angella Polino, a former witch doctor, standing second from left, with his family, near Lira.

Charles Mukuru stands beside one of the death chambers where cult members in Kanungu, Uganda, were forced to drink poisoned soda.

Opening to the acid pit known as Noah's Ark where Kanungu cult members' bodies were thrown.

A pot seller, Daniel Emora, front, with a friend, stops about twenty miles from Soroti, Uganda. He said he was happy that the local militia defeated the rebels.

Men playing *omweso*, an ancient African board game, in the village of Arasi, about twenty miles from Soroti.

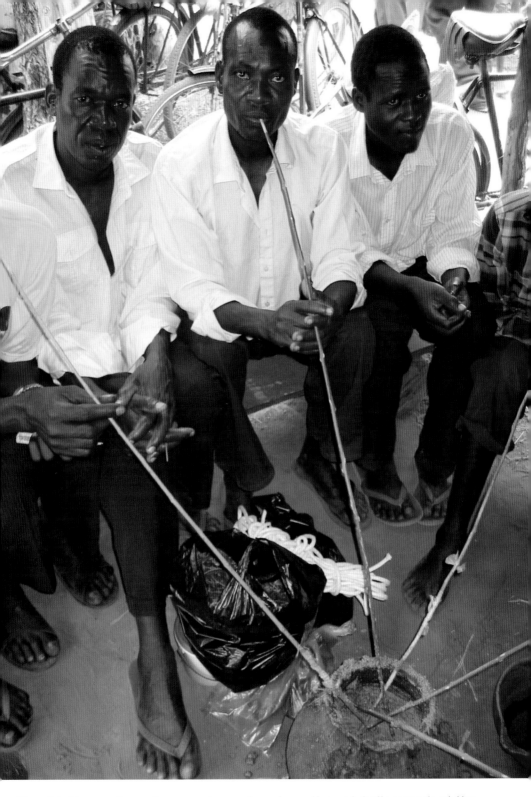

Men drinking *malwa*, a homemade sorghum beer, through hollow reeds at the Arapai market.

(LEFT) Bagging and selling cut and dried cassava root at the Arapai market.

(BELOW) Women selling dried peanuts at the Arapai market.

(ABOVE AND LEFT)
Hutu refugees from Democratic Republic of Congo (DRC) at a camp in Kisoro, Uganda.

Severino Lukoya at his church in Gulu, 2006.

Bullet holes and bloodstains on a pickup truck that was attacked south of Juba, South Sudan, by suspected members of the LRA, July 2006.

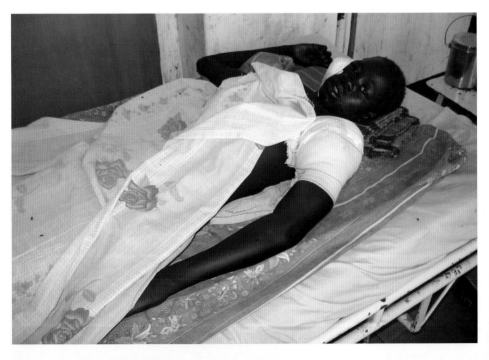

Cecilia Ulum, sixteen, was wounded in the attack.

Paul Agoth, a guard on the truck, returned fire.

Sign along the road in Juba, South Sudan.

Three women near Gumbo village stand at the grave of a friend killed by unknown bandits.

Peter Loting, chief of Gumbo village, about seven miles from Juba, South Sudan.

Villagers at Nabanga, on the border between South Sudan and DRC, standing with a former soldier with the South Sudanese forces, who handed his weapon to the young boy for the photo.

Author with guards on the border of South Sudan and DRC waiting for rebels of the Lord's Resistance Army to arrive for a meeting with Riek Machar. (PHOTO BY MATT BROWN)

Contingent of Lord's Resistance Army rebels, led by deputy commander Vincent Otti, seated, with brown boots, meeting at the DRC and South Sudan border.

Deputy Commander of the Lord's Resistance Army, Vincent Otti, widely reported to have been executed by LRA leader Joseph Kony in October 2007.

Walking through the jungle with LRA rebels, on the border between DRC and South Sudan.

a fat bag of it. One of the sellers gave me a couple of leaves to try. It was an acquired taste.

Beyond Mbale and on the other side of the mountains was Nakapiripirit, a windblown town in southern Karamoja, the lawless lands of the Karamajong. This tribe of notoriously violent cattle rustlers would rather shoot than talk, and their conduct was based on their conviction that any cow on the planet was theirs, regardless of whose corral or field it was in. Also known for disdaining clothes, the Karamajong had swapped their spears and arrows for AK-47s, thousands of which they appropriated from government armories when the Idi Amin regime fell. These same warriors opened fire on an armed convoy protecting President Museveni during his one and only campaign stop in the region.

On my previous trip to this region, I had been traveling with Sam Gummah, and after several hours on bone-jarring roads, we had reached Nakapiripirit, where we'd met with a freelance reporter to discuss stories over bowls of stewed goat and bottles of warm beer. We had eaten in a dirt-floor restaurant with walls of plywood and sticks, the tables covered with worn oilcloth. It wasn't advisable to stay after dark, so we had abandoned the town of brick shops and mud-and-clapboard shacks just as the sun set. As we climbed high into the foothills of Mount Elgon, we had entered a vicious downpour that turned the clay road into a sea of sticky mud. When a couple of hulking dump trucks had suddenly appeared in our headlights, having buried themselves in the sucking ooze, we veered off the road and into axle-deep mud. I had expected a long night in a stuffy car. But a couple of local villagers rapped on our window to offer assistance. After lots of shoving, shouting, racing engines, spinning tires, and dispensing a fistful of cash, we had miraculously found ourselves back on the road.

But this day, however, was clear and sunny, and Aziz and I were in good spirits. Aziz was overjoyed because the gasoline station where we had filled up had been giving away packets of laundry detergent with every purchase. Our fill-up had cost about seventy U.S. dollars, which translated into twenty-eight packets of the stuff. As we rolled along the empty stretches of road, I perused the newspapers to keep up with machinations of the 2006 Ugandan presidential political campaign, which was well under way. The major Kampala newspapers only sporadically mentioned the ongoing catastrophe in the north. For the most part, newspapers reported only announcements from the Ugandan military about the number of LRA rebels killed in the skirmishes across the north or in southern Sudan. There was virtually no coverage of the thousands of people who had lost limbs in the appalling violence. The Ugandans south and west of the Nile River, long since numb to the war, suffered compassion fatigue. They were tired of hearing and reading about it. They wanted to get on with their lives. For all practical purposes, the war was taking place in another country. Ugandan life revolved around the capital of Kampala, which looked and felt like a modern city with towering office buildings, glittering hotels, and classy restaurants far from the misery and squalor of the refugee camps.

One of my tasks on this trip was to conduct a voter survey ahead of the coming election, set for the end of February 2006. It was unscientific by most polling standards but would be useful as a guide for what Ugandans viewed as important.

The results confirmed my suspicions. In the regions directly affected by the war with the LRA, the vast majority of people were not only distraught over the war, they were resentful. The war had robbed them of their past, present, and future. The economy was virtually nonexistent except for subsistence farming and foreign aid. Village markets consisted of fruit and vegetable stands selling produce picked from the few places where crops could be gathered during the day before growers had to scurry back to their refugee camps at night. For people in the south and west, however, the war seemed a distant concern. Jobs and the economy were the most important issues in their lives.

The people's presidential preferences reflected these divergent concerns. Southerners supported the status quo as represented by incumbent president Museveni, who belonged to the ethnic southern tribes. People in the north, east, and northwest supported opposition leader Kizza Besigye.

Ironically, Museveni and Besigye had once been close. Besigye had served as Museveni's personal physician during Museveni's rebel war against the Obote regime during the early 1980s. But the two had split when Besigye married Museveni's childhood friend and reputed former paramour. Besigye ran for president against Museveni in 2001 but lost, and Museveni had forced him into exile.

Yet Besigye returned to try again, despite having to face trumped-up charges of terrorism and attempts to overthrow the government, and he quickly developed a strong following. People in the war-torn regions of the north and east blamed Museveni, not just Joseph Kony and his LRA, for the twenty years of war. Though Besigye was unproven as a political leader, he provided an alternative and promised a negotiated peace with the LRA. This was welcome news to people whose lives had become a daily battle for survival. The northerners knew that their hopes for peace and prosperity did not rest with Museveni.

Outside of Mbale we stopped at another gas station, where I bought a soda from a man with a Muslim skullcap who pried off the cap with a flick of an opener. He asked if I was going to leave the bottle with him. No. He charged me another seven hundred Ugandan shillings, which made the bottle worth as much as the contents. As we waited for the slow-moving pump to fill the tank, a man approached with a rack draped with women's lingerie in one hand and a platter of toothpick containers in the other. He thrust the lingerie toward me, the silky slips in black, red, pink, and blue fluttering in the breeze, then pleaded with me in Karamajong to give him money. This was the future, I feared, of this warrior tribe of cattle rustlers who were cousins of the Maasai in Kenya. Museveni was waging another low-level war against these people, a second front in this pearl of Africa.

As we headed north, I asked Aziz why people didn't plant more mango trees and set up orchards.

What they like here is cattle, he said, and they view farming—or "digging"—as a lowly occupation. But it is hard to tell who is poorer, the cattle herders or the farmers. We passed small herds tended by lean men who whacked their animals out of the road with sticks polished smooth by calloused hands, men draped in rags, seemingly oblivious to harsh sun.

A couple hours later we rested in the cool darkness of the restaurant and lounge of the Golden Ark Hotel in Soroti. CNN blared from a television hanging on the wall and secured inside a box of welded angle iron. The news story was about a discomforting skin condition contracted by American women in some California spas.

I grew anxious. In most corners of Uganda, sanitation and soap are luxuries. Many villages have only recently received water wells from aid groups, and they have to be convinced to keep their cows from defecating beside the pumps in order to keep the water clean. The growing gap between the developed and undeveloped worlds is obvious on every corner, on every street, down every country road. It can be crushing. Generous donations are but bandages on gaping wounds. Yet a questionable skin condition in California spas is news for CNN. The story might have been about a different planet as far as most Ugandans are concerned, one where people have the kind of income that allows them the luxury to visits spas, where laws exist to protect people and their health, and where police and courts enforce those laws. Out in the street here live people who have not bathed in weeks, who are dying of AIDS, malaria, dysentery, starvation, abuse, and neglect. A couple of hundred miles to the north, people had been bludgeoned to death for no reason except that they had been born. But that is not news.

Next door to our hotel was one of the town's only Internet access points, a cramped and airless room with four computers managed by a tall girl with knotted hair extensions. On the wall a poster announced a Christian revival in the local stadium featuring a visiting *muzungu* from the United States, a man with a square jaw, bright eyes, and a thick head of hair who grinned like only a religious zealot or cult leader could. This man would fly in, deliver his message of positivism to people who lived in fear and poverty, collect contributions, and then fly back to a world of comfort, convenience, and cash machines.

The next morning I was on my way deep into the country to find a member of the former commanders and founders of the Arrow Boys militia. I traveled with Joe Elunya, one of the news agency's correspondents, a savvy and talented journalist. The Arrow Boys, a homegrown militia of some five thousand fighters, had been Uganda's most formidable force against the Lord's Resistance Army. They had done what the Ugandan army had been unable to do: they had driven the LRA out of their region. After the Ugandan army's Operation Iron Fist offensive into southern Sudan in 2002, Kony responded with a vicious and far-reaching counteroffensive that sent his units streaming south into the Teso region. Two years later, after conducting countless killings and kidnappings, the LRA units had retreated in defeat. By late 2005, they were all but gone.

Our road looked like it had not been graded since the LRA roamed the region. Yet it was crowded with bicycles and people, men herding clusters of goats, women balancing bundles on their heads, children clinging. We dipped down and around potholes the size of bathtubs, threading our way through the throng. Today was market day here in Arapai, Elunya explained, and I decided we would return after our search for the Arrow Boys. People here live much as else-where in the Ugandan countryside, in small and remote clusters hid-den by the tall elephant grass, usually with just three or four mud and thatch-roofed huts surrounding a larger thatch-roofed structure.

The larger huts are Pentecostal churches, Elunya said, and are very popular. Pentecostalism has the right mix of kooky Christian conven-tions and spooky spiritualism that intoxicates rural people, most of whom have never strayed far from their basic belief in spirits, living and dead.

This jarred my own memories of wandering a Navajo reservation in the American Southwest, researching the devastation wrought by uranium mining. I had stumbled across large white tents in some remote and windblown corners, set against the sculpted red sandstone buttes and under the turquoise sky. The tents housed Christian revivals. If one of the local Navajos was the slightest bit charismatic, this provided a venue to collect contributions. Both there and here, such "spiritual" experiences provide locals with a certain amount of entertainment and amusement—and something to help explain the unexplainable in a tenuous and violent world.

We stopped at a collection of concrete and brick stores, a trading center called Amuria, and found ourselves caught up in a political parade featuring some of the region's local favorites, who were demon-strating their power with an escort of armed men in pickups, trailed by a horde of screaming children. We parked in front of a building set aside from the rest and inside found the district chairman, Robert Adiama, the equivalent of a regional governor. His concrete-floored office consisted of a wooden bench, a visitor's chair, and a wooden desk stamped with large black letters—TESO COACHES—the name of a local bus company it had come from. A small map of the district dangled from a nail hammered into whitewashed plaster.

Adiama was talking to a couple of German doctors but waved us in and motioned for us to sit. He grilled the doctors about what they were doing, which was providing basic health care to thousands of people who would otherwise not get any. After a long pause, Adiama earnestly told them how much he appreciated their work and that their safety was his utmost concern.

If anyone could guarantee their safety, it was Adiama. As one of the Arrow Boys' founders, he served as their chief intelligence officer. He was composed and confident, if not cocksure, of himself. It was refreshing to meet someone like him in a place where passivity predominates. People like Adiama make this country click.

After dismissing the doctors, Adiama nodded patiently as I asked him what accounted for the Arrow Boys' success against the LRA.

"We have our contacts," he said. "When the LRA is going to move south from Pader, we know about it three days ahead of time." But it was more than that. The Arrow Boy's secret, he explained, was a coordinated alert system, a network of informants who quickly spread the word that the LRA was on the move, when, where, and in what numbers.

LRA activity in the Teso region had stopped, however, with the most recent incident taking place on September 29, 2005, just four months before my visit, when the Arrow Boys proclaimed they had killed one of the LRA's most notorious commanders, Dominic Ongwen, who was among the five LRA commanders indicted by the ICC. The report eventually proved false. The overly enthusiastic Arrow Boys had misidentified a subcommander's body.

"We put him out of action," Adiama growled through clenched teeth. Arresting people like Ongwen and the others and putting them on trial for several years in The Hague were outrageous to Adiama. The LRA leaders would live well in that setting compared with life in the African bush, and he didn't like that. Adiama did not support any policy that took men responsible for the atrocities committed by the LRA and kept them alive in comfortable surroundings while highly paid lawyers argued over evidence, only to render a judgment that would never result in a death sentence.

Adiama looked at me with burning eyes, then sighed. "The LRA faced their first blow in Teso," he said calmly. But it was more than just a blow. Adiama said the Arrow Boys killed more than forty LRA commanders in the Teso region. Though no numbers are kept of total casualties, it is not unreasonable to project that many times that number of LRA soldiers were killed and wounded. And this would not include the deaths that the LRA inflicted on the kidnapped child soldiers and child brides.

Although the Teso people are Nilotic, they have culturally and linguistically distanced themselves from the Acholi and the Langi and considered the LRA incursion an Acholi invasion to be repulsed by any and all means. The Arrow Boys formed a local support and intelligence network that extended to the most far-flung villages.

"We help the population to own the problem," Adiama said. "We prepared the community to respond and asked the government for help in doing it."

Government support came in the form of weapons distributed throughout the villages, with some fifty guns distributed to each subcounty, the smallest unit of government. When the LRA attacked, the grassroots militia quickly assembled and pursued the rebels.

"The only way to control the situation was rapid response," Adiama explained.

Because the Arrow Boys had been so successful, they were incorporated into the ranks of the Ugandan military.

Why hadn't a similar system been put to use in the north?

"The commanders in the north have to step up their relationship with the community," he said. "The army can't do much if they are not helped. The commanders have to go the extra mile. It was the will of the community [in Teso] that caused the LRA to be rooted out, not the professionalism of the army." But in order for the LRA to be defeated and finished, their support from Sudan needed to be cut, he said. "Sudan should denounce the LRA," he said, something it did a year later when the LRA proved no longer useful. "When the rebels have a fallback position, it is difficult to defeat them. The government of Sudan has a lot to do."

Adiama thought the LRA problem would eventually end, but that hope rested on politics. "I have a lot of hope the security will improve as long as the government remains stable." Because the LRA was still at large, the Arrow Boys remained critical to the area's defense. "While the LRA is active, the region is vulnerable."

Adiama had a more immediate problem than the LRA: the Karamajong cattle raiders. Just a week earlier, he had issued an order for the Arrow Boys to shoot Karamajong cattle rustlers on sight. Adiama had been roundly criticized for this by human rights groups, but he did not back down.

"Armed men stealing cows should be shot," he said, grinding his teeth again. Just as gardens are vital, so are the cows vital to the health and well-being of the Teso people. "They kill our people when they come. They steal our cattle. They say we should be sympathetic." He shook his head in disgust. "We are not aggressive. We are a peaceful people. If [Karamajong] want our cows, they can buy them. If they think we have their cows, take us to court."

Because of the continual raids by the Karamajong, and the LRA invasion of the preceding years, refugee camps dotted the Teso lands. As traditional cattle herders, "the people of Teso are not used to camp life," he said. "It is like being in a prison." He looked forward to the day when the Teso people could vacate the camps and return to their rural life. "Give them implements for production and you will see success," he said. For the vast majority of the Teso people, the war is now history. The refugee camps there were dismantled in 2007, and those displaced by the LRA are once again farming and raising cattle. Only those still affected by the Karamjong cattle rustlers remain in a few scattered camps. And, here again, the Arrow Boys have helped. Many in the Arrow Boys militia have been incorporated into a special Anti-

Stock Theft Unit of the Ugandan military; their job is to prevent rustling and protect Teso cattle growers.

We headed deeper into the countryside, and after half an hour of bumping along dirt roads, we came across a couple of men on bicycles piled high with large, low-fired pots, expertly tied with ropes so they wouldn't crack or break despite the jarring. They stopped as we stopped. The pot peddler was Daniel Emora, who was unsure of his age but figured he was about forty years old. A slight man with a friendly but wary look, his eyes lit up at my question.

"The Arrow Boys rescued me from the LRA," he said, explaining that they had killed his wife's family, including her father, and kidnapped many children from his village. The fate of the children was still unknown because they had never returned. He enthusiastically explained how the militia had driven out the rebels and said that, yes, he felt safe now. "The rebels are no longer in the area."

Emora lived in a nearby town and hoped to return to his village but would wait until after the elections. He did not support President Museveni, whom he blamed for the ongoing problem of the LRA and its invasion of Teso territory.

"The Arrow Boys should remain," he said. "If they are disbanded, the rebels will . . . come back."

We continued our drive through the savannahs of high grass and stopped at the village of Arasi, a collection of huts circling around a couple of brick stores. A dozen men huddled in the shade of an open thatch-roofed pavilion watching a couple of men play the traditional African board game *omweso*, as it is called in Uganda; elsewhere the game is called *mancala*. It is the oldest board game in the world, and though it is most often played on a slab of wood with a series of depressions in which beads are placed and moved, it was originally played in the dirt with pebbles. The game resembles backgammon, and the stones, beans, or beads are moved around the board with the strategy of capturing the opponent's stones and territory.

The men paused in the midst of the game to tell me that two years earlier the LRA had killed twenty villagers here and kidnapped four children, one of whom was still missing. The Arrow Boys drove the LRA out.

"If possible, they should increase their numbers," one of the men said, otherwise "[our] security will disappear." The other players agreed.

When I asked why the LRA persisted in the north, they chortled. "Maybe the community has sympathy" for them.

———————

We returned to Arapai, where the market was bustling. Mounds of dried white cassava root were jammed into large plastic sacks and sold for the equivalent of several dollars, enough to feed a family for a month. Long stalks of sugarcane were stacked and sold in bundles. A bleating goat, tied to the back of a bicycle, would provide enough meat for a week or more. Several dozen of the long-horned Anchole cows were tethered near a half-dozen men haggling over prices. Shoes, shirts, pants—all manner of clothing—were piled and hung in the makeshift stalls. A man had rigged up a large grinding stone to the back of his bicycle, and it whirled as he pedaled, drawing a steady clientele who waited to get their *pangas* honed to a fine edge.

Seated under a small covering was Jacki Okurut, a forty-five-year-old man who patiently wove plastic rope. He loved the Arrow Boys. "They have worked hard. So we are now in peace because they did good. Let them continue their work, because the Karamajong are still bothering us."

Did he agree with Adiama's order to shoot the Karamajong cattle rustlers on sight?

He shook his head. "The law should be followed."

It was a heartening response and one of the few times anyone had mentioned the rule of law. That this simple man sitting at a market on the dry plains of Teso argued for it was refreshing. If only the belief permeated the society.

On the far side of the market were the *malwa* pavilions. *Malwa* is a homemade beer made of fermented sorghum, served in clay pots and sipped through long, hollow reeds. It is a potent brew if you sip enough of it. The proprietors regularly add warm, fresh brew to each pot, which has several straws, keeping the customers such as Celestino Elibu happy and well supplied.

Elibu's eyes were red, and his breath smelled of stale beer as he explained that for the equivalent of about twenty-five cents, he could sit and sip for several hours. It was a good way to while away the day, catch up on gossip, and spend time with friends. About a third of the customers were women. Elibu and his fellow imbibers exuded gratitude for the Arrow Boys and hatred for the LRA.

"We feel safe, but we are still haunted by the memory of our dead relatives," he said.

At the mention of the dead, an eerie silence fell over this *malwa*-drinking crew. Each dutifully nodded. The LRA was neither forgotten nor forgiven. This market out here on Uganda's eastern plains owed its existence to the Arrow Boys. They understood this.

———

The Arrow Boys frequently were in the national news as they stepped up their encounters with the Karamajong, who continued as they had for centuries raiding cattle in Teso territory. The Arrow Boys conducted regular sweeps to the north and east, focusing on villages and trading centers where the rustlers tended to congregate. The sweeps were part of an ongoing operation to disarm the Karamajong, who liked to hide their weapons by burying them in the ground under their corrals. Several months after I visited Amuria, more than three hundred Karamajong were captured and an unknown number were killed after a running gun battle not far from the northeastern city of Kotido.

The Ugandan units routinely confiscated hundreds of the Karamajong's weapons. While this was an obvious way to end their ability to steal cattle, disarming the Karamajong created a second problem. The LRA had not ventured into the Karamajong region because the cattle rustlers were well armed and more than ready to fight. There were strategic reasons as well. The Karamajong caused nearly as much trouble for the Ugandan army as the LRA did. So why bother them?

But the fact that the Karamajong and the Teso were well armed raised serious questions about the government's long-standing policy of disarming and forcing the northerners to live in the internal refugee camps. Clearly, this made the Acholi and Langi more, not less, vulnerable. Their vulnerability became all the more apparent when the danger to camp refugees came from within as well as without.

This became abundantly clear when several months later I traveled to the northern fringe area of the Teso region and to the Ogwete camp for internally displaced refugees, some seventy-five miles east of Lira— a no-man's-land caught between LRA and Karamajong control. It lay in a wide and open region of thick grass and spotty stands of forest. It was here, on Sunday, May 21, 2006, that a militiaman assigned to guard the Ogwete camp went on a drunken rampage that left eleven dead and fourteen injured. Three days after fleeing into the night, he was shot to death by the Arrow Boys. They claimed the soldier was caught in crossfire. Others said he was executed. It was the worst massacre ever in a refugee camp that was completely unrelated to the Lord's Resistance Army. And it exemplified the explosive tensions that roiled below the surface in northern Uganda, the result of the refugees' wretched and seemingly endless gulag existence.

I visited Ogwete camp shortly after the killing spree. A thick cloud of depression still hovered over the camp. The residents were in shock.

As they slowly told their stories, they pieced together a mosaic of jealousy and madness born out of years of camp life.

Peter Okulu was a member of the Amuka, or the Rhino militia, the same paramilitary group that protected the Orem village I had visited nearer to Lira. Since the LRA had dwindled in the region, camp life had fallen into a lethargic, listless routine. Although the militia lived separately near the camp, they were part and parcel of daily camp life. Okulu fell in love with a fifteen-year-old girl named Susan, the daughter of the camp leader, Moses Ogwang. Ogwang had a position of prestige and sent his daughter to a private boarding school some thirty miles away. Ogwang's high hopes for his daughter did not include her marrying one of the Rhino militia. On holidays and breaks, she returned to her family in the camp and spent time with her best friend and cousin, Rose Ochen. The relationship with Okulu happened easily, since Rose, who was much older than Susan at twenty-two, was seeing Okulu's close friend Rashid Okello.

No one took much notice of the two couples until some builders from Lira arrived to construct bathhouses near the camp, a project funded by an international aid organization. Susan and Rose were hired to prepare meals for the workers for the duration of the construction. Okulu immediately became jealous, camp residents said, and began accusing one of the builders of having an affair with Susan. Whenever he saw the builders, Okulu insulted them and threw stones, the construction supervisor told me.

Early one Sunday, Okulu and his friend Okello started drinking beer. Although it is unclear what happened next, Ogwang eventually complained to the militia commander, who had Okulu arrested. Just hours later, inexplicably, Okulu was out and drinking again, but now he was armed. He had escaped his confinement to quarters after telling the commanding officer that he had done nothing wrong. That would soon change.

From his grungy bed in the Lira hospital, Ogwang described how a quiet Sunday evening turned into a night of blood, death, and horror. "He came and fired at us at close range," he said of Okulu. "I was sitting outside with three others. One was shot in the neck. He died instantly." Ogwang was riddled with bullets, one ripping through his right thigh and shattering the bone. The rampage continued for several hours as camp residents hid from the madness. Some tried to defend themselves, and other militia members got involved, turning the camp into a free-fire zone. Okulu later fled into the night.

Ogwang said he was baffled by the massacre. "I have no idea what caused this. The military man [Okulu] never spoke of his feelings." He was unaware of his daughter's affair because she was away in boarding school most of the time. When he was well enough to leave the hospital, Ogwang said he would try to figure out what had happened. But he would find a troubled situation.

Johnson Ogongor, another camp official, said the killings had a drastic effect on the camp. Many blamed the two girls for provoking the incident, implying that neither Ogwang nor his daughter would be welcomed back. But, more important, no one trusted the guards anymore.

"There is a lot of fear," Ogongor said. He had lived in this camp for nearly two years and agreed that this kind of tragedy would not occur if people could return to their farms and cattle. "There is a need to go back, but there is no security," he complained. A unit of the LRA still operated in the area, as did a couple of bands of Karamajong cattle rustlers. Most refugees had been unwilling to leave the camp before the killing. Now they wondered which was more dangerous, life inside or outside of the camp.

8

Degrees of Darkness

THE REFUGEE CAMP OUTSIDE of Kisoro, a town in the far southwestern corner of Uganda, sat on a broad and grassy field surrounded by towering volcanic peaks collared with clouds. Sporadic eruptions over the past decade were an apt metaphor for this deadly nexus of Uganda, Rwanda, and the former Zaire, now the Democratic Republic of the Congo. Here the region's bloody ethnic cauldron bubbled over, stoked by a miasma of armed militias wielding machetes and blasting away with machine guns, grenade launchers, and assault rifles. At one end of this placid field was a large UN truck dispensing paltry supplies for nearly five thousand people who had poured across the border from the Congo in the past few days. Their shelters from the frigid mountain air that swept into the valley most nights were thin green plastic tarps thrown over hastily made stick frames. Half a dozen portable toilets stood at oddly tilted angles at the outskirts. Knots of hungry, hollow-eyed children roamed aimlessly, many barefoot and wearing dirty, threadbare clothes. The parents sprawled on the ground, expressionless, exhausted, using a rolled-up jacket or an arm for a pillow. Human feces littered the field.

These were the Rwandese Hutus, who twelve years earlier fled their country for the Congo in the wake of the 1994 Rwandan genocide, an event that shocked the world with its intensity, efficiency, and depravity. In the span of several months and in one of Africa's smallest countries, an estimated eight hundred thousand Tutsis were killed as UN peacekeepers stood by, crippled by the UN's bureaucratic dithering. It had been sparked by the April 6 death of Rwandan president Juvenal Habyarimana, a Hutu whose plane was downed as it descended into the Rwandan capital of Kigali. Emotions flared as Hutus blamed Tutsis, who in turn blamed Hutu extremists for provoking an excuse to launch their genocidal plan.

Despite composing less than 20 percent of the population, the Tutsis were long considered the country's elite, a notion espoused by the Germans who first colonized the area in the late 1800s and later reinforced by the Belgians who assumed control of the country after World War I. The Tutsis are a Hamatic people, thought to have migrated from the Horn of Africa. Many have distinctive physical characteristics, being tall, possessing somewhat light skin, and having narrow facial features.

The Hutus are generally Bantu peoples, originating in western and central Africa and making up an 80 percent majority. By the time of Rwanda's formal independence from Belgium in 1962, government rule based on majority representation gave the Hutus sweeping power.

But ethnic hatred was well entrenched. The first massacre of Tutsis occurred during a revolt in 1959, and over the ensuing years similar but lesser mass killings took place until the explosive events of 1994. The genocide was conducted by police, paramilitary organizations, and ordinary citizens armed with machetes who turned on their friends and neighbors. These loosely organized militias were called the Interahamwe, which roughly translated means "those who strike together." These groups held sway for three terrifying months until they were driven out by Rwanda's current president, Paul

Kagame, who led his Tutsi army into Rwanda from Uganda, curtailed the genocide, and took control.

Though the worst seemed over for Rwanda, the fighting moved across the border into the Congo. Hutus of the former Rwandan army joined with the Interahamwe and roamed the jungles irrespective of borders and immune from the government of Mobutu Sese Seko. This allowed the Interahamwe to conduct retaliatory and harassing raids into Rwanda, which they hoped would destabilize and topple Kagame.

Fed up with the lawlessness and persistent threat, the Rwandan Tutsi army invaded the Congo in 1996 in a joint operation with Uganda, since both countries had been under attack from various antigovernment militias based in the eastern Congo region. The Rwandans and Ugandans also funneled weapons and money to the rebel forces fighting Mobutu, led by Laurent-Désiré Kabila. Rwanda was particularly embittered and armed the ethnic Tutsi Banyamulenge militias, which also operated in eastern Congo as a force to counter and subdue the Interahamwe militias. The invasion and support of Kabila were denounced by Mobutu, but his government was so hopelessly corrupt that it was helpless to stop the invasion. Kabila's forces included many Rwandan Tutsi soldiers and officers, and they eventually took Kinshasa. But Kabila shed his Rwandan military core, realizing that he needed to unify the newly renamed Democratic Republic of the Congo under Congolese control, and so he expelled the armies from Uganda and Rwanda. This did not go down well with the resentful Rwandans, who rightly feared a resurgence of the Hutu militias.

Rwanda's fears were well founded, since Kabila, whom they had helped put in power, turned to the Hutus in the eastern Congo for help to push the Tutsi-led Rwandan army out of his country. This sparked an even greater war as the Ugandan and Rwandan armies, and the militias they backed, began another drive into the Congo, this time to overthrow Kabila.

Kabila enlisted the support of his neighbors, such as Angola and Zimbabwe, sparking the largest and most bloody war that Africa has ever endured. Some 3.5 to 4 million people died, making it by far the most deadly conflict since World War II. (Among other atrocities committed during these chaotic years, the Interahamwe were found to have been responsible for the 1999 killing of eight foreign tourists tracking mountain gorillas in Uganda's Bwindi Impenetrable National Forest, including two U.S. citizens.)

Though the UN inserted more than five thousand peacekeepers into the Congo in early 2000, the fighting continued. In January 2001, Laurent Kabila was assassinated by one of his bodyguards, and it was widely suspected that Ugandan or Rwandan forces played a part. His Western-educated son, Joseph Kabila, was sworn in as president, and this resulted in the deescalation of hostilities. Uganda and Rwanda began pulling troops back from the front line.

But there was more to the war than politics and ethnic animosities. In April 2001 a UN panel released a report that accused the governments of Uganda, Rwanda, and Zimbabwe of using the war as cover to exploit diamonds, cobalt, coltan, gold, and other valuable resources in the Congo. In 2002 Rwanda and Uganda signed peace agreements and withdrew again, denying the accusations.

The ethnic fighting continued throughout eastern Congo, however. Laurent Nkunda led the Tutsi Banyamulenge into the jungles of eastern Congo where they conducted periodic attacks on the Hutu communities in the Goma area. It was these thousands of Hutu men, women, and children whom I encountered in this makeshift camp. More were coming.

"The rebels are still fighting," a woman wailed as she stood on the edge of a crowd waiting to receive some meager supplies from the United Nations. In all, an estimated twenty thousand Congolese of Rwandan origin had poured into Uganda the previous week. Most had crossed into Uganda about sixty miles to the north at Inshasha, where conditions were just as desperate. Here UN workers handed out plastic containers for water, to be collected from who knew where, a few cups, thin gray blankets, and packets of high-energy cookies. The recipients were family heads, usually men, who clutched these items to their chests and disappeared through the crowd.

I was with another of our news agency reporters, Goodluck Musinguzi, a native of the area. The refugees were badly frightened. "They'd rather die here" of starvation than risk a return to their homes, said refugee John Hukiza. When I asked him why the Banyamulenge had attacked them, he said they were trying "to create their own country" inside the Congo.

It seemed an unlikely scenario, but Musinguzi explained that it wasn't. The Congo is roughly the size of Europe, and the seat of the Congolese government is far to the west in Kinshasa. Vast expanses of roadless jungle lie between here and the capital, and transportation is virtually impossible except by foot or air. Kinshasa holds a tenuous grasp on these lawless eastern provinces. Except for the presence of the large UN force, which had swelled to seventeen thousand, government control over the region is nonexistent. At that moment, the Banyamulenge controlled the region across the border toward Goma. A Tutsi-controlled Rwandese state in the Congo was an attractive notion for the Rwandan government, Musinguzi said. It would relieve the agonizing pressure on the limited amount of cultivatable land in tiny Rwanda, a land of terraced and intensely cultivated hillsides. Having fled Rwanda, and now forced from the Congo, the Hutus had nowhere to go except Uganda.

Theodore Sebdul, forty-six, said his family of six had been chased out of their home by the Banyamulenge fighters and barely escaped with their lives. He and his neighbors had been caught in crossfire. They were warned of the approaching Tutsi fighters, but the nominal Congolese army assured them that it could control the situation. When violent fighting erupted near his village, it was not clear who was shooting. But "when the [Congolese] soldiers ran away," people knew. "The villagers followed," he said. He and his family walked all night through the rain and cold. Some of the Congolese government soldiers also fled across the border into Uganda, but the Ugandan military rounded them up and returned them to the UN in the Congo. The Tutsi militia was recognizable, Sebdul said, as the same that pursued the notorious Hutu Interahamwe in the Congo. The refugees ran because "they saw the same [Tutsis] who were killing them before. That is why they cannot stay there."

The Ugandan government planned to move the Rwandan Congolese about ninety-five miles to the interior and into an existing refugee camp operated by the UN with an estimated one hundred thousand Hutus who had fled Rwanda more than ten years earlier. The government promised the new refugees food and shelter if they agreed to settle in the camp. But transportation to get these new refugees to the interior was slow in coming, and as the refugees waited, conditions grew grim.

"They go begging [in town] for food," said one refugee. "If you get something, you eat. If you don't . . ."

Eliberata Nyirazabominga, age thirty-eight, a mother of three carrying an infant on her back, said she had gone three days without a meal. She had fled the fighting in the middle of the night and had not seen her husband since then. Some refugees were crossing back into the Congo during the day, she said, trekking long distances to their villages to retrieve food and returning in the evenings. Many suffered from diarrhea and dehydration in addition to cold and hunger.

Musinguzi and I drove a short distance to the border and walked into the Congo to see for ourselves what was going on. A no-man's-land of fifty yards, marked by a wobbly wire fence, separates the two countries. On the Congo side, soldiers clustered at the base of a communications tower with a commanding view a couple of hundred yards up the mountain. Civilians lounged at what served as an immigration office.

We asked who was in charge, explaining that we wanted to walk through the village, but got nothing but blank stares. Eventually, a man who seemed to speak for the office told us to wait. He refused to give his name, but insisted, "The situation is normal here. There is no problem." A couple of young men appeared, both of whom spoke English and stank of beer. They would accompany us, they said.

Shops were boarded up, and people huddled quietly, stealing glances as we passed. At a makeshift market, some people displayed cabbages, potatoes, and a few slabs of fly-covered goat meat on a board. Farther on, heavily armed irregulars sporting berets, fatigue pants, and T-shirts—some toting thirty-caliber machine guns—watched us and fingered their weapons. Others held rocket-propelled grenade launchers on their shoulders. These soldiers were the freshly occupying force and expected another fight at any moment. Were they Banyamulenge or Congolese forces? Our questions were met with hostile stares. We left.

Several months later I encountered some of these same Hutu refugees who had moved inland to the sprawling refugee camp at Nakivale, not far from Uganda's southern border with Tanzania. Some of the Hutus had returned to the Congo, having been told the situation had settled. They had been killed. Those who relocated to this camp had survived, but had that same forlorn, suspicious, and often hostile stare. Yet, here in the heart of Uganda, the tensions between the Hutus and Tutsis had resurfaced as explosively as ever. During the 1994 genocide, many of the Tutsi cattle herders had fled the massacres by driving their cattle east into neighboring Tanzania. Some had mingled with Ugandan cattle herders, who had also taken their animals across the border into Tanzania about the same time to escape a drought in southern Uganda. A dozen years later, competition for Tanzania's northwestern grasslands had become fierce, and in early 2006 the Tanzania government forced them out. Instead of returning to the densely populated and hilly lands of Rwanda, the Tutsi cattle herders migrated north into Uganda. These Tutsi cattle herders encountered thousands of their hostile former neighbors, the Rwandan Hutus who had been living in the crowded Nakivale refugee camp nearby. Traditionally farmers, many of the Hutus had cultivated plots in the vacant land surrounding the camp. With the arrival of the Tutsi cattle herders, cows trampled and devoured the Hutus' gardens. Violence was imminent. The local law enforcement officer, James Mugisha, was unarmed and understandably very scared. Fights had already broken out between the Hutu farmers and Tutsi cattle herders. He had asked for reinforcements. None were forthcoming.

Though the genocide of Rwanda had occurred a dozen years earlier, I found myself in the midst of a potential clash. For an outsider, a *muzungu,* the distinctions between tribes can be difficult to recognize or comprehend. When it comes to the Rwandans, or the Ugandans for that matter, many have intermarried, and resulting physical characteristics blend. These differences are nothing as obvious as the broad racial distinctions I have experienced in America.

But Americans have not necessarily transcended racial stereotypes either. Segregation in the United States was not outlawed until the 1960s, just fifty years ago. Most American communities still divide themselves ethnically and racially and remain unofficially exclusionary. Neighborhoods in the United States are further refined by nationalities, as each retains its own religious practices, stores, restaurants, and language. The idea of the American melting pot has its limits. And it is not just America. Racially motivated riots erupted across France in 2005, exposing the raw reality that undercuts France's vaunted phrase *Liberté, égalité, fraternité.* Germany's domestic workers live in ethnically separated neighborhoods victimized by white supremacist skinheads.

Despite the seemingly glacial speed of integration, I know that often, within a generation or two, those degrees of separation melt away as foreign languages and traditions fade and children are caught in the tsunami that is American culture.

What I was seeing here was something different. In Uganda I heard friendly ethnic banter in our newsroom among the staff, which represented the various ethnic groups that the country comprised. I had seen and heard the banter elsewhere, though sometimes it sounded more hostile. The divisions were largely based on degrees of darkness and appearance, separating the taller, angular, and deeply dark Nilotic northerners from the shorter, more rounded Bantu southerners. At its root is racism, the notion that the lighter-skinned people are somehow better than darker-skinned people. It undoubtedly began during the distant centuries of raids by Arab slave traders and was only further compounded and solidified by the arrival of the Europeans with their weaponry and technology.

What had been going on in Rwanda and eastern Congo resembled the ethnic and intertribal rivalry behind the conflict in northern Uganda. More than once the word *genocide* had been attached to Uganda's twenty-year war with the LRA. The accusation at first seemed outlandish. The numbers of dead were nowhere near what had happened in Rwanda. Yet the war had persisted for some twenty years; despite the fact that Museveni's forces were far better equipped, far better paid, and better disciplined, they had been unable to defeat the LRA or capture Kony in all this time. Museveni rarely addressed this failure, preferring to blame it on a host of other issues over which he had no control. Finally, on May 4, 2006, while talking to a room of foreigners pressing him to help with the disbanding of the refugee camps, Museveni offered his idea of what was behind twenty years of war with the LRA.

Museveni admitted that he had underestimated the tenacity of the LRA and had not put enough men and resources into the war to win it. "The aggravating factor was the underspending by us on defense for a number of years until 2002, when we said, enough is enough."

His answer raised the question: why did it take so long to realize that? Museveni had been fighting in the north since 1986, some sixteen years before he apparently became fed up. Despite this admission, Museveni denied that the war was a conflict between Uganda's northern and southern tribes. "Another lie is that it is a conflict between the north and south. But who are the people who have been killed by Kony? They are not southern; they are northern. Almost 98 percent to 99 percent of the people killed by Kony are not from any other part of Uganda except the north. So why would the north-south conflict result into [sic] mainly northern victims [at the hands of northerners]?"[1] Museveni had offered up the most obvious reason to dismiss the underlying ethnic conflict, yet the perverse reality lingered just below the surface.

When I arrived in Uganda, an estimated 95 percent of the Acholi lived in the refugee camps for internally displaced people. This was incredibly convenient for Museveni. Each camp was protected and guarded by the Ugandan military and/or a detachment of militia. A population of nearly two million traditionally rebellious and unsettled people were confined to gulags under the watchful eyes of the Ugandan army's northern command. All Museveni's government had to worry about was fighting the LRA, and even that seemed beyond its abilities. The refugees, meanwhile, were being fed and cared for by the United Nation's World Food Program and a battalion of international aid agencies and their loyal workers.

The archipelago of camps left the north virtually void of humanity, an open range where the two armies could engage in running gun battles. As long as the skirmishes remained far from the eyes of a questioning press and populace, the army could claim body counts that no one could verify. The open bush country also allowed the LRA to roam relatively freely and neatly avoid full-scale confrontations with

Museveni's army—the key to any guerrilla war. Since few people were left in the villages or countryside, this forced the LRA units to attack the refugee camps to find their victims, food, and other supplies—the exact places that had been created to protect the Acholi from the LRA. The LRA raided these protected camps at will, demonstrating the embarrassing weakness of Museveni's tactics and raising the question as to why these people were held in the camps in the first place. Clearly it was not for their protection, because they simply were not safe.

The Ugandan army's heralded Operation Iron Fist of 2002, in which the army pursued Kony into southern Sudan, did not diminish the LRA attacks on the camps or the abductions. Instead, attacks increased. It was the opposite of the intended effect. The peak of the night commuters phenomenon, where children migrated nightly from the refugee camps to fortified children's shelters in the towns, took place in 2004, two years after the offensive and the same year when LRA attacked the town of Gulu, the headquarters of the northern command.

In his May 2006 address, Museveni deflected attention from his failures by claiming that his true enemy was a much larger and broader force—Sudan and the Congo—an assertion of ego more than reality. As leader of an army that had put him in office and that had invaded the Congo and controlled much of northern Congo for several years, he could not admit failure in confronting a wily renegade in the bush. "We had to confront Sudan and the [Congo's] Mobutu regimes because you could not defeat the agent without disciplining the sponsor."[2] Sudan had been disciplined? The Ugandan army had entered Sudan with the purpose of pursuing the LRA, not under the threat of confronting the Sudanese army, which simply stepped aside.

Museveni said Kony had been a tool, but it was true in more ways than one. If Kony was a tool of Sudan, he certainly had been a tool of Museveni as well. Sudan had supported Kony, given him refuge, and provided medical care and weapons. But Kony's perpetual existence had also provided Museveni with the perfect excuse to maintain a massive military presence in the north. This army not only battled the LRA, but limited its growth by making recruitment of more soldiers difficult. It also prevented other hostile forces arising from among the Acholi or Langi. Yet Uganda's tactic against the LRA never achieved the intensity of an all-out ground war with a hope of defeating this elusive enemy. It simply limited the LRA's effectiveness. It was a cat playing with a mouse, swatting it, batting it, biting it on occasion, but never killing it. Ending the war meant opening a new chapter in the north and for the Museveni government, which also risked that Kony and the LRA could be replaced with something worse. The continued existence of the LRA was a useful evil. It gave Museveni the excuse he needed to exert near total control over the Acholi and Langi. Why kill the mouse and end the war?

There were other benefits. The international status of Kony's LRA was raised by the U.S. government when in 2001 it listed the Lord's Resistance Army as an international terrorist organization. As Uganda's lingering problem, the LRA provided a sound reason for Uganda's appeal for foreign aid. The United States spent $77.5 million in 2005 in northern Uganda and provided 60 percent of the food aid to northern Uganda, valued at an estimated $47 million, while other programs worked on improving living conditions, mainly through sanitation and water services.[3] But a portion of the U.S. aid, as well as that of other European countries, came in direct cash contributions to the Ugandan government budget. To what extent this money went into the military budget is unclear. But as long as the LRA remained alive, it justified increasing expenditures in the Ugandan defense department. Unfortunately, not all of that money earmarked for defense went where it should have gone.

In 2003 the Ugandan government conducted a wide-ranging investigation of fraud in the military and uncovered appalling abuses. Untold thousands of fake soldiers filled the military payrolls. The money meant for these "ghost soldiers" had apparently gone into the pockets of generals and their deputy commanders. The full extent of the fraud was never revealed because prosecutions were conducted in closed courts-martial, but it was easily many millions of dollars.[4] Some of the blame for the ghost soldiers was due to the thousands of Rwandan soldiers who had once been on the payrolls and had played an integral role in the combined military force that had helped Museveni topple Obote. These soldiers had stayed on, but they left in 1994 to follow their leader, Paul Kagame, who liberated the Tutsis from the Hutu genocide. While this ghost-solider larceny of the defense budget may have been appalling, it exposed the raw underbelly of Uganda's failure to defeat Kony and the LRA for so long. While Uganda claimed that a certain number of soldiers were fighting the LRA in the north, in reality these numbers were far less. The strategic implications were obvious. The war was halfhearted at best. There was no interest in victory, only in the perception that a war was being fought. Continuation of the conflict meant money for commanders and their cohorts. Why end it? After all, the Acholi were decimating themselves. Why endanger Ugandan soldiers?

There were other abuses, including the purchase of decrepit Russian-made helicopters from the Ukraine at outrageously inflated prices, the sale of which profited Ugandan officials hundreds of thousands of dollars in commissions. There was also the purchase of Chinese-made military uniforms that didn't fit the long and lanky Ugandan soldiers. Museveni eventually dismissed his top command in the north, who faced ongoing courts-martial that were closed to the press. But even these actions didn't stop the abuse. As recently as the spring of 2007, thousands of ghost soldiers continued to be "discovered" by investigating generals who reviewed the annual military budget and expressed their shock and dismay.[5]

One of Museveni's harshest critics was Morris Latigo, a prominent member of the Ugandan parliament. He led the opposition caucus, a loose coalition of legislators from several parties that had attempted to break Museveni's stranglehold over the government, which he orchestrated though his National Resistance Movement Party. That an opposition existed at all was because in mid-2005 Uganda had adopted a national referendum calling for multiparty elections. The vote took place at the behest of foreign governments who had threatened to withhold aid, prompting Museveni to rail against foreign interference in the affairs of his state. But he had to listen. Foreign governments provided fully half of the Ugandan government's operating budget. After two consecutive elections under his one-party system, some semblance of democracy in Uganda was necessary. But Museveni got even by strong-arming his puppet parliament into removing term limits from the constitution, effectively handing him the presidency for life. The government hampered opposition parties with a dizzying array of restrictions and last-minute requirements imposed by a capricious national elections board. Museveni then engineered the arrest and jailing of Kizza Besigye, his major political rival, for some fifty days during the peak of the campaign on trumped-up charges. The election was over before it began.

———

A modest man with an infectious smile, Latigo is a soft-spoken Acholi duly proud of his doctorate in agriculture from Ohio State University. Having been touched by the LRA atrocities, he has an acute understanding of the Acholi mind and the dynamics of the LRA's longevity.

I met Latigo on June 7, 2006, a gray and rainy day, as he was moving into his new parliamentary office, just days after the parliamentary elections, the results of which had exposed the deepening divide between the north and south. Across the north and east, Museveni's handpicked party candidates had been voted out of office and replaced by opposition candidates. It was not a rout but had handed the opposition a full one-third of the Parliament, a huge step. Legislators now followed Latigo's lead, and his three mobile phones buzzed and beeped throughout our interview.

The war had changed and mutated over the years, much like a chess game, yet Latigo blamed Museveni for the persistence of the LRA. "The real origin of this war is not like many people [think], that the Acholis wanted to come back to power," he said. "The perception is that there was a northern hegemony in this country that had to be destroyed." It was not true, he said. However, "Everybody knows very well, that if there is any group that can undermine [Museveni] militarily, it is the Acholi. When he took over power, he was politically very, very vulnerable. The greatest challenge was the potential military might that went with the Acholi running away from Kampala with huge military equipment and guns, etc. He deliberately went about devising a strategy to handle that situation. And one of the things he did was to provoke . . . because many Acholis had run to Sudan."

After Museveni and his National Resistance Army took over in 1986, the situation in the north seemed to settle down, Latigo said. "You could find . . . soldiers drinking together with NRA. Some thought, for once, this is a good change." But it was a deceptive peace. Museveni's forces used the lull to chart a final conquest. "All that president's team did was to stay calm, gather intelligence, and prepare to move. They started arresting people. The [Acholi] reaction was, this time we're not going to die like pigs. Because that's what happened under [Idi] Amin. Nobody anticipated [Amin's purge], nobody was prepared for it collectively, and people just died as individuals." When the brutal arrests began, a call went out to the Acholi in Sudan: "Look, there is a crisis and we have to fight."

Museveni's tactics were deliberate. "His strategy was to draw out this military force and alienate it, just destroy it. And once you have done that, then you are militarily secure. And the president's obsession with military security is known to everybody. There was no way he was going to let twenty thousand Acholi sit in southern Sudan with guns." Museveni's calculated gamble went very wrong, however. Since the Ugandan army had defeated Lakwena's Holy Spirit Mobile Forces in some six months, Museveni doubted that the north would support another guerrilla war, let alone an extended one. "Some of the assumptions about whether people will actually fight, whether the environment in Acholi[land] can sustain a guerrilla war . . . were wrong. Acholi are the last people you want to pick a fight with. You'll fight for years. Really, this is what has happened. And, so, the war, which I think the president had calculated would last six months and would have finished with these people, became a very chaotic war."

Yet if the Acholi had suffered the brunt of the LRA violence, the kidnappings, and the mutilations, why hadn't they risen up and said enough is enough?

"Kony, in his own madness . . . has been a very successful strategist." In the early days of the war, Latigo said, "People would go to town or to the [Ugandan] military units and . . . they would tell them, oh, these people [the LRA] are in this place. Kony knew the risk of this. And so . . . if he was attacked . . . having operated in some village, he would come, round up the guys in the village, [and] cut their lips. So, the immediate reaction from the people was, even when you see [the LRA], you don't say [anything]. Even when they have done something wrong, you don't criticize . . . because when they come, they will either cut your lips, cut your ears which you use to hear them, [or] cut the arm you use to point where they are. That was the symbolic thing about cutting the ears, cutting the mouth, cutting the hands."

It was a horrific practice, Latigo agreed. It had "a terrible psychological impact. People just would not talk about these guys. Even when they were suffering, they wouldn't talk because the risk was too big." It grew worse, however. "Later it even moved beyond this and

[they] started killing. If they thought that the reason why they were attacked was because somebody from a village reported them, they would come wipe out the village, and villagers just kept quiet."

I listened in a stunned silence. People were hacked to death because they had the courage to say, Hey, there go the bad guys. They had been silenced by a band of self-proclaimed rebels said to be fighting the government and justifying the killing and mutilation of innocent villagers with their own ghastly delusions of grandeur. This was the plying of primitive psychology, manipulation of the most fundamental emotion: fear. Fear of injury, fear of death. It has worked since the dawn of time and is alive and well around the world. It is the weapon of choice among the armed militias throughout Africa, the Islamic fundamentalist militias across the Middle East, in central and southern Asia. It is used by gangs across America, by the Mafia, by Central and South American militias and drug lords. It is everywhere. The only available antidote is the rule of law, which in some places still holds sway. And it is from this very thin thread that the civilized world dangles in raging wind.

As long as the war stayed in the north, Museveni had occupied himself with rebuilding the government and the economy. But as the war dragged on, the government changed tactics, Latigo explained. Because the Acholi were willing to support the guerrilla movement, Museveni "had to create camps, to take people away from the environment, then deny the LRA a source of recruitment, whether forced or voluntary, and deny the LRA food, which is critical to the war."

Despite the violence and intimidation by the LRA, which soon alienated the LRA from the northern population, the Acholi eventually also turned against the government. "Ultimately there was an understanding as to who to blame," Latigo said. When the Ugandan army first battled the LRA, the Acholi had turned to them for help, and said, There is this Kony who is growing out the in the bush. We need to work collectively to eliminate him, otherwise this conflict will be very dangerous. People said, give us guns. Instead, the government said, No, we can't give you guns. And people then decided to mobilize with arrows and spears to hunt down these people. Now that further alienated the LRA and they became even more vicious. Now ultimately, if you try everything and all the support you expect from government doesn't come, then you begin to believe that government really wants you to suffer. And from that moment, people looked at Kony as just an instrument that government uses to subjugate them. And therefore, they could not spend time blaming Kony. They must blame the source of that suffering, which is government. And that is really the mind-set of our people. This thing is like a cancer that has become malignant. It will take generations to address this problem."

But the spirit of the Acholi has not been broken, Latigo said. "The Bible says Fear not one who wants to destroy you physically, fear the ones who want to destroy your spirit. That has been central to this conflict. That is why we can't complain about the physical suffering, because if we did that, we would be diverted from fighting to uphold our spirits. Thousands will die, but thousands more will be born. But if they are born to an empty culture, they are as useless as vegetation or animals. To us, that is the most critical." When the war has ended and rebuilding begins, Latigo said Acholiland will be quickly restored to past glories. "You will be surprised."

———

At the time of that interview, stirrings of peace talks between the government and the LRA were in the wind. South Sudan's vice president, Riek Machar, had met in secret several times with Kony to lay the groundwork for talks the following month in Juba. Latigo was hopeful because Machar, himself a former militia commander, had cultivated Kony's trust, something that Museveni did not understand how to do. In Kony, Latigo said, "You have some illiterate, who, through this military campaign, has become so powerful and has built a kind of self-belief that makes him a demigod. That means the ego is so huge. You cannot address the objective mind of such a person unless you address the ego factor first. Machar's approach is to say, yeah, you're powerful, but you also have a responsibility in that power to end the suffering of the people and to let the country move forward." If the talks ultimately failed, Latigo said, it would be because of Museveni. "For him this war must end his way and he must be the sole winner. It is not about getting the quickest respite to the suffering of the people, it is just who wins. If the brinkmanship continues, we still have a problem." And that, he predicted, meant a dark future. "The shortcut is . . . kill the man," he said of Kony. "But if you killed him, there is no guarantee that war will end. Absolutely none. You could even have a more vicious thing because there will be so many [Acholi] warlords all striving to prove themselves."

9

Back to the Land

OVER TWO HUNDRED INTERNAL refugee camps were scattered across the north, and after a while they blended into a dismal sameness that numbed the senses: densely clustered mud and thatch-roofed huts where neighbor bumped against neighbor, children scampered, babies cried, and the smoke of cooking fires clouded the air. In the back-country, where rebels stepped from the tall grasses to gun down passing vehicles, abandoned schools sat dark and empty, their walls pock-marked with bullet holes, the windows shattered, the doors ripped from the hinges, the rooms devoid of desks and chairs. Mile after mile were filled with abandoned farms, overgrown pastures, and once cultivated fields now choked with thick and tangled brush. This was a war for the Acholi people? But where were they now? Where was the government that was being resisted? There was nothing here but desolation and destruction. Despite Latigo's optimism, reoccupying the land would be one thing, rebuilding the villages another, and resurrecting the lost life of the Acholi in the north yet again something else.

"How can we go back?" asked Albino Awule, a forty-seven-year-old farmer living in the Walela refugee camp, some twenty miles northwest of Lira. "We are afraid of Kony." We sat on small wooden folding chairs situated on the swept dirt outside his mud and thatch-roofed hut along with two Ugandan journalists. We had attracted a crowd as we meandered through this camp of fifteen thousand displaced people, trailed by about a hundred barefoot children with protruding bellies and dressed in little more than rags. They crowded around, curiously attentive. We were drawn to this camp by reports of a killing that had taken place over a parcel of disputed land, which turned out to be false. Someone had mistakenly claimed his land, Awule said, but it had been resolved without bloodshed. It was indicative of the future, he said, now that he and other camp residents were venturing back to their long-abandoned garden plots. More such land disputes would certainly arise, he suspected, and would not be resolved peacefully. He felt lucky.

Rumors swirled of some seven deaths due to land disputes in recent months, the deadly fallout of decisions by the regional Land Tribunal based in Lira. The tribunal was a government panel established now that refugees were being urged to return to their villages. They had been promised resettlement packages that included seeds, hoes, and corrugated metal roofing to reconstruct their huts. Little of it had materialized, prompting complaints of the expected government graft and corruption. And why not? The machetes that were part of the resettlement packages were so cheap and flimsy they easily could be bent in half.

In June 2006, because LRA activity had dwindled and peace talks were approaching, the government had optimistically announced that 650,000 of the approximate 1.8 million people living in the camps would soon be on their way home. It was yet another example of the wildly overstated optimism propagated by the government. The reality was that camp residents were revisiting their villages during the day to reclaim their family plots and begin cultivating their gardens to supplement their meager diets, then returning to the camps at night. It was nearing the end of the rainy season and the land felt abundant again. Corn stalks grew tall and leafy, the sweet potato plants were thick and green, and the red cassava stems waved in the wind. The roads were clogged each morning as farmers lugged their thick-bladed hoes to and from their gardens, often several miles from the camps. But by late afternoon, those roads were again populated by weary gardeners heading back to the confines of the camps.

Not until a peace deal was signed and Kony was under control would they go back, the villagers told me. Too many people had died horrible deaths over too many years for them to forget their fear of the rebels. Pronouncements of peace by government officials in far-away Kampala carried little weight among the villagers.

"The rebels killed many people here," Awule complained. The most serious recent rebel attack had been in late January 2005 when the rebels had burned villages in the area, attacked the camp, bludgeoned many people to death, and stolen all the food they could take. "Some were burned in their houses," Awule said. "Some were cut by axes. Others were killed by a gun. They raped women," and young boys and girls were kidnapped. The rebels were still around, he said, and residents were not about to abandon the collective security camps. Most mornings these past days the farmers had found the stalks of uprooted cassava plants—the same plants they had cultivated the day before. Boot tracks pocked the freshly tilled earth—imprints of the same calf-high rubber boots favored by the rebel fighters. He nodded his head with grim certainty.

Awule's personal land problems began because he had stayed away from his village for several years, moving his wife and eight children from one refugee camp to another. When he finally ventured back to his village one day, "I found somebody cultivating my land." The interloper, he said, "felt the land was his. He knew me. I knew him." But it was an honest mistake because the boundaries had disappeared, he explained. Wanting to follow the law, Awule took his claim to the head of the local council and then the police. They only shrugged, so he went to the regional land tribunal, where his claim was finally honored.

Awule said he and thousands of others in the camp couldn't wait to go home. "We are in a very bad condition here. Some are dying of hunger and diseases." Even if the problem with the rebels was finished, it would take time to rebuild, he said. "There is no property left," he says of the village structures. "It was burned by the rebels. There is the land, but we are afraid to go back. The rebels are still there. When they are gone, we will be going back home."

———

Ciprian Okello, a lean man with a quick smile and energetic eyes, was the leader of the Walela camp, created only two years earlier. "These people are ready to go back, but they fear. The rebels are malingering around."

The camp residents survived on emergency supplies of corn and sorghum from the UN, but it was just enough to stave off starvation. The situation in the camp was desperate, and the Ugandan government was to blame, he said, and he scoffed at the government's claims that people were returning to the land. "If the government wants the people to go back and resettle, we want to hear clearly that no rebels are around." And he added, "We want enough materials to start living [again] in the villages." No one in the camp had ever seen any government assistance. Neither had they been assured the rebels were gone.

As most refugees spoke fondly of a return to their lands, yet another land war loomed on the horizon with grave consequences for the already battered and decimated north. With the villages abandoned, the clans scattered, and the leaders dead and gone, the traditional Acholi system of land management was disintegrating. Like much of Africa's communal system, lands had been managed and supervised on the local level by clan elders. Clans knew whose land was whose because they lived on it every day. And families within the clans also knew the boundaries of their lands because granting land was a decision made by the clan. It ensured that, as one generation followed another, the families would retain their rights to grow as large a garden as they needed and would have a place to house their goats and cows. Grazing lands were communal property, and as one clan and its herds grew, grazing land could always be a source of conflict. But it was a fully functioning system in which the clan made sure that any family's lands were passed equitably to the next generation. Disputes were settled by the clans, and life moved on. There was enough room for all. If a family moved away, died, or disavowed its claims, the land reverted to the clan for the elders to redistribute. The system guaranteed the survival of the families and the clans, as everyone had a place to live and a place to grow their food. No one got richer than his or her neighbor, and no one starved.

But after twenty years of guerrilla warfare in the north, like most of everything else in Acholiland, the traditional system of land management had fallen apart. The clans were dispersed. Clan leaders had been killed or had died or, if alive, had now scattered to various camps. Traditional Acholi life had fallen into disarray. In the midst of this chaos, the government proposed a new system of land management in the north, providing land titles for returning villagers. The individual deeds would be recorded with government land agencies and would give one person something of value that could be used as capital or collateral. The land could be kept, transferred to children, or sold.

Supporters of the idea said that this would be the catalyst for an economic resurgence in the north. Some considered it a critical step toward modernity, an entry into the capitalist system of free enterprise. But others felt sure that a system of deeded land would only lead to the impoverishment and subjugation of the north and the ultimate destruction of the Acholi.

Judy Adoko, an activist with the Land and Equity Movement in Uganda, said the government's back-to-the-land movement subverted traditional landownership and would precipitate yet another social catastrophe in the north. At best it would create confusion, and at worst it would result in a colossal land grab by the country's ruling elite, leaving more than a million people homeless. The government's resettlement plans, she was convinced, would put the north in a state of permanent chaos.

The government's land tribunals were not necessary because traditional procedures in place among the Acholi clans guaranteed equity of land distribution, resolved disputes, and ensured continuity. "The land can be managed by custom," she said. Creating a new system that did not respect ancient Acholi practices and traditions would only further subvert those who had already suffered severe losses due to the fighting with the LRA. The traditional system secured the survival of each generation because the land could never be sold. If you were entitled to land for your family, you needed only to ask the clan.

"In the north with the Acholi [the destruction of the clans] is a serious matter," she said, because the LRA fighters routinely executed village elders and kidnapped children for child soldiers, the same children who would traditionally inherit the land. With clan elders gone, no one was left to manage and maintain the process, and an entire generation had grown up in the refugee camps and knew nothing of village life, farming, or animal husbandry.

"The new generation does not have the same values, and we have many widows," Adoko said. If the government proceeded with the land title plan, which excluded women, Adoko predicted, "what we will have now is a potential land grab" by speculators who will offer attractive sums to title holders, most likely men. "The phrase that 'women don't own land' is the excuse they use. When the clan is not there to protect her, the widow is the most vulnerable."

If land in the north was for sale, Adoko said, the result would be concentration of the land in the hands of a few, most likely wealthy southerners. The landless would then flock to the cities, exacerbating problems in the already overcrowded urban areas. Customary tenure, she said, "is a good system, but it doesn't lead to economic growth." Once titles are issued, "it will be survival of the fittest," and the fittest, she said, are those who already are in the country's power elite.

Adoko and others were convinced the new system of landowner-ship had nothing to do with the noble notions of privatization and economic development. "Many feel that the real reason behind the war was that the government wanted to take their land," she said. Since the cattle-herding culture held sway across much of Uganda, the growing herds and growing population in the south put pressure on the vast amount of communal grazing land in the north traditionally held by the Acholi, Langi, and Teso clans. The situation was ripe for a legitimatized land grab. "The law protects anyone who has a title," legal or not, and if the government-appointed land tribunals recog-nized and upheld those titles, there was little an individual landless Acholi could do to stop it. "If our forefathers sold land, where would we be now?" she asked. "The poverty that will come [will be] worse than any poverty we have ever known."

At the crossroads of this conflict were the land tribunals. They operated much like the circuit-riding judges of the American West, traveling from town to town settling land disputes. In early June 2006, I caught up with one of the tribunals as it was wrapping up several days of hearings in the town of Lira. It was chaired by Charles Opio Ogwal, a pleasant and affable lawyer who complained that the tri-bunal's work would be simplified if only land in the north had been registered with the government. But most of it hadn't.

"It is a problem," he said, because most of the land in the north is governed by "customary tenure." Without any formal records of boundaries of family or common lands, the tribunal relied on witnesses and testimony. In some cases, clans had been battling with other clans over communal grazing land.

He disputed Adoko's claim that the clan system helped protect widows. Often the opposite was true. "They may not favor the widow and her family if she wants to sell the land," he said. For example, "the brothers [of her late husband] may stop her or insist on her marrying one of them." In such a case, the new husband could then claim title to the land. "It is not easy to deal with them," he said. And even if a clan made a decision, it was not legally binding. A decision by a tribunal was, however, and "the solution is usually more long lasting."

One member of the tribunal, Sam Ocula, of Gulu, advocated the traditional system of customary tenure. "It is very protective of the tenants. The system is there to protect the whole community," he said. "The communal attachment to the land is very strong."

But, he said, the trend to private ownership was critical to the future economic development of the north in a postwar environment. Ocula favored documentation of land ownership, even if that documentation affirmed clan or communal control, since people's memories could be flawed or prejudiced. With certificates of common tenure possession by a clan, or with individual land titles, landowners or clans could approach banks for loans for farm equipment or other capital equipment that would help them generate income. Having records other than a neighbor's memories to define things, such as the land on which schools had been built but abandoned due to the war, would ease the rebuilding of the north, he said. Already the tribunal had been wrestling with conflicting claims due to destroyed or missing land boundary markers. "People have not yet started to go back to the villages," he said, but as they do, "we anticipate very big problems."

Many of the land disputes created by the war could not be solved by the clan system, Ocula argued. The new generation that had grown up in the refugee camps had never seen the land they supposedly would inherit from the clan, and likewise most were not known or recognized by the clan leaders. Some were known, but had been gone for years, and more often than not, many did not know if the rightful owners were alive or dead.

But even more complicated was the reality of those who had been born in "captivity," which is how Ocula described the refugee camps. These children were born of parents from different clans. "What clan do they belong to?" he asked. It was a serious question because the answer would determine which family's land could be claimed. "This will be a major source of conflict," he feared. In the coming years, he said, "People will go and organically fight out the ownership of the land."

Despite the lack of legal standing of the clans, Ocula preferred the clan and communal system of landownership to the issuance of private, individual land titles. "Private ownership will increase the problem," he said. "Those with money will always come and seduce people in various ways. The stronger person takes it," he said of the land. "The widows and children are the most affected." Already many refugees had realized that their gardens and grazing land had a value beyond the clan, and they had already begun to claim ownership of indistinct parcels of land that may or may not have been theirs. Land fraud was on the rise, he said, because, "land boundaries have never been there." The land tribunal was caught in the middle of this looming problem. "We now have cases with those who have sold their land, spent the money, and are landless. They go back to the clan and reclaim the land."

Franco Ojur had recently been elected chairman of the Lira district when we met in late May 2006. The government had targeted Lira to be among the first regions to receive the resettlement packages for long-awaited evacuation of the camps. As we sat on red fabric couches in his modest office, he shook his head pessimistically when I asked how the movement back to the land was going.

"Not much is being done by the government," he said with resignation. He thought the situation was political punishment for him. He had been a member of President Museveni's National Resistance Movement party but had lost one of the party's preelection primaries, a result he disputed. Confident of his popular support, he declared himself an independent candidate and had won handily.

"People got fed up with living in the camps," Ojur said, and "slowly were leaving the camps, but they don't leave the camps completely." They tended their gardens by day but lived in the camps at night. "Resettlement is not something that can be done in a short period of time." Some corrugated metal roofing was delivered to the region, but it was useless unless people had the material to rebuild the walls that support the roofing, he said. Since most camp residents were unemployed, they would need money to buy tools, wood, nails, and hoes. "People are patiently waiting," he said.

Ojur doubted the legitimacy of the government's plan to provide private land titles to individual landowners. "The customary system we have is quite sufficient. If the government insists people have titles [to land], it will create a lot of tension." Land, he said, "is a very sensitive matter" in the north. He made the remark with the kind of gravity that told me that the situation could mean serious problems in the future if not handled properly.

But land boundary and ownership disputes were only part of the problem, Ojur said. Vast herds of cattle and other domestic animals had been lost. The rural education system was nonexistent. Hundreds of rural schools had been abandoned, some destroyed and most badly damaged. They lacked desks, tables, chairs, windows, and, most important, teachers and teaching materials. Health care did not exist. Backcountry roads had not been graded for years, were overgrown, and now were nothing more than washed-out footpaths. The reconstruction of the north would be expensive and lengthy.

"We shall be working for some time," he said drily.

Camp residents across the north, especially in the Lira region, were reluctant to begin a mass exodus of the camps because some of the most horrific mass killings of civilians had taken place here. These memories, and the resulting widespread fear they caused, were seared on the community's collective consciousness. Two years earlier, on November 11, 2003, rebels had killed scores in the Lira suburb of Ngetta, the location of Father Fraser's church and radio station. The brutal slaughter had sent people fleeing into town for protection.

Albertina Adongo, one of the few survivors of that massacre, recalled that at about 11:00 P.M. that night she was roused by her son shouting that the LRA rebels were coming. Moments later, rebel fighters filled her hut, grabbed her husband, and sent her outside. The last time she saw her husband alive, he lay on the floor of their hut, she said, and, knowing he would soon die, he made the sign of the cross. She waited outside and listened as the young soldiers smashed her husband's skull with a hoe. When the soldiers left, she crawled back in.

"I gathered the pieces of his skull. They were scattered like peels of oranges. The hens ran away with some pieces. I sat next to his body, paralyzed. My brain had stopped functioning," she said.

But the nightmare was not over. About 2:00 A.M. the rebels came back with a dozen captives, who were ordered to lie on their sides with their heads resting against a log. "They were told not to scream," Adongo said. "Then their heads were smashed with logs and pounding sticks. Those who resisted had their necks slit with knives. One had his tongue removed. The killings were done with intervals and lasted for four hours. 'It is very nice to kill Lango,' the rebels said. Those who cried were ordered to keep quiet and told, 'We are just helping you to reach the other side.'"

Adongo eventually reunited with her children, who had fled. In what the newspaper called "an absurd twist of fate," the boy who had killed her husband later attended the same school in the same class as her daughter. Adongo said she was not bitter. Instead, she forgave him. "He was abducted and ordered to kill. I forgive all of them. Their leader forced them. They are all lost children."[2]

A year after the attack on Ngetta, the LRA struck again, this time more viciously. On the night of April 21, 2004, a much larger unit of LRA fighters launched a massive attack on the Barlonyo camp, about six miles from Lira. The attack came in the evening, according to survivors, and began with mortars mercilessly raining on the camp. Several hundred heavily armed rebels swarmed into the camp, overrunning the thirty or so hopelessly outnumbered and outgunned militia members. The defenders fled. Rebels wielding machetes and clubs screamed at the people to return to their huts, then promptly set them on fire, burning them alive. Those who fled the flames were shot, hacked, or clubbed to death. The next morning residents pulled nearly three hundred bodies from the smoldering ruins.

Camp leader Moses Ogwang was one of the survivors. Nearly four years after the 2004 massacre, I visited the Barlonyo camp, and as Ogwang and I stood in the waning light of day, not far from the white marble monument built just months after the tragedy, he pointed to where the LRA rebels had attacked and swept into the camp. Ogwang had fled that night, which is how he survived. "So many people they killed," he said, explaining that he had lost his mother, his brother, and a nephew. He described to me how the rebels circulated through the camp, setting the huts on fire and grabbing people as they ran out, then held them as others killed them with machetes.

One of the first people to visit the site the morning after was Father Fraser, who saw the wreckage, the burned and mutilated bodies. He said the army moved quickly to bury the bodies; he suspected this was so people would not know the full extent of the tragedy. The camp had been a creation of the army, he said, because they wanted to consolidate the scattered villages into a larger one that supposedly was easier to defend. Fraser said relatives later exhumed the bodies and reburied them in family plots. It was one of the most horrific episodes of the twenty-year war. "Kony should be taken to the international court for just Barlonyo alone," he said.

Over two years after the Barlonyo massacre, refugee camp residents in the Lira area were justifiably wary about returning to their lands, despite the government's insinuations that the LRA was in hand and that peace was just around the corner. Shortly after I spoke with Ojur and just a day after I spoke with Awule and Okello at the Walela refugee camp in 2006, the LRA attacked the Alito camp in the neighboring Apac district, killing one person and abducting seventeen, including a priest from the Alito Catholic Mission. The attack began about 8:00 P.M., the camp leader said, and continued until 1:00 A.M., a full five hours, until the military detachment nearby finally responded, chasing the rebels away. The rebels were pursued by the Ugandan military, and in the confusion of the pursuit, ten of the seventeen escaped from the LRA.

As with most others in the north, Ojur blamed the government for much of the suffering in the north. The Ugandan army and the militias were woefully undermanned and poorly equipped, due to the debilitating deception of the ghost soldiers. Where a unit of seven hundred Ugandan and militia soldiers was reported in position and protecting an area, only one or two hundred soldiers existed in reality, Ojur said. This had allowed the LRA units to strike at will. If counterattacks were launched, they were too brief to be effective and rarely inflicted substantial damage on the LRA. The LRA survived. "We can never relax," he said.

After a year and a half of being away from Uganda, I returned to northern Uganda in December 2007. Little had changed despite eighteen months of almost no rebel activity and the ongoing peace talks. It was the dry season, and again the great plumes of white smoke from the burning grass roiled skyward, and I found an odd satisfaction in seeing the repeat of this perennial cycle. The equatorial sun burned hotly as we bounced north out of Lira on the dirt roads that had once been the province of the LRA's lethal fighters. I traveled with a couple of Ugandan journalists, my friend Joe Wacha and Julius Ochen, a video journalist and entrepreneur who ran a cramped Internet café off the main street in Lira where he taught computer skills to eager locals. Just a couple of miles from town, however, they joked that not so long ago, this would have been a deadly trip. Indiscriminate ambushes had long been the order of the day. But not all of the vehicles were hit, they said, since the LRA and the sympathizers had devised a notification system as to who was friendly and who was not. Either a yellow plastic jerry can or a few fish were tied to the front bumper as a signal to LRA fighters not to shoot, they said.

As we moved steadily northward, the land dried, and brown grasses mingled with the green to give the land an amber hue. But I was taken by something else: patches of green dotted with white. Cotton. Fields of it on both sides of the road. Small fields, of course, and cultivated by hand, but still sprouting a product about to go to market. Wacha and Ochen talked about the latest controversy swirling through the land, which was not the LRA but the price of cotton. That it was a topic of discussion was remarkable. In just a couple of growing seasons of peace in the north, the region had taken a step toward normalcy. A cash crop was suddenly abundant. Maybe, I thought, northern Uganda would recover more quickly than anyone imagined.

We bounced along the roller-coaster roads, eventually arriving at the dusty town of Pader, a place that resembled the set of a spaghetti western. The main dirt street sprouted signs for aid groups, a few "hotels" offered grimy concrete rooms, and a couple of gas stations pumped petrol at inflated prices and sold warm soda and dusty packets of stale cookies. We drove north, then veered off the main dirt road to a smaller track flanked by tall grass. We were headed to a place that Ochen described as a former LRA base, a strategic location surrounded by high hills from which the LRA had fought off the Ugandan army and savaged the local population, stealing food and plucking its children. I gazed at the largely vacant landscape, recalling Ochen's description of the area from the night before as the region through which northern Arab slave traders of centuries past had routinely swept to collect their human cargo. This same slave trade had brought a horde of proselytizing Christian missionaries to eradicate that particular scourge but also to convert the "heathens." No wonder the Acholis had assumed the mantle of the warrior tribe. This is where Saharan Africa meets sub-Saharan Africa in a clash of cultures, values, and ethnicity as alive today as it was centuries earlier.

We turned off the road where clusters of conical thatched roofs spread out below towering mango trees and extended to the base of the nearby ridge. This was the Lataya camp, a spread of hundreds of homes for more than six thousand people. The arrival of our four-wheel-drive attracted immediate attention, and moments later the packed dirt in the shade of a tree was swept and chairs and benches provided. David Ocaya, the leader of this part of the camp, joined us with two of his friends, Alfred Anyar and Richard Logai.

Are people going back to their villages, I asked, now that the peace talks have been under way for eighteen months and the LRA violence is all but gone?

He shook his head no and uttered the all-too-familiar refrain: "People are fearing because of the rebels." Of the thousands in the camp, only about thirty families had left permanently. The rest still visited their original villages by day and returned to the camp at night. The latest rebel activity had taken place just a few months earlier when a rebel remnant of some six soldiers had exchanged fire with the Ugandan army. A couple of rebel collaborators supplied the rebel unit from the camp, he said, and they had been arrested. The clash was just enough to keep the camp residents on edge because the camp had been attacked four times between 2004 and 2006, with thirty people dead and about one hundred people, mostly children, abducted.

But the LRA was not the only problem, Anyar explained. Whenever the LRA attacked, the camp residents would flee. At the time, the Ugandan army used helicopters to chase the rebels, he said, and on one occasion, the fleeing camp residents were mistaken for rebels. Fifteen camp residents were killed, he said. Since some rebels still roamed the area, "it is not yet completely comfortable."

And there were other lasting effects from the war, said Logai. "People are fearing the land mines. You never know where the rebels [put] these things. That is why people are moving back [to the villages] slowly." Despite the fear, it is unclear exactly how extensively most areas in the north were mined, he said, but the government had actively been warning people not to pick up anything they didn't recognize, particularly unexploded ordnance.

Despite their worries, the vast majority of people enjoyed the benefits of the past eighteen months of peace as the talks in Juba continued, Ocaya said. "It is allowing them to renew their lives and do things to make money for school fees. Now, because of the talks, the roads are open. We are praying for a peaceful conclusion to the talks." Until a peace agreement is signed, and Kony has formally quit the war, Ocaya said, most residents are sitting and waiting. Once peace is formalized, he said, the families would have to reassemble, since many had been scattered during the war, had been killed, or were living in various camps, and then they could return to their original homes.

But some people, such as Ellen Abwo, age forty, and her friend Helen Lalam, age fifty, did not have far to go. The Lataya camp had been their village, and others had moved in. Abwo said she hoped to collect compensation from the government for hosting several thousand of her neighbors, but she doubted whether such a payment would ever materialize. Regardless, she and Lalam had devised a way to make it pay. About ten yards from where we talked, a fire crackled below several stacked pots where they were making a distilled liquor called *kava*. It was a variation of the word *cover,* Wacha explained, which was the topmost plate where the distilled alcohol condensed into a pot. The alcohol came from fermented sorghum or corn, she said, which they heated. She sold a cup of the booze for about a nickel and a half liter for about fifteen cents. Lalam had been making *kava* for twenty years, she said, and it paid her expenses for her two children, a girl, thirteen, and a boy, sixteen, who had been abducted by the LRA but was now back and trying to reclaim his life.

Just about a mile from the camp, however, Cisto Odongo, age thirty-five, and about a dozen of his friends toiled in the hot sun, each building a new thatch-roofed hut. It would take about three weeks to complete, he said, because getting the right materials was time-consuming. In part they were motivated to act now because the tall grass they needed for the thatch was dry, and soon most of it would be burned, clearing the way for new growth. Six-inch-thick logs were taken from the trees that grew on the hills, he explained, then were buried upright and used for supports. They were connected with pliable sticks and bound with strips of stringy bark. The roof supports consisted of long bamboo poles that he and his friends had walked about fifteen miles to find. With the help of friends, they secured and tied each conical frame, then tied bundles of thatch to it. The huts felt remarkably cool in the afternoon sun and provided ample protection from the rains. The circular mud-brick walls would have to come later, because water needed to make the mud was scarce. For the time being, however, a thatched roof overhead was enough.

After five years of living in refuge camps, Odongo was ready to enjoy the peace. "As long as I can live peacefully and till my soil without having to pay rent, that is the best," he said. He longed for the days when he could relax in his own house and raise a family and domestic animals.

He felt confident that the traditional life of the Acholi would be restored, if they only could return to their villages. "People used to make a fire and the whole family would sit around it. The elders would tell stories, and that's how the young people would learn." Communities gathered for dances and shared stories and trade. "I believe it will be easy to get back to traditional life. Families are fewer [in the villages] than in the crowded camps, and you can follow someone's behavior more closely," he said. "That is what we are looking for."

———

A few days later, in Gulu, I met with Yusef Adek, one of the senior members of the LRA's peace-negotiating team. We had met more than a year before in the Nabanga camp on the border of the Congo and South Sudan. We had been part of the entourage brought by Riek Machar, and, though we had talked, he was reluctant to answer the myriad questions I had about the war. Partly because the rest of the LRA's delegation was there watching, it was impossible to speak in private. He had, however, promised me a full interview later in Gulu. Now was the time.

Adek was an Acholi elder who largely operated out of the public spotlight. The government was well aware of him, however, and had identified him as an LRA sympathizer. His home bore the scars of several army attacks, he said, and he had been arrested thirteen times. He had been stripped of his animals by the Ugandan army, but allowed to keep his house on the outskirts of Gulu. He was forced to report regularly to the authorities in Kampala. "I am still a prisoner," he said. "They call me a rebel collaborator."

While he talked extensively about the war and the peace talks, which he said were virtually irreversible at that point, he also talked about the future of the Acholi. He tried hard to put me at ease about the damage done during the war and the resiliency of the Acholi people. With an air of dismissal, he quoted an oft-used phrase in Acholi. "When two elephants struggle, it is the grass that suffers," he said. "We are the grass."

Once peace is secured, it will not take long to rebuild the north, he said. Even as Adek spoke, evidence of this was apparent in Gulu. A number of new banks had been built during the year that I had been gone, gleaming new edifices with ATMs. If the banks had arrived, it meant money had arrived, and the long lines of people waiting to use them proved it.

"It will not take five years" to rebuild the north, Adek said. "We will catch up with the others." Adek was also well aware of the heated emotions that bubbled up around the questions of landownership in the north. There was no doubt that he favored traditional landownership schemes as opposed to private land titles. "In Acholi we are left with two properties: our lives and our land." If either one was disturbed any further, it would only bring more war, he said bluntly. And in the same breath, he seemed to end the debate over the government's proposal to issue private land titles. "If you want to touch anything about the land, we will go to war," he said, poking the air with his finger.

10

The Call for Peace

ARCHBISHOP JOHN BAPTIST ODAMA smiled calmly as he sat on a large white sofa in the cool dimness of the reception room of the Gulu Archdiocese in mid-March 2006. Only months earlier he had suggested that he be arrested and tried by the International Criminal Court in lieu of Joseph Kony. I asked him to explain.

"People have been in a cage," Odama said of the Acholi. Outside the cage the Ugandan army roamed the countryside and chased the LRA rebels. Inside the cage nearly two million people lived in the internal refugee camps, among them the night commuters, the displaced children who migrated nightly from the camps to the protected shelters in town. "This military approach has not been able to break the walls of imprisonment," he said. "It is not bearing fruit."

Odama was among the Acholi religious and cultural leaders in Gulu who had urged peace talks and reconciliation between the government and the LRA since the early 1990s. Failure followed failure, as Kony's forces rejected and sometimes killed peace emissaries. The religious leaders achieved a breakthrough in 2002 after the Uganda Parliament approved an amnesty program for LRA soldiers, a move that Odama and others had lobbied for strongly. The idea of amnesty, particularly for the kidnapped soldiers, was universally known and extremely popular; the Acholi did not want their children to be prosecuted for crimes they had been forced to commit against their will. The program resulted in an estimated fifteen thousand child soldiers and commanders turning themselves in. Odama was clearly pleased with the result, though it had done little to blunt the impact of the war or to end it. Amnesty, however, gave the fighters an alternative to prolonged membership in Kony's army. The kidnapped soldiers could flee the forced brutality of the rebels and not face prosecution.

On the surface, amnesty for the LRA seemed like a plausible and welcome idea to end the malaise of war. Historically, amnesty has been widely used to entice combatants to lay down their weapons with the understanding they would not be prosecuted for being part of a defeated army. But some problems surrounded this logic when applied to the LRA, in particular to the entire command structure. First of all, the LRA lacked an important ingredient: credibility. Kony's commanders claimed they were fighting to overthrow the Ugandan government and establish a new government ruled by the Ten Commandments. Yet their modus operandi was to kidnap, kill, pillage, and plunder—violate everything they claimed to stand for. Second, their primary victims were not the Ugandan army but the Acholi, the very people for whom they claimed to be fighting. Third, by victimizing their own people, they lost any legitimate claim to represent the Acholi or the interests of the north. They represented only themselves and were a self-perpetuating group of killers. In any other society, they would have been hunted down and the survivors prosecuted. Why should the Lord's Resistance Army be granted amnesty?

The answer, of course, was that the north was war-weary. They were sick and tired of fear, of fighting, of bloodshed. Amnesty was not a cop-out or a convenient way to avoid punishing criminals, Odama insisted. It was a last-ditch effort, and, to the religious leaders in northern Uganda, it had the potential to bring about an end to the madness. It was part of a two-pronged approach, extending an olive branch with one hand and a hammer with the other. When the Ugandan army surged into southern Sudan with Operation Iron Fist, Odama and friends had asked for peace talks, offering themselves as mediators between the government and the rebels, he said. They had met with President Museveni and asked, "Why don't you push more for peace?" They urged dialogue with the rebels, saying it would "create room for reconciliation." In practical terms, a peace accord would save money and halt the destruction of lives and property. Museveni assented, but did not withdraw the military.

In 2002 and early 2003, the leaders and their emissaries met with the rebels at least six times, he said. Odama proudly handed me a photo of him and the LRA's former negotiator and rebel commander Sam Kolo, taken on March 6, 2003. Despite the elation surrounding the meeting with the rebels and the resurgent hope that peace talks finally could be on track, the mood quickly soured after the Ugandan army attacked rebel forces near the meeting site, which outraged the Acholi leaders. Although the government later admitted its mistake, calling it an "uncoordinated move," the peace effort was sabotaged. "The rebels were suspicious of us," Odama said, "and the government was accusing us of supporting the rebels."

Late the following year, however, the leaders reopened talks via yet another group of mediators that included, among others, Betty Bigombe, a Ugandan working with the World Bank, and Gracie Mandela, the wife of Nelson Mandela of South Africa. Meanwhile, the International Criminal Court worked intently in northern Uganda to gather evidence and testimony for its pending indictments against Kony and his top commanders. Odama and the other leaders worried that if the indictments were issued at this juncture, the renewed peace efforts would be subverted yet again. Kony would never sign a peace deal if he knew that he and his top commanders would land in an international court.

"We advised the ICC to slow down," he said. "The peace process could be jeopardized."

With the ICC indictments pending, a cease-fire was arranged, and talks proceeded. By December 2004 Kony and his commanders were reviewing a memorandum of understanding for a cease-fire and peace talks. When the December 15 deadline passed without an agreement, Bigombe and the religious leaders appealed to Museveni for an extension, saying the elusive peace was within reach. Museveni set midnight December 31, 2004, as the final deadline.

"People were very hopeful now that everything would be finished," Odama said.

But again the deadline passed with no word from Kony. On New Year's Day the Ugandan army attacked LRA units in the area where the meetings had been taking place. It was as close as the government had ever gotten to a peace deal with the LRA.

Ten months later, in October 2005, the ICC indictments against Kony and his top commanders were unsealed. While the international community applauded the court's first formal act after five years since its creation, Odama cringed. As far as he was concerned, the door to peace had closed.

Wearing a neatly ironed ivory robe and cap, Odama waved his hands in frustration at all the attempts to end the war: escalation of military action, amnesty, peace talks, and now international court indictments. "None of them has succeeded to stop this war," he said. "If the arrest of Kony and his commanders was to bring peace to the people as a last approach, and because it has not happened, and [because] we are not sure they will be arrested at all," Odama explained, "I offer[ed] myself to be arrested for the sake of peace." He would be the sacrificial lamb on the altar of international justice.

Was he serious? Wasn't this yet another delusion, not that far removed from Kony's own proclamations that he was a prophet, a demigod sent to lead the Acholi into a new world? Here was a Catholic archbishop nailing himself on a cross because the outside world demanded a trial. With someone, anyone, on trial, Odama said, "the people in the camps can go free; the night commuters can go free; and then Kony and the [Ugandan army] can go free . . . so therefore the war can stop."

It was a Catholic archbishop's modest proposal from the heart of Africa. But a trial was not a theatrical event. Defendants did not audition for the part. A trial was supposed to determine the guilt or innocence of the accused, not surrogate volunteers. Did Odama not understand this? Rather than clamoring for justice more loudly than anyone else, the Acholi instead grumbled that the ICC indictments made things worse. But were they truly prepared after twenty years of war to throw up their hands in resignation and tell the LRA that all was forgiven? I doubted it. Too many child soldiers and young women returning from the LRA told of being ostracized, of being labeled as killers, criminals, and deviants. Though the rank-and-file fighters escaped prosecution for their war crimes, the Acholi community dispensed sympathy but not forgiveness. They hated the LRA. Yet the ICC was criticized for perpetuating the war. By implication, the Acholi were saying that the concepts of war crimes and crimes against humanity were foreign, an invention of another world, another civilization. They suggested that justice had nothing to do with the thousands of victims in northern Uganda.

The core of this Christian cleric's call for peace was forgiveness of the LRA. He took the New Testament dictum to turn the other cheek, easily the most vexing of all Christian beliefs to accept or follow, literally. But Kony and the LRA had not asked for forgiveness and apparently did not want it. Someone or something else was always to blame for their actions. This unwanted and undeserved offer of forgiveness was motivated by fear—fear that the killing and mutilation would never end. It amounted to extortion. This offer of forgiveness might have been intended to lure the LRA out of the bush, or it might have been a way for the Acholi to achieve a sense of peace about the decades of horror. But it did not wipe the slate clean. More precisely, it was an opportunity for the Acholi to understand what in themselves and their culture had given rise to Kony and the LRA. By convention, forgiveness came from God via the church, but only after a confession, a plea for mercy, and penance. None of this was forthcoming from the LRA or its leaders. As much as Odama resisted it, he and the rest of the Acholi existed in a world of crime and of punishment. After twenty years of heinous war waged for no clear reason or purpose, it was ludicrous to suggest that Kony and his army should walk out of the bush and be treated as if nothing had happened. The word *amnesty* derives from *amnesia,* an ancient Greek term meaning "not to remember." It was what Odama and others were suggesting for the Acholi, that they not remember. In reality, it was moral amnesia.

Would the war ever end?

"There is a time for war, and there is a time for end of the war," Odama said, offering an overworked biblical paraphrase.

When I pushed him for an answer, he admitted that peace was up to the Acholi themselves. "If the people unite and declare that this war should not continue, it will stop."

Why hadn't that been done already?

He shrugged. "It is a puzzle to me. With God's help, this will end, but when, I don't know." Odama was genuinely perplexed by why the endless suffering had not prompted stronger efforts to end it. "The war has . . . grandchildren, and it is still going on." He had even offered a public apology to the children of the north on behalf of Ugandan society and its institutions. "For you peace doesn't mean anything," he had said to the war's children. None of the population under twenty years of age had ever known peace.

He fell silent for a long time, then lifted his eyes. With a note of sadness, he said, "I feel I could have done more, but because [the war's end] has not happened, forgive me." Finally, Odama was being real. I didn't know what to say.

⎯⎯⎯⎯⎯

Not far from Odama's offices and along one of the rough streets of Gulu was the modest Islamic center where I found Sheik Musah Kahlil. He represented the Islamic 20 percent of the north's population. His participation in the peace process had been part of the refracted reality in northern Uganda.

Kony had acknowledged Islam in his amalgamated religious practices by forbidding the use of drugs and alcohol among his soldiers. Kony also reportedly respected Friday as the Islamic holy day of rest, and I wanted to know how this Muslim cleric viewed Kony and the war. Kahlil had just returned from visiting a crowded refugee camp in the Pader region east of Gulu, and the visit had left him troubled and anxious.

"We saw hundreds of malnourished children," he said, waving his hands. "We fear the situation will be worse." A week earlier, in the midst of the dry season, fire had destroyed hundreds of the camps' densely packed thatch-roofed huts, which were always vulnerable to an errant spark carried on the gusting winds. Once a roof ignited, the fire spread quickly, leaping from one hut to another. With the coming rainy season, Khalil said, these now-homeless refugees faced disease and exposure.

The peace initiative grew out of a day of prayer arranged by religious leaders in the north in 1997, he said, on the tenth anniversary of Kony's war. "Since the beginning, our people were suffering," he said. "Our people were dying." By appealing for peace, "we served as the voice of the voiceless," he said. "It is important that we throw away our differences and work collectively for a peaceful solution."

The religious leaders had produced several books advocating peace, he explained, and the heart of their message was forgiveness.

One was titled *Forgive Seventy Times Seven,* but he didn't have a copy handy. When their efforts culminated in face-to-face meetings with the LRA's top leaders, Kahlil was among the negotiating team members in the north on the fateful night of December 31, 2004. "People were celebrating already. We thought that peace had succeeded."

The ICC indictments that followed ten months later threw a wet blanket over any further peace efforts. "If only the ICC could wait and give peace a chance, it would end the conflict," he said. "But peace needs patience. When the ICC issued the warrants, [we] were handcuffed." Much of what the international community has tried has backfired, he said. The indictments, like the reward offered for Kony's capture, only hardened Kony's resolve to fight on. "It resulted in innocent people dying," he said. "Things have become very difficult. We had to change our strategy." He reflected on the peace initiatives. The war has "made our community hopeless. The only way to end the conflict is through peaceful means." Despite the setbacks to the peace initiatives, he said, "We will continue."

Besides backing the amnesty program, Kahlil said he and other religious leaders had asked that the Ugandan army establish a "safety corridor" whereby captured child soldiers and child brides could be released by the LRA without fear of attack. I first heard of the proposed safe zone from Kony's deputy Vincent Otti, who was the call-in guest on talk radio in Kampala shortly after I arrived in Uganda. It was a rambling, disjointed discussion in which Otti repeatedly called Kony a prophet. Otti said that the LRA would not give up unless and until it received guarantees of a "safety corridor" through which it could make an escape.

Where did Kahlil think Kony and the LRA would go?

"He's somebody who knows very well he will be tried," Kahlil replied, apparently unable to guess or predict. With the ICC indictments, the LRA had nothing left but to fight and die, he said. "What is their future if they come out?"

If Kony was not getting the support he needed from various sources, I suggested, he would have to quit.

"We don't know who is supplying him," he said, despite the fact that pro-Kony information had recently surfaced in the Sudan press of Khartoum's support for him. Support for the LRA came from the Islamic fundamentalists who controlled the Sudan regime, he agreed, but Kony had distanced himself from them. That support had become an open secret just a couple months earlier when Hassan al-Turabi, the former Speaker of the Sudanese Assembly, had defended Kony and the LRA in an interview with a British journalist. Turabi admitted that Sudan had supported the LRA for many years, saying, "It's natural. In all wars people do the same. If there's a state of war between you and the other side, then you arm the other side's opposition, don't you?"[1]

He also denied that the LRA committed atrocities against civilians and children. "They don't kill them by the way, they don't murder."[2] Because Uganda had backed the rebel Sudan People's Liberation Army led by Museveni's close ally, the late John Garang, Khartoum retaliated by arming the LRA.

Because the conflict had gone beyond Uganda's borders, Khalil urged that an international peacekeeping force be brought in. "There is an international dimension to this war." Kony had been quoted as saying "We are fighting America," Kahlil explained. The connection, however, was obscure because the United States was one among many foreign countries that provided direct cash support to the government. The international community should be pressing Sudan and Uganda to make peace, he said. If the United States and other foreign players in the region will not seek peace, he said, then northern Uganda should be declared a "disaster zone" and UN troops should be placed here.

But the military solution that Kahlil and others had criticized, not the peace process, controlled the situation, I suggested. It had been relatively quiet in the north for months.

Kahlil disagreed. The relative calm in the north was deceptive. "They are not people who are easily defeated militarily," he said of the LRA. "It will be difficult. Kony knows how to disperse his forces." As he has done in the past, Kony would bide his time to regroup. "When the rain stops and the grasses are green, Kony is back." With a Museveni victory in the presidential polls, that was all but assured, he said. "They will come full swing and fight seriously. Kony is a man [that many] underestimate," he said, suggesting that Kony was stronger and more determined than most people realized. "I don't think [Kony and the LRA] are militarily weakened."

———

David Onen Acana was the Acholi *rwot,* or traditional and lineal Acholi chief. Unlike the Acholi religious leaders, he supported military action against the LRA as well as the pursuit of a negotiated peace. With some satisfaction, he noted the Ugandan army was "at it each day, chasing these people." Onen spoke as if the LRA rebels were not Acholis, not his would-be subjects, and distanced himself from the force. Yet Onen agreed that "the best way to end this is through dialogue."

But a dialogue about what? I asked. Whatever political agenda the LRA may once have had was gone.

He agreed, saying that the war had gone on so long that the LRA had become a self-perpetuating militia. But no one wanted more Acholi children to die. "We all failed to protect them," he said of the thousands of kidnapped children and adults. "So we can't recommend that they be killed out there. Many hope our daughters and sons will someday return home."

Onen called the failed peace negotiations of late 2004 a wasted opportunity because of the mistrust on both sides. The LRA doubted the sincerity of the government, and vice versa. Because the Acholi leaders strongly influenced the Acholi community, they provided a unique ability to negotiate with Kony. The LRA was keenly aware that if they signed a peace deal, it would solve the rebels' situation only vis-à-vis the government. The Acholi community at large would still reject the returning soldiers and, worse yet, exact revenge. Onen said he had tried to convince the LRA otherwise. "We told them the community, because of the camps and uncertainty in their lives, wanted to go back to their villages and be free again." Onen said that they discussed forgiveness for past evils by using traditional techniques, cleansing rituals, and healing ceremonies. One such ancient Acholi ceremony called *mato oput* involved the drinking of a bitter concoction made from the leaves of an oput tree. The offender apologized for misdeeds, then was forgiven and welcomed back into the village. Under the watchful eyes of elders, the guilty party stepped on a raw egg, the symbol of a break with the past, then jumped over an *opobo* (bamboo) stick, which represented a leap from the past to the present. Both the guilty and wronged parties drank the tea to show that they accepted the bitterness of the past and promised never to taste such bitterness again. Each returning LRA soldier would be dealt with on a case-by-case basis, Onen said. Despite the overtures of peace by himself and the religious leaders, "It was up to [the LRA] to move as soon as possible to show they want peace." But they hadn't.

Rarely had I encountered anger or disgust among the Acholi over the LRA, but it surfaced in Onen. Meeting Kony and his commanders to talk peace had given him a chance to confront Kony.

"I knew it was a risk," Onen said, but "I told them all the wrongs they were doing. If they were fighting the government, they should confront the government directly." Instead, they were attacking defenseless villagers. They listened, he said, but nothing changed. When the first deadline of December 15, 2004, arrived without an agreement, Onen said he went to Museveni personally and asked for the extension. The peace talks unraveled on the eve of the deadline, he explained, when Kony demanded to know who had drafted the agreement. When he learned it had been drafted by an outside party, he rejected it outright. Despite that, Onen thought an agreement could have been reached with more time. "It was too [little] time [for Kony] to consult with all of the commanders," he said.

But one wasted opportunity did not explain why Kony had survived for more than twenty years. The war with the LRA has been prolonged because the government had made serious miscalculations and badly mismanaged the war, Onen explained. Museveni had underestimated the size of the LRA problem and the tenacity of the fighters. "It started out small, but after twenty years, the damage has been done." Onen compared the LRA war to a dung beetle that starts out with a small piece of waste that over time becomes enormous. But he saw progress against the LRA with the amnesty program. More and more LRA fighters were coming out of the bush. "They realize what they have done [got] out of hand." Despite that, Onen thought a peaceful end to the war was possible. "I know they have the capacity to talk," he said of the LRA. "What I feel is important is to meet with Kony. He is the one who is giving the orders to the commanders in the field. I'm offering myself [as a negotiator], but he can choose. So long as they're still out there, we should not lose hope." That chance to meet Kony would come soon.

Hope was something that Betty Bigombe had a lot of, but it was running out. As the former designated negotiator with the LRA for the Ugandan government, she had been at the center of the struggle to bring the war to an end. Bigombe's involvement with the north began with a 1988 appointment to the Ugandan prime minister's office, where she oversaw pacification programs in the north. At the time, Alice Lakwena's Holy Spirit Mobile Forces had just been defeated, but a malevolent new militia had replaced it: the Lord's Resistance Army. As a senior fellow at the U.S. Institute of Peace, she had provided technical support to the Carter Center in the peace efforts between the governments of Uganda and Sudan. After years of work, she was able to arrange talks with Kony in mid-1993. The talks continued for six months but collapsed in early 1994. Kony intensified his war. Bigombe left for the United States, where she studied at Harvard University, eventually becoming a consultant with the World Bank.

But ten years after her contact with Kony had broken off, while traveling in Africa she was stunned by the brutality of the Barlonyo massacre near Lira in February 2004, which left more than three hundred refugees dead. The fifty-two-year-old took a leave from the bank, returned to Gulu, and obtained authority from Museveni to reopen negotiations.

Although she represented the Ugandan government at the time of our meeting in the spring of 2006, Bigombe bluntly expressed her doubts as to how the war had been handled in the north. What has been done to stop the clandestine support the LRA continued to receive from Sudan? she had asked. Has the Ugandan military "done its best"? Have the Acholi people been mobilized in their own defense? Has the government attempted to understand the group's mystical beliefs? Has the community been involved in pursuing Kony?

Her questions echoed the concerns of Arrow Boys commander Robert Adiama that lack of community involvement allowed the war to continue. Bigombe had other explanations as well. "Poverty at this level fans the war," she said. When people live in desperation, joining a militia looks like a viable option. When survival is at stake, moral prohibitions fall away. In her mind, this went a long way to explain some of the support for the LRA among the Acholi.

Bigombe stayed in constant contact with Kony at the time, perhaps one of only a few people. "My conviction is that only through talks can we have sustainable peace. A military victory [for Uganda] is a defeat," she said, because "the defeated people feel disgruntled." Renewing talks, she said, would create "an opportunity for people to air their grievances. Northerners have an ax to grind with Museveni."

Did the LRA have a legitimate political agenda?

To understand Kony, she said, one has to understand "how the spirit works on Kony," who had convinced his fighters that he was only an instrument of a larger, more powerful force.

Did she agree with that?

She shrugged. "Sometimes he talks perfect sense."

He is fully aware that he has only three options now: death, prison, or exile, she said. Because of that, he is likely more motivated than ever to negotiate.

But with Museveni's victory in the February presidential election, coupled with a renewed agreement with Sudan for the Ugandan army to pursue the LRA there, wasn't Kony's fate sealed?

"The LRA is weakened," she agreed, but the rebels always seem to regroup and came back with renewed brutality. Until Kony is captured or killed, the door should be left open to talks, she argued.

But for how long? I asked.

"As long as it takes."

Meanwhile, the relentless call from the Acholi leaders for dialogue and forgiveness had fallen on deaf ears in the Ugandan capital. President Museveni seemed to slam the door on peace talks in his May 4, 2006, address to foreign donors helping to restore normalcy to the north. There was no need for a negotiated peace with Kony, he said, because the Ugandan army had all but defeated the LRA.

"Some [people] continue to peddle the lie that there can be a peaceful solution involving Kony—even at this stage. [For us] there is a solution. We have chased Kony out of Uganda; we have chased him out of southern Sudan. If they allow, we shall get him in [the] Congo." Museveni spoke as if peace were at hand and Kony would soon be on trial. "We want to capture Kony and a few of his associates and hand them over to The Hague so as to end impunity," Museveni crowed. "If for some reason the International Court of Justice did not want to prosecute Kony, we would prosecute him ourselves. After all it is our law he is breaking."[3]

Two months later, Museveni would sing a different song.

11

Armed Conflict Is a Health Risk

JUST BEFORE THE LIGHT went out, I was warned about the rats. It was my first night in Juba, South Sudan, and I was in a metal-roofed mud house in a crowded corner of the regional capital. Once a simple, elegant community on the banks of the upper Nile, Juba had been overrun and pulverized by decades of war. Yet this gritty town's mean existence stood as a testament to human tenacity and endurance. Maybe it was just because they were alive and could suck in a breath of air or sip a warm soda, but the South Sudanese strode along the broad and sandy boulevards with a casual disinterest that I found appealing. They had seen it all, including the swarm of *muzungus* who now flowed into the town in their SUVs—UN and foreign aid workers, international journalists, peace activists, and other flotsam that moved with the ebb and flow of the looming peace talks between representatives of the Lord's Resistance Army and the Ugandan government.

Lubang Galaya, aka Moses, had met me at the airport. Moses, a meek young man with aspirations to journalism, had attended one of our news agency's weeklong workshops. He insistently shouldered my bag and waited as officials stamped my visa and pocketed a fistful of dollars. I was permitted to travel within the borders of South Sudan, an autonomous region that had gained legitimacy with its January 2005 Comprehensive Peace Agreement with the Sudan government in Khartoum. Several local journalists loosely aligned with a local radio station happened to be meeting someone else, and with relief Moses and I clambered into the bed of their compact pickup and bounced and splashed through puddles and potholes into town. We were dropped off near Moses's abode, which he explained belonged to his sister and her husband who were out of town, and he described it as "quite nice" as he fiddled with the lock to the stick fence. Though beastly hot, the inside seemed harmless enough: dark, with a neatly swept dirt floor, a couple of single beds with clean sheets, and free-standing cupboards.

Later we waited beside the road for a ride in one of the many battered and crowded minivans that provided public transportation. We extracted ourselves from a van at the town's center, which consisted of a cluster of still-standing commercial buildings, one of which housed the Nile Commercial Bank, a chaotic and crowded business where I exchanged dollars into Sudanese *dinars*. We ambled down what was left of a sidewalk and then a muddy and garbage-strewn lane fronted by an abandoned building with a portal where a dozen bedraggled people sprawled on the dirty concrete. A large and elderly woman with elephantine skin, naked except for a rag around her waist, bellowed like a sea lion at no one in particular as a couple of children stood nearby and stared. I bought a mobile phone card with a couple of hours of airtime in a concrete bunker below a telecommunications tower that connected my calls to Kampala. As long as I stayed within town, it relieved me from having to rely on costly satellite phone service. After visiting a couple of the local radio stations, we learned of a press conference scheduled for later that day by the key players in the pending peace talks: South Sudan president Salva

Kiir, its vice president, Riek Machar, and Ugandan internal affairs minister Ruhakana Rugunda.

The peace process had begun in secret several months earlier but became very public when a video recording of these clandestine meetings in the jungle along the Sudanese–Congo border was leaked to the press. The hour-long video captured Kony and his key people, specifically his deputy Vincent Otti, a couple of Dutch peace activists, and an entourage of officials from the fledgling government of South Sudan led by Machar discussing their willingness to talk peace. Machar had been forcefully blunt with Kony.

"Our people are being killed by you," he said. "Stop it. Our people are being abducted by your troops. Stop it. Stop killing any of our people." Kony and Otti had simple choices, Marchar warned, stay and talk peace, or leave the country. "If we see you killing our people, we will fight. If you rape our people, we will fight. If you are looting our people, we will fight." Machar went to great lengths, however, to assure Kony and Otti that South Sudan was motivated only by its desire for peace and had no intention of coercing the rebels into a trap or possible capture for trial before the ICC. "We are acting independently. We have no hidden agenda. We are not puppets of anybody." While Kony and Otti said they urgently wanted to talk peace with Uganda and had no quarrel with South Sudan, they were clearly tentative. Machar urged them to assemble the strongest delegation possible for the talks. "It is like sending someone into battle," he said, "a battle of words." After twenty years of fighting on the run, it turned out to be a battle for which they were ill equipped. Then, in a highly controversial move, Machar reached into his briefcase and handed Kony twenty thousand U.S. dollars in cash. "Buy food with it, not ammunition," he said.[1]

Weeks later a delegation of more than a dozen Acholi, most of whom had had little contact or direct relationship with Kony, gathered in Juba as the official negotiation team for Kony and his LRA.

The composition of the delegation threatened to derail the talks before they began; it did not include anyone from the LRA's command structure who could speak authoritatively on Kony's behalf—if such a person existed. It is common protocol, if not common sense, that negotiations take place between ranks of equals on the opposing sides. Uganda's Rugunda was a cabinet minister close to Museveni who spoke for the government. But the LRA delegation lacked anyone of similar rank or stature, and none had any experience in negotiations. It consisted largely of Acholi expatriates, five from the UK, one from Germany, a Kampala lawyer who told me he had only spoken to Kony years ago, an Acholi elder from Gulu, an English teacher named Obonyo Olweny of Kenya, who became the delegation spokesman, and Martin Ojul, an Acholi who had lived in the United States and emerged as the delegation leader. While the composition of the group attempted to put an educated, articulate, and international face to the LRA, it could not mask Kony and Otti's reluctance and inability to function outside of their militia's brutal and bush-bound existence.

On the way to the press conference in the government headquarters at the western edge of town, we negotiated one of the roundabouts where a faded and rusting sign caused me to do a double take. It read ARMED CONFLICT IS HEALTH RISK. It depicted a child being wheeled in a stroller, something I had not seen anywhere in this part of Africa, and was underscored in Arabic script. This painfully obvious and absurd statement was the work of some well-intentioned aid group. In the lower corner was the unmistakable logo of the United Nations International Children's Emergency Fund (UNICEF). Did people here or anywhere need to be told something like that? But what was more worrisome was that *someone* thought that people here needed that sign and that UN money had paid for it. Why not give people a sack of corn, a cow, or a goat? Why not dig a well? Why not do something useful? No one could have been more disconnected from the reality of South Sudan.

We passed barracks abandoned by the Sudanese army only months earlier, now crawling with the ranks of the Sudanese People's Liberation Army. The continuous presence of military units underscored the reality that South Sudan had been as much of a battleground for the LRA as northern Uganda—in effect the LRA's second front. Moses and I showed press credentials at the gate, then meandered to the air-conditioned reception room where we joined a dozen or more soldiers and senior aides snoozing on couches.

After huddling behind closed doors for a couple of hours, the trio of officials emerged, with South Sudan president Salva Kiir announcing that Uganda had agreed that South Sudan would mediate the talks and had urged a "speedy conclusion to the conflict" that had plagued the region for two decades. Rugunda echoed Kiir's optimistic appraisals for success for the talks, due to begin the following week, despite the fact that critical and unresolved issues lingered ominously in the background. The International Criminal Court's indictment prowled on the periphery like a hungry lion. Rugunda dismissed that concern with a wave. "We are focusing on a peaceful conclusion," he said, not wanting to dampen the growing prospect of peace. "We are confident answers will be found to all outstanding questions," he said, because, "this time the LRA means business." The remark was meaningful because Rugunda had been burned before by the LRA as the top government official at the aborted peace overtures two and a half years earlier. This time, he intoned, "We are confident of success."

Rugunda later told me privately that he was indeed skeptical about the talks but had convinced Museveni that it was worth a try, especially in light of the international attention focused on them. "We are skeptical because of previous behavior," he said, but quickly added, "We want to give peace a chance."

That skepticism mixed with optimism was echoed by Busho Ndinyenka, the Ugandan consul general to South Sudan, who was candid and frank. "Many times we have been taken for a ride" by the

LRA, which often insisted that it wanted to settle the war. Like many others in Juba in those days, he was now optimistic, too much so as it turned out. "We want them to quickly get organized," he said, and that "the end of the month is not impossible" for a conclusion to the talks. "Why should it take two years?"

But it would take years, in part because the LRA had other ideas, a different notion of organization, and a timetable of its own born of the bush and seemingly unrelated to calendars of the outside world.

Ndinyenka recognized the trepidation on the part of the LRA. "Quite a number of these people are scared," he stated, and confided that the LRA's options were limited. "Khartoum has reduced its support" for Kony, he said, who had become increasingly desperate since the Sudanese army had withdrawn to the north and left Kony to fend for himself. To prevent Kony from withdrawing deeper into the Congo and, worse yet, reigniting his war in South Sudan, Machar had arranged for convoys of trucks to keep the LRA forces supplied with water and essential food supplies. When word leaked of these supplies, as well as Machar's videotaped handover of twenty thousand dollars in cash, it set off a storm of protest. Ndinyenka said the move by Machar was "flawed" thinking, but Machar "wants to build confidence. His objective was noble." But Ndinyenka cautioned, "Knowing what Kony is, I wouldn't have done it. It is like throwing steaks at a tiger to get him to stop eating meat."

Both Kiir and Machar knew that if peace were to come to South Sudan, it would have to be of their own doing, not that of the international community. The time was ripe, Kiir said, because "the LRA has . . . been on the run." With the Sudanese Armed Forces (SAF) out of the picture, the dynamics of the war had changed. Kony was essentially cornered. To the north, east, and southeast were units of the Ugandan army and the Sudanese People's Liberation Army. A massive UN force was positioned south of Kony's camp in the Congo's Garamba Park. Combined with growing international pressure, such as the listing of the LRA as a terrorist group and the ICC indictments, as well as Khartoum's curtailment of supplies, Kony had begun to talk. The talks, Kiir said, "will stop the bloodshed in South Sudan and northern Uganda." There was something else at stake: oil.

As part of South Sudan's comprehensive agreement with the north, painstakingly negotiated by the late leader of the SPLA, John Garang, South Sudan would receive 50 percent of all revenues from oil extracted in the south. The south had a substantial amount of oil and, if properly developed, could be a major new global source and theoretically transform this abysmally impoverished and conflicted corner of the globe. According to a report issued just a couple of months before the talks, anywhere from three billion to as much as twelve billion barrels of crude lay under the swamps and savannahs of South Sudan. Some had already been tapped, and hundreds of thousands of barrels of crude were being pumped each day via pipeline to the East African coast.

Many critical details were unresolved, however, such as which wells were in the south and which were not, and no formal agreement had been reached between Sudan and South Sudan over these oil fields. Leases had been granted to different oil companies for the same properties by each government. Sudan's Khartoum government had awarded drilling rights in South Sudan to the major French oil company, Total. The South Sudan government had awarded rights to the same plot to a British oil exploration company. Meanwhile, Chinese, Malaysian, and Indian companies were also busy in the region. But none of this lucrative activity could be sorted out as long as a group like the LRA was rampaging around the region, shooting up convoys, raping women, and kidnapping children. South Sudan's appetite for oil revenues had been whetted with the receipt of eight hundred million dollars, which had filled its coffers in late February 2006, just four months earlier. In a region that had been ruled by militias, chaos, and civil war for twenty years, that kind of money caused problems. In fact,

South Sudan had trouble figuring out how to spend it all. No government structures existed: no finance department, no public works, no health office, and so on. The government was in the process of being formed, staffed, trained, and equipped, all within a matter of months.[2] If South Sudan would have a future, it needed peace.

Among the many things that Juba needed was a water and sewer system, a couple of conveniences I'd overlooked when we returned to Moses's abode that evening. I shrugged as I stuffed a towel, bar of soap, and a toothbrush into my day pack and followed him down the feces-littered path to the dirt road. We stumbled over rocky outcroppings that would challenge the best of SUVs, groping our way through the darkness broken by an occasional kerosene lantern tended by a tireless vegetable and soda vendor. Like moths, we were drawn to bright lights at the end of the street, a well-lighted café and bar powered by a humming generator. While Moses settled into the coolness of the Internet café behind the bar, I took advantage of the concrete shower stall beside the toilets to rinse away the day's sweat and dirt. After a dinner of stewed goat and rice served on a paper plate, I watched numbly as a creaky Internet connection opened pages inch by inch.

At Moses's borrowed home, I fell into bed exhausted and wished my host a good night. He responded by saying, "Don't let the rats bother you. They're a little noisy." I grunted, rolled over, and had almost dozed off when the skittering across the metal roofing intensified. It soon escalated into a noisy invasion of rogue rodents bent on reclaiming the place. I could not see their beady eyes in the pitch black of night, but I could hear them. They were everywhere, scratching and clawing their way up and across and down the few pieces of furniture, the cabinets and chairs, squealing as they fought and battled over God knows what. At one moment, late in the night after I had drifted into a troubled sleep, a couple of the creatures dropped onto my bed in a ball of screeching fur, each sinking its diseased fangs into the other, claws groping flesh. I thrashed madly, kicking and banging whatever was nearby, then sat up, gasping the stale, rodent-infested air. It was quiet for a while, but I couldn't sleep and rose just before the dawn I thought would never come.

I shook hands with Moses at the guarded gate of a ménage of pre-fab, plug-in portable air-conditioned housing units operated by RA International, a global company that specializes in providing housing and catering in some of the world's most troubled regions. The place had become an enclave of Westerners, Sudanese generals, aid work-ers, peace negotiators, and researchers that included the negotiating team of the LRA. There was a common shower hall and cavernous dining tent with a bar and couches at one end and a large flat-screened TV hanging at the other that alternately broadcasted CNN, the BBC, and British Premiere League football. Here I bumped into Matt Brown, a former Peace Corps worker in western Africa who'd become a scrappy reporter writing for Agence France-Presse. We'd met the day before at the press conference, and we soon realized we had landed in the lion's den. In every corner, private conversations were whispered, hands cupped over satellite phones, and eyes glanced furtively, always avoiding contact. We teamed up, in part I suppose because we were the only U.S. journalists on the scene at the time.

I recognized a man I'd seen in the pirated video of the clandestine meetings between Kony and Machar as one of the peace negotiators. I introduced myself and said I'd seen him in a movie, which raised a laugh on his part, but he then cautioned me that he never talked to the press. I was taken aback, but I grudgingly understood. His group, Pax Christi, was Catholic and operated exclusively behind the scenes. Their efforts, along with a substantial amount of cash that paid for food, housing, transportation, and satellite phone cards, had launched these talks. If they were ever perceived to be gleaning publicity or tak-ing credit for the quest for peace, they would not be trusted. I could only nod and wish him well, knowing that reportage was too often the voyeuristic exploitation of human weakness and depravity.

Later that day I spoke with Obonyo Olweny, who leaned on his meaty forearms, occasionally wagging a finger and shaking his head to emphasize a point. We sat at a white plastic table shaded by a towering tree and sipped sodas against the stultifying heat as this former high school English teacher–cum–LRA spokesman explained to me why the rebels had finally agreed to talk peace.

"The local people of the northern Uganda have always wished for peace," he said, and this desire had been expressed to Kony via the Acholi elders. How and when this had occurred was a detail that went unexplained, as did most everything about the LRA. "The LRA leaders saw the need for peace," he said, as if the realization had finally come after twenty years of bloodshed. "It is time to have the talks."

Did the ICC have anything to do with this realization?

"The ICC has not been a factor," he insisted, charging that the court's investigation was biased and lopsided against the LRA and had failed to look at the crimes committed by the Ugandan military. "The indictments by the ICC [are] not a complete reflection of the situation in northern Uganda. The government of Uganda is responsible for a lot of the suffering. Why no ICC indictments against the government? More atrocities were committed by the army than [by] the LRA ever since 1986."

He then offered a warning that could ultimately sabotage the talks: "The ICC should not focus on five people at the expense of the suffering of 1.5 million people in the camps," suggesting that the gulaglike life of the northern Acholi was a criminal and indictable offense. But it also implied that freedom for the LRA leadership—withdrawal of the indictments—could lever the end of the war and the freedom for more than 1.5 million interned people. Was that a condition? He shook his head no and said that the indictments "were not an impediment to peace. It's not part of the bargaining." Rather, the LRA was fighting on behalf of the Acholi people against the army, he said. Museveni's National Resistance Movement "had an agenda to destroy the economy of the north," which it did "in a very short time" by killing and stealing most of the livestock. The situation in the north was a "humanitarian crisis" for which the government should "acknowledge its part." That acknowledgment also was not a precondition to the peace talks but would help resolve the lingering resentment by the Acholi, he said. Ultimately, "We want the government to agree to a just and lasting peace," but what constituted "just and lasting" went undefined. When a definition did finally emerge, it consisted of a laundry list of demands as unrealistic and contradictory as Kony's claims to be fighting on behalf of the Ten Commandments.

How long did he expect the talks to go on?

Olweny shrugged, saying that a "deadline is inappropriate" and that they were working under directions from Kony to "talk as long as necessary to bring peace."

The word *peace* was bandied about with regularity and a deceptive sense of certainty. Yet just a couple of miles from Juba, random and bloody attacks on convoys and villages by rebels were part of the daily routine. Most people blamed the roving bands of the LRA, but the identity of these groups was difficult to pin down. With pronouncements of peace echoing in our ears, Brown and I drove across the long and narrow metal bridge that spanned the Nile. A thin gauze of high clouds softened the equatorial sun in the relative cool of the morning as we pursued details of an attack on a truck a couple of days earlier by what most said was a renegade unit of the Lord's Resistance Army. The attack had left five dead and eleven wounded. Rebels had ambushed workers of GTZ, a German company rebuilding roads and dikes in South Sudan under a UN contract. In the local offices of GTZ, we watched as Julius Mono, a Sudanese supervisor with the company, spread out a map and grimly explained that a couple days earlier a driver had taken a company surveyor along with three armed guards to a site some twenty kilometers away. As was the practice, the truck stopped to pick up hitchhikers along the way, and soon the truck labored under a load of fifteen people, mostly young women and children. When they entered a lonely stretch of road, around thirty heavily armed soldiers emerged from the bush and opened fire. The truck swerved to a stop as bodies riddled with bullets fell to the road. Others leaped for cover in the forest thickets. Among those who ran were the surveyor and driver. The guards returned fire, Mono said, and some of the attackers fell. A nearby unit of the Ugandan army arrived at the site some two hours later, but gave scant pursuit of the attackers, Mono said, claiming that they didn't have the supplies they needed for an extended search. The hunt for the driver and surveyor had continued for a second day, but without success. While it should have been the SPLA's job to track down the rebels, they had been ordered not to engage the LRA units as long as the peace talks were under way, I was told later.

"We blame the LRA," Mono said matter-of-factly, explaining the evidence he had gathered. A letter had been found at the attack site, apparently left on purpose, announcing that the LRA had arrived and the local villagers "should not run away," Mono explained, because "they are here to monitor the peace talks . . . and after that would be back." The letter stated clearly in Acholi that "we are LRA," he said. Among the documents left behind by the attackers were receipts for cash withdrawals from a Ugandan bank. A local woman had been abducted from her village several months earlier, he said, but had escaped from this same group. She confirmed that the kidnappers were the LRA and were responsible for several other attacks in the area in recent months, one of which was a running gun battle just a hundred yards from where we sat, that she had witnessed before she had escaped.

"How many more people do they want killed?" Mono complained, his eyes burning with anger. "You see a young child lying on top of his [dead] mother," he said, referring to a young woman who was killed in the attack, yet her six-month-old child had lived. "It's a terrible thing and something must be done." His eyes began to water and he turned away. "It affects me deeply."

Project manager Herbert Kremeier, a stout and modest German man, shared Mono's frustration. "Security has been an issue all the time," he said, but now "it's a bit out of hand." The company had completed work on seven hundred miles of road in South Sudan in the past two years without incident, but now work would stop. "This hit us very badly. We don't know if we are in a position to continue."

No one was closer to the scene than Paul Agoth, an agile and unassuming twenty-four-year-old corporal in the SPLA who had been in the back of the pickup when it was attacked. In the midst of the chaos of the attack, Agoth jumped from the truck, cocked his gun, and returned fire at close range.

"There were many bullets. They were shooting everywhere." Agoth said he was not particularly frightened because he'd been a child soldier himself, having first been kidnapped to fight with one of the Sudanese militias at the age of ten. "I wasn't afraid because I was quite ready," he said. Most of the passengers who could ran quickly into the bush. Those who couldn't were shot on the spot by the attackers, he said. He was convinced that he killed two of the attackers but could not prove it because the bodies were dragged away as the rebels fled. He was also convinced the attackers were LRA from Uganda from the way they spoke and dressed, wearing their trademark rubber boots and dreadlocks. When Brown and I produced cameras, Agoth insisted on donning his uniform. He returned moments later and posed while thrusting his bayoneted Kalishnikov, saying, "I'm ready to fight them again."

Brown and I later visited the Juba hospital where the wounded from the attack had been taken and were being treated. There we found Cecilia Ulum, a sixteen-year-old who had been in the back of the truck when it was attacked. She had been shot in the upper chest, and from her bed in the hospital she looked at us numbly, unable to talk about the experience, as if still not sure whether she was alive or dead.

The booted and dreadlocked fighters of the LRA were known in the area as the *tong-tong,* which meant "chop-chop," a reference to their fondness for wielding machetes, explained Peter Loting, chief of the nearby Gumbo village. He was neither a Dinka nor a Nuer, the two dominant ethnicities in South Sudan, nor was he an Acholi, which was one of the approximate fifty ethnicities in the region. He came from the Lokowa tribe, was fifty-four, and had been educated in Addis Ababa. He had returned to South Sudan for an administrative career with the government of the Sudanese state of Central Equatoria, and he had recently retired, having accepted the role of village chief.

Life deteriorated for people in his area about six years ago when LRA units began raiding villages, he said. "They started stealing their property, stealing their food, raiding their animals, reaping their food," Loting said of the victimized villagers. "They were robbing and killing people." The LRA finally attacked Gumbo and killed a policeman. "People panicked," he said, some fleeing to Juba, others to Uganda, and some running as far away as Khartoum. The killings had been more or less regular for the past six months, prompting the SPLA to station a unit on the banks of the Nile at the eastern end of the bridge to prevent an attack on Juba. A nearby village had been hit a couple of weeks ago, Loting said. More than just the *tong-tong* roamed the region, he said. "There is also another gang," he said, often seen by farmers and wood collectors. "We know some gangs are there. They are using the *tong-tong* as an umbrella," he said. This gang consisted of former fighters, some once with the LRA, some formerly with the

SPLA or other militias who had left for one reason or another. Their motives were simple, he explained, because some had been captured and forced to talk. "They confess they do this to earn their living."

Lean and lanky and wielding a thick cane, Loting gladly climbed into our vehicle and took us to a cluster of huts a few miles away that had recently been attacked. There we found seventy-year-old Raphael Lado, who stood near his hut and leaned unsteadily on his cane as he recalled two weeks earlier when bandits broke into his mud hut in the middle of the night. He had just returned to his village from Juba to console his son-in-law, Anatolio, fifty-one, who had lost his wife recently. The two had cleared her grave that day and retired early that night, with Anatolio sleeping on the floor mat and Raphael taking the cot. Some hours later, the attackers entered, shouting and flashing lights in their faces, Lado recalled. Shots were fired, and Anatolio slumped, blood spurting from his neck. Lado said the attackers apparently had mistaken his wooden cane propped against the wall for a gun. Lado waited to be shot, frozen with fear. But as he looked at the killer, the man slapped his face and said, "Sleep, uncle, sleep," then disappeared into the night. Lado fell back, keeping silent as the rebels moved from hut to hut, shooting, killing, and looting.

Were they LRA?

Lado shrugged. "It was night," he said, "and [I] did not know them." By the time it was over that night, three women had been killed, and a seventeen-year-old boy was shot in the back trying to escape. Loting showed me where the boy had fallen. The grass and ground were still caked with blood.

We walked up a gentle slope under a now-cloudy sky to a nearby cluster of huts where several women stood beside three freshly made graves marked by paltry sticks. The women wore long one-piece cotton dresses, waved their hands wildly as they talked, and smelled faintly of beer. Loting later explained they had been drinking their homemade brew and had complained that he had done nothing to help them recover the pots and pans that the attackers had stolen. Loting shook his head sympathetically as we left, the women's ranting unabated by our departure.

"This area is a chest of problems," Loting explained as we climbed back into our vehicle. "People here are bad." He shook his head at the plethora of deadly militias that plundered the area. "They are very troublesome people. This is a troublesome area." Despite the town's proximity to Juba, he said, security and protection were woefully poor. Most villagers now spent their nights across the river in Juba, protected by the natural barrier provided by the Nile. He was anxious that the peace talks with the LRA be successful. They were long overdue.

"The people are losing," he stated. "Peace talks will make it a bit milder," he said of life here. Kony should quit his rebel life. "He should not waste his time in different places killing people. It is unnecessary." If Kony did not reach a peace deal, Loting said, he should be arrested and put on trial.

Trials for Kony and his commanders became increasingly unlikely the next day as Ugandan president Museveni surprised the negotiators when he announced that the Ugandan government would extend amnesty to Kony and his command—something that he had previously ruled out. It was an unusual and unexpected step that at first glance seemed to bolster the prospects for peace by opening the door for Kony and his fighters to surrender and return to northern Uganda as free men. But the response from the LRA was equally unexpected. Rather than welcoming Museveni's offer, the LRA slammed the door on it.

"Amnesty has not helped solve the conflict in the north," Olweny said, shaking his head in disgust. Furthermore, neither Kony nor the LRA wanted amnesty. Accepting amnesty was an admission of guilt, Olweny said, which neither Kony nor the LRA would do. Instead of talking about amnesty, the Ugandan government needed to look at the causes of the twenty-year conflict. "We should sit down and talk about the grievances of the people of the north . . . how the current government has marginalized the people of the north and how the government systematically impoverished the people of eastern and northern Uganda . . . how the [Ugandan army] has been used and mis-used by the government to oppress people and commit atrocities. Why should the government order people into camps, and as a result thou-sands have died?" Forget amnesty, Olweny said. "We're going to talk about a genocide that has been taking place. It is a genocide that has gone unnoticed by the world."

Olweny's unequivocal rejection of amnesty was a harbinger of the confusing twists and turns, stops and starts, that the talks would take and exposed the immense distrust that the LRA had for the govern-ment. Olweny said it was a distrust based on history and noted that Museveni's government was founded on deception and broken agree-ments. In 1985 the Acholi government of Tito Okello reached an agreement to end Uganda's five-year war with Museveni's National Resistance Army. But instead of honoring it, Museveni moved on Kampala and forcibly took control. "By reneging on that agreement," Olweny said, "he sowed the seeds of this war." Olweny's words con-tradicted those of Professor Latigo, however, who had claimed the Acholi were not interested in recapturing control of the government. Olweny insisted that Kony's fight embodied the Acholi struggle to reassert its control over the government. "The Kony rebellion became the most successful . . . resistance against oppressive rule," he said with pride. He described Kony as "a person who has a serious political grievance." I noted that most of the former LRA commanders I'd met insisted that the LRA movement was more spiritual than political. Olweny disagreed, saying, "The LRA is not a mystical organ. They believe very strongly in God and God's power and inspiration." But the LRA routinely committed atrocities and violated its professed adherence to the Ten Commandments. How could he contend that the LRA fought on behalf of the Acholi people when they were the army's primary victims? Olweny bristled at the question. "Mutilations were not committed by the LRA, I can assure you." Instead, these atrocities were the work of the Ugandan army, he said. How, then, did he explain the LRA's frequent attacks on villages and refugee camps? The LRA had to go through the villages and camps in order to attack the army and militia units, he said. That the camps existed was because "there is a secret policy of the Museveni government to destroy the people of the north," he said. The refugees were killed in the camps, not by LRA rebels, but because the Ugandan soldiers were "using the people as human shields."

It was critical, after all, that the LRA be presented by people like Olweny as a credible political force, not a vicious rebel cult. An edifice of expectations had been built around the peace talks that could not be easily dismantled. Many people had much at stake. The people of northern Uganda, first and foremost, who had borne the brunt of this uncivil conflict. There was the government of Uganda, which had invested so much time and effort to control and contain the marauding rebel units. There were the aid organizations and the UN, which struggled to contain the scale of the humanitarian disaster. Then there was the LRA itself, which had devolved into loosely linked bands that continued to lurk across northern Uganda, southern Sudan, and now whose main force was camped out across the border in a remote corner of the Congo. It was now an army composed of young soldiers who had grown up with guns in their hands and who knew no other life except running, raiding, and following their mystical leader. Assuming a peace deal was reached, would they and could they adapt to a civilian life?

A credible force, be it military or political, needed organization and discipline. If the attackers at Gumbo were who they seemed to be, the LRA lacked both. In truth, the LRA had both. So why would the LRA disrupt the talks by attacking an unarmed group so close to Juba when they had much more to gain with a peace deal than without? Something else was afoot.

Olweny assured me that the attackers were not LRA and that Kony had told his units to stand down. I described the evidence found at the scene, clearly indicating LRA presence.

"Those are not LRA," he insisted. "We have no LRA units in the area."

I asked him about the widely rumored presence of a renegade unit of the LRA that had broken away from Kony but that dressed and looked the same and was bent on waging its own militia war.

He just shook his head. "There is no separate faction of the LRA. They are not LRA in any way. We are at peace with the government of South Sudan. There is no reason we should attack anywhere." But, he conceded, forces were at work trying to disrupt the talks. "I think there are groups trying to derail the peace process," he said, and he accused the Ugandan army of acting on behalf of the government in this regard.

Why? I asked.

So the government can continue its policy of destruction in the north, he said.

I wondered if Riek Machar could shed some light on the attacks and tracked him down in his office. He had been the true mastermind of these talks and appeared to be willing and even eager to do whatever it took to make sure the talks took place. Machar seemed as surprised as anyone that Museveni had proclaimed amnesty for Kony and his command.

"He has gone further than we suspected," Machar said, and the result was quite the opposite of Museveni's earlier refusals to talk peace with the LRA. "To us it was a very shrewd move. . . . This enhances the peace process."

But something else was afoot, I said, because attacks on villages had been a constant problem here and in other parts of South Sudan. All indications were that it was the LRA. Could the LRA be trusted? I asked.

Like Olweny, Machar just shook his head. "I was informed of those attacks," he said, and they were being investigated. "The LRA has confirmed they have no people on the east bank of the Nile."

The evidence found at the scene clearly seemed to implicate the LRA, I argued, but Machar discounted it all as fake. If the LRA was already engaged in talks, he said, then why would it go to such lengths to identify itself as clearly breaking the unofficial cease-fire that was in effect? "They wouldn't do a stupid thing like that," he said.

Could it be the work of other renegade militias?

Although he refused to answer the question that day, Machar later privately confirmed that a renegade militia, apparently backed by the Sudan government, may have been behind the GTZ attack. And a brigade of ex-LRA fighters was also at large in the Equatoria provinces. The Sudanese government had a motive for derailing the talks, and it had to do with oil. As part of the Comprehensive Peace Agreement, South Sudan would vote on independence in six years. But if peace was unachievable and lawlessness ruled, the government of Sudan had the excuse it needed to cancel the referendum and possibly invade, thus reclaiming the oil fields in southern Sudan.

These attacks would not derail the talks, Machar insisted. For too long South Sudan had been a battleground, and he, like everyone else, looked forward to the end of fighting. "It is a war that is not ours," he said of the clashes between the LRA and Ugandan army. "Maybe it is best to have talks." Those talks were due to start the following week and would, it was hoped, include Vincent Otti, the number two man in the LRA. But within days that hope had fizzled. Machar headed back into the jungle to meet with Kony and to keep the talks on track. This time I went with him.

12

In Search of Joseph Kony

Two DAYS LATER, A rugged Russian Antonov passenger plane, chartered for the occasion, sat baking in the sun on the cracked concrete runway in Juba. Several dozen people lingered under the shade of some trees outside the VIP lounge: the LRA negotiating team, a handful of peace activists and monitors, researchers, and journalists, and a dozen or so members of Riek Machar's security unit and entourage. We waited as our names were checked against a list of those headed to the jungle enclave of Nabanga on the Sudan–Congo border where Machar was to meet with Kony and collect a couple of LRA commanders to bolster the rebel's negotiating team. It was to be a quick trip so the team could be back in Juba for the late July 2006 launch of what most thought was the best hope for a breakthrough in a long and bloody war.

But it was anything but quick. The departure time ticked past without the slightest murmur. Most of us had been in Africa long enough to know that things happened when they happened, especially flights into the jungle. We eventually clambered up the portable steps into a sweltering, airless cabin, clutching our bottled water, and waited for Machar's arrival.

In the bootlegged recording of the clandestine meetings, Kony had complained about his distorted image in the news media and the eyes of the world. He declared that he was a victim of Uganda's propaganda because he had been in the bush so long and, lacking a base, could not properly present his agenda. Dressed in green fatigues with Ugandan army epaulets and rubber boots, and sporting a light blue beret, he had attempted to paint himself as a righteous and beleaguered guerrilla leader.

"I am not a terrorist," he pleaded. "I am a human being like you. I'm fighting like you for the right cause. What has happened there [in northern Uganda] is very bad. You can't stay in the bush for twenty years for nothing. We are here for something that is good for our lives." His complaint was well founded, yet he was aware he was to blame for his dismal reputation. "Journalists don't know me because I am hard to get."[1]

Despite a war that had lasted for two decades and had burned across the borders of two countries, and now threatened to spill into a third, Kony was perhaps the least known and most mysterious rebel leader on the continent. His public reticence had worked against him, leaving the abhorrent acts of his semi-independent guerrilla units to speak for him. A month earlier I had traveled to his home village of Odek, some thirty miles southeast of Gulu. The army normally restricted travel to the village to protected convoys, but because of the relative quiet due to the pending peace talks, we had no delays or troubles.

The morning was fresh and bright from the previous night's rain. Farmers crowded the road, making their daily trek from the camps to their distant gardens, patches of leafy green corn, beans, and cassava that filled the expanses between occasional stands of forest. I was again with Columbus Onoo, the Gulu journalist who helped me when I visited the region, and who relished his role as translator and guide and worked with pride and flair. We passed through the town of

Opit, the home of Alice Lakwena, now a busy community with a large refugee camp. It lay close to the defunct railroad line that wound its way from the Kenyan coast to the banks of the Nile River some seventy miles farther to the west, the steel rails a mute testament to the doomed dreams of colonial entrepreneurs.

Odek, a modest place near a meandering stream, was dominated by a refugee camp protected by a small army unit. Nearby was the site of Kony's home, long since razed, I was told, but still a monument to Odek's now-infamous son. As we chatted with one of the camp officials, a couple of men ambled by, each with a spear and one with a handmade net draped over his shoulder. They were hunters who, except for their contemporary clothes, could have stepped out of the bush similarly equipped a thousand years earlier. One was Jakayo Odora, Kony's closest friend from childhood, on his way to hunt for *duka*, a small antelope native to the region that was traditionally hunted with a net and spear. He delayed his hunt to talk, and we settled onto low-slung wooden chairs beside the mud hut that was the camp's administrative office.

Odora had recently been elected the local community council head, and his mild manners and casual friendliness made this understandable. "He was my best friend," Odora said of Kony. "We always shared ideas." The two had also shared a desk from the third through the sixth grade. Kony was friendly and well liked, he said. "He didn't provoke anyone. He didn't disturb his fellow students." Although he described Kony as "a good student" who excelled in history, he qualified his assessment by saying Kony "was not very bright" when it came to English and math. Not known for athletic ability, Kony, however, "liked traditional dances. He was good at music. The best in school." Kony formed his own dance group that performed the *larakaraka* for holidays and special occasions. Odora appreciated "the way he talked with people. I liked it. He was a very polite man. He started to live as a peaceful farmer."

The turning point for Kony came during his teenage years, Odora said, when Kony began his apprenticeship as the village witch doctor under the tutelage of his older brother, Benon Okello. "When his brother died, he took over full responsibility." Kony was good at the work and seemed more interested in herbs and healing than casting out witches but did enjoy dabbling in the occult. He collected herbs from Awere Hill, a tree-covered mount that dominates the local landscape. Kony would often spend the night there and return in the morning. "He was purely a witch doctor. He was well known. If he said something would happen, it would. He was very respected for what he did. He had no political interest." Although that clearly changed for Kony, Odora did not know why or how. "He never told anyone he was going to form a rebel group," but he did. "He started urging people to come join him. He told them he had guns." He also "told people he had a spirit," Odora said, that would allow them to fight unharmed, and that he could "turn stones into bombs." Kony's claims clearly echoed Alice Lakwena's militaristic mysticism. "I was very surprised," he said, when Kony took his new army into the bush, but others weren't. "People joined him willingly," Odora said, and some eighty fighters formed the nucleus of his rebels. In 1988, more than a year after Kony had amassed his group, he "sent soldiers to take me." Odora refused.

Kony made an annual pilgrimage to Awere Hill because it was a sacred place. "He comes there to pray," Odora said. "There is water on the hill and they take it. He considers it holy water. He still now sneaks back to that hill for the water." Knowing Kony's attraction to Awere Hill, the Ugandan army had reinforced its outpost at Odek, apparently thinking they had a chance to capture him plucking herbs or drinking the water.

Odora was dismayed at what had become of his childhood friend, a man he never imagined could lead a brutal army. "I miss him, but I don't miss his deeds. I'm not happy with what he is doing now. Even his two brothers were killed by his soldiers" when one of the LRA units in the area, considered one of the LRA's most vicious, attacked Odek mercilessly. Not only had Kony apparently lost a friend, the violence had alienated most of the villagers as well. In the early 1990s, the Acholi elders from the area once appealed for Kony to cease his fighting, Odora recalled, but "he never responded." Unlike many with whom I had talked who resented the meddling of the international community and the indictments of the ICC, Odora thought these legal actions were appropriate. "The ICC should indict and prosecute him," he said. "What he is doing is contrary to what should be done." Despite it all, what would he say to Kony today if he had the chance? His eyes lighted at the thought. "I'm asking you kindly . . . two of your brothers [were] killed. I do request you to come back and join us, as we always stay at home. Nobody will disturb you if you come back." If Odora delivered those words, I doubted Kony would listen.

We'd sat for an hour on the Juba tarmac when the twin engines of the hulking plane finally coughed to life. Air moved through the cabin as Machar climbed onboard. An hour later we landed on a red dirt airstrip in the rural town of Maridi in the Sudanese state of Western Equatoria. Soldiers emerged from the shoulder-high grass and towering acacia trees that flanked the strip as our bags thumped heavily on the ground. Under cloudy skies we walked a short distance to the local compound operated by the international CARE agency and settled into some hastily arranged chairs under a tree. We waited while a convoy of Toyota Land Cruisers and drivers was rounded up for the next leg of our journey.

Machar had done this many times and, settling into a chair, leaned back and spread his arms magnanimously. "Welcome to my palace," he said with a laugh. There was time to kill, and the disparate group mingled. The finals of the World Cup soccer match were approaching, and we talked about the various teams, prompting a joke by Crispus Odongo, a Kampala lawyer and member of the LRA negotiating team.

"Why don't the [India] Indians play football?" he asked. "When they find an empty corner someplace, they put a shop there." It was common among Ugandans to criticize and joke about the enterprising Indian community, referred to as the *wahindis,* who were the backbone of the country's economy and who owned the vast majority of shops and stores.

In my attempts to unmask the mysterious Kony before my trip to Juba, I had visited the church of Severino Lukoya, Kony's uncle and the father of the late Alice Lakwena. Lukoya had known Kony from childhood, and if anyone had a sense of Kony's mind it would be Lukoya, who had led his own religious movement and had inspired his daughter, who converted her spiritual calling into an armed rebellion. After Lakwena's defeat, Kony, not wanting any competition, had captured Lukoya as he attempted to resurrect Lakwena's army. Lukoya now had his own church, tucked away in a back alley of Gulu, and he called it the New Tribe of Melta. Inside, several young women lounged on mats with babies and small children and listened reverently as Lukoya answered my questions about the possibilities of peace with the LRA and its leader, Kony. Wizened with cloudy eyes and white hair, he wore a white robe and had an otherworldly look.

Lukoya explained that he spoke "on behalf of the spirits" but did so "in human form." He said that God had been telling him that people should "go away from killing and come to him. The time has come for people to live and love themselves. The spirits of those who died are crying to me every night." He had visions. "I have given my life so people can live," he said. "I have put myself on the rock so they get life." Lukoya had seven spirits who communicated through him, he told me, including a number of biblical characters such as David, Elijah, Moses, and Abraham, among others. He claimed responsibility for giving the spirit messenger Lakwena to his daughter so she could lead her rebellion. "It was wise for me to send the spirit to my daughter," he said, which enabled her to speak to "animals and the mountains." But, he confessed, "she failed," not because her army was decimated but "because she was ordered to stop" by the spirit. She had been killing too many people, he said, and "the spirits disagreed with those killings and decided to leave her." But those who died with his daughter's army would be blessed in heaven, he assured me.

Had he also given the spirit to Kony?

He shook his head. "The spirit with Alice is different from that of Joseph Kony," he said. "Joseph Kony is using the spirit called 'destroyer.' I see Joseph Kony as a destroyer. He doesn't care. That is why he arrested me." Lukoya said Kony incorporated his followers into the LRA units. His voice rose; he was still bitter about the encounter. "He arrested me and was beating me" with his own staff, or shepherd's crook, several of which Lukoya had propped in corners of his church. After beating him, Kony burned the crook, which made him angry. "By scattering my followers and breaking my stick, I became annoyed with him."

Lukoya said that his daughter and Kony had been close cousins, but when they both launched their movements, at nearly the same time, they fell apart. Kony "didn't want to be under the control of a woman," he said. An encounter apparently took place in early 1987, just before Alice launched her war, detailed in Behrend's *Alice Lakwena and the Holy Spirits.* That spring, Lakwena's movement had gained incredible momentum and attracted huge donations and volunteers. Her temple in Opit became a focal point for the various resistance groups, including Kony's. At the time, Kony was claiming that the spirit Lakwena had also authorized him to set up an army, and he was attacking various government installations. Kony went to Opit to meet with his cousin Alice and to consult with the spirit Lakwena who had possessed her. The meeting did not go well. Lakwena told Kony that he was possessed by a spirit that made him a good healer and doctor, but not a good military commander. She chided Kony for not knowing which stones would make the so-called stone grenades that exploded on impact. She asked Kony then to submit to purification ceremonies and join Lakwena's Holy Spirit Mobile Forces. Kony reportedly left without saying a word, later saying he had been insulted. The depth of this insult may have affected Kony deeply, causing him to spend a lifetime proving it was false. The bitter rivalry between the two began there and resulted in clashes between Lakwena and Kony's forces in late June as Lakwena launched some vicious punitive attacks against the other competing and uncooperative rebel groups. But she was diverted suddenly when the Ugandan army attacked her forces and inflicted heavy casualties. In early July she launched her drive toward Kampala, leaving Kony and the others to their own devices.[2] When she was defeated five months later, in November, the field had been cleared and left open for Kony to consolidate the remnants.

When I met Lukoya, peace talks between Kony and Uganda were in the wind. I asked if he thought the talks would succeed.

"I know the war is soon coming to an end," he said, but he didn't know who would win or lose. "The government should accept that the shedding of blood should stop."

Did he think Kony was serious about peace, or, like so many previous efforts, was this just a time for him to resupply?

"What he is interested in is power," Lukoya said. "That is what he wants up to now."

Did he hate Kony for what he had done?

Lukoya shook his head. "I love him as my child sent by God. I tried to bring him to me but he refused. He rejected being close to me because I told him to stop." Should Kony be punished? Lukoya refused to talk about Kony any further, and instead said, "The government should not treat me like an enemy." He had a lot of work left to do on earth. "I have not yet purified the people of Uganda."

Back in Sudan, as rain threatened, we finally pulled out of Maridi, bouncing and chugging along some incredibly rough roads through the forested and swampy savannahs. The road repeatedly dipped into small ponds of mud capable of swallowing the vehicles. Each vehicle was packed with passengers and piled high with luggage tied to robust roof racks, and the weight lent desperately needed traction. The external, roof-high air intakes for the engines proved vital as we splashed and churned our way from one gaping mud hole to the next.

Several hours later, in the waning light of day, numb from the bounding and banging, we turned in to a forlorn community at a crossroad in this corner of nowhere. Lanterns and candles lighted the brick shops that lined the roads where local villagers milled about in darkness. Though we were hungry and hollow eyed, it was late, and food was scarce. After downing a soda and packet of cookies, and longing for a stiff drink that I knew was days away, I unrolled my sleeping bag on a foam pad in the corner of a thatch-roofed hut and promptly fell asleep.

The next morning, sunlight seeped through broken clouds in this verdant land and gave way to a drizzling rain that did nothing to lift anyone's spirits. The minimal amenities were welcome: an outhouse and a washbasin. For breakfast, someone handed me a stubby cob of roasted corn. I bit into it hungrily. It was the corn I'd seen women roast over little charcoal fires all over the region, but it was far from the juicy sweet corn I knew from my Midwest upbringing. This was tough and crunchy and required patience and time to soften enough to swallow. Yet it was remarkably efficient at staving off hunger and left the sense of food in the stomach. We were soon rolling again through increasingly dense terrain, on roads that were little more than ruts flanked by swamps. A tape of Acholi music played again and again, and I soon found myself singing to lyrics that I did not comprehend in the slightest. I finally asked. One song was a man singing about how much he missed his hometown of Gulu. Another was of a man lamenting that his crops had been stolen by Ugandan army soldiers. The gut-level disgruntlement with the state of affairs in northern Uganda was being expressed via the popular medium of local culture and song, a form of protest by the Acholi people. The songs gave an unspoken credence to these members of the LRA delegation who were on this trip to meet and consult with Kony, and who carried themselves with a sense of mission and urgency.

Three hours later we turned down yet another rutted road and stopped at a compound of well-kept huts at the edge of a jungle forest. This was the SPLA outpost at Nabanga, a village on the Congo border. The outpost huts were for Machar, his guards, and a few select others, and the rest of us were sent a hundred yards down the road to a school. Although it was in use most days, the school was like those I'd seen in the countryside of northern Uganda. The doors and windows had long since been removed, frames and all, leaving the mud brick walls exposed. The corrugated metal roof was rusted, admitting nickel-sized holes of light. I dropped my bag on the gritty pitted concrete. This was home till further notice.

A soft rain started to fall, forcing us all inside the empty rooms where we gazed at the surrounding forests and listened to the soporific drumming of the rain on the leafy canopy. The *muzungus* among the entourage descended into their accoutrements, fiddling with laptop computers, digital cameras, sat phones, pens, and notebooks while others lapsed into conversations and stretched out on the concrete for naps.

The school was arranged in a U shape, with about a dozen soldiers occupying a building in front of which they parked a four-wheel-drive extra-cab pickup mounted with a machine gun, which they covered with a piece of green plastic tarp. For the most part they kept to themselves. I had become accustomed to this society of ever-present semiautomatic weapons and shabby uniforms. They served as our protection, but it would be paltry protection if in fact we became embroiled in a confrontation with the LRA.

I wandered from building to building, each with different char-coal scrawls adorning the cracked plaster walls. One room had been a prison where a captive had left his mark: "Omer Kpete James Babari . . . I was arrested into this prison on 23 May 1992." In another, draw-ings of AK-47s decorated the walls, and a collection of flat stones served as seats. It was a classroom. The blackboard consisted of a patch of black paint on which had been written: "Polio Eradication Program South Sudan, 20/2/06." In another room a third-grade English lesson had stopped. "Today Madi is going to see her. . . . Some do not see them very often. My grandmother and my grandfather live in a vil-lage near . . ." I was told that the school had been built by an aid organ-ization in the early 1970s but had been destroyed in late 1990 by the SPLA. Yet, sixteen years on, this shell of a structure still served its pur-pose. I thought of the thousands upon thousands of schools in the United States and the millions upon millions of students and their par-ents who would rail against even the thought of "letting" their chil-dren be taught in such a building. What little education there was to be dispensed was found here.

Waiting soon became an exercise in patience, if not a medita-tion in what people like Riek Machar will do to achieve peace and to what lengths journalists will go for a story. Besides Matt Brown and myself, there was Matthew Green with the Reuters news agency in Nairobi, who shared a fixation on the LRA and was accompanied by a Reuters contributor based in Juba. Two video journalists with al-Jazeera news agency who were based in Khartoum and a publi-cist working for the South Sudan government rounded out the news media people. Others included Nico Plooijer, with the Pax Christi organization based in Utrecht, Netherlands, whose organization was helping underwrite the peace effort; Mareika Schomerus, who was studying the LRA in South Sudan for her doctorate at the Lon-don School of Economics; and Fabio Riccardi and Jiancarlo Penza, both members of an Italian peace group based in Rome called the

Community of Saint Egidio, which had been working for an end to the war for years.

We all owed our presence to Machar, an amiable if not charismatic man in his own right. An ethnic Nuer, he was born in 1952, the twenty-sixth of thirty-one children fathered by the chief of Ler, a town in south-central Sudan. At the age of eleven, he was sent away to learn the ways of the *turuk,* or "foreigners," consciously groomed to become the kind of man who could lead the tribal Nuer into modernity. They traditionally wore little more than leather loincloths and used cow dung for cooking and to dress their hair. The Nuer were similar to the Acholi in that theirs was a loosely organized society of clans with reputations as fierce warriors who protected their people and property with swift violence. Their traditional lands had been wrested from the Dinka, with whom they had shared an uneasy alliance. Although the Nuer acknowledged an omnipotent God, they also accepted lesser divinities who occasionally communicated with humanity via special people. One such person was Machar's grandfather, and the communicating spirit was Teny, whose name found its way into Machar's full and formal last name: Teny-Dhourgon. And when necessary, Machar would remind people of his semicelestial linkages. Because of this background, Machar had a unique understanding of Kony and his mind.

In his youth, however, unlike the other boys in his tribe, Riek went unmarked, which meant he did not undergo the traditional horizontal scarring of his forehead that identified him as a clan member. At his first school he wore shorts and a shirt, sat in a chair, and slept under a blanket and a mosquito net—something his childhood friends had never experienced. He did extremely well and eventually graduated from the University of Khartoum, where he studied engineering and was awarded scholarships to study in Britain. In early 1984 he completed his doctoral work at Bradford Polytechnic in Yorkshire. [3]

But his mind was political, not technical, and burned with a desire to lead the liberation of South Sudan. In 1983, while at Bradford, he had formed a group called the Sudan Revolutionary Congress, which manifestly supported a rebel group of former Sudanese army officers, all Neurs, who called themselves Anyanya II and sought independence for South Sudan. Meanwhile, another former Sudanese army officer, Colonel John Garang, a Dinka commander, had also led his army unit in a revolt and fled to Ethiopia, seeking to ally with the Anyanya II. Garang did not want independence for South Sudan but rather a united Sudan under a socialist secular government. This difference erupted into fighting between the two groups, resulting in many Neur dead, since Garang had the support of Ethiopian leader Colonel Mengistu Haile Mariam, who shared Garang's ideas. This also drove the Nuer back to Sudan.[4]

When Machar went to Addis Ababa in 1984 to join Garang, it was not the first time they'd met. While finishing his doctoral work, he and some members of his Sudan Revolutionary Congress had been flown to Tripoli by Libya's Muammar Gadhafi to meet with Garang. Machar warmed to Garang's ideas and wanted to rise above tribal divisions for the greater good. He had also found something of a kindred spirit in Garang, who had not only received advanced military training in the United States but had earned a doctorate in agronomics from Iowa State University. Garang made Machar his office manager, and, by the following year, Machar was a brigade commander with three thousand soldiers. In the next year, he had recaptured his hometown from the Sudanese government and set up his own administration there. By 1989, Machar had assumed control of most of the western and northern portions of South Sudan and effectively governed more than one million people. Though thousands had died in the struggle, the Neur were finally united. Some people believed a prophecy had been fulfilled that said an unmarked and left-handed man would save the Nuer. Machar was that man.[5]

Garang and Machar had a tumultuous relationship, and their forces eventually clashed more than once, taking and retaking territory in southern Sudan. The life of this man and the events of this complex time were ably recounted in the book *Emma's War*, by journalist Deborah Scroggins, which tells the story of the adventurous British aid worker Emma McCune and her marriage to Machar.

During a quiet moment several days later, I caught Machar alone and asked him about the split with Garang. He flared at the question and denied there had been a split.

"We disagreed on the approach," he said. But "we were one movement from the very start." But most were oblivious to that unity, since it disappeared in 1991 and only reappeared in 2002 when "we reunited," Machar said. It was a pivotal year, largely due to international pressure for the Sudan and Uganda to withdraw their support for each other's enemies: Uganda for Garang's SPLA and Sudan for Kony's LRA and for Machar's SPLA faction. The agreement threw open the door for Museveni's army to pursue Kony's rebels but also paved the way for talks between Garang and Sudan, which resulted in the January 2005 peace agreement.

Finally, after twenty years of factional warfare, both Garang's and Machar's goals were met. Garang would become vice president of Sudan, thus ensuring a semisecular state, but after six years, the South Sudanese would vote on their complete independence. The government of South Sudan, in turn, was a tribal power-sharing arrangement led by a Dinka president (Garang) and a Nuer vice president (Machar). Following Garang's untimely death in 2005 in a freak helicopter accident while returning to South Sudan from Kampala, Salva Kiir became president. The agreement was clearly a milestone, but peace remained elusive. Four years after Uganda's first invasion of Southern Sudan, the LRA was as lethal as ever.

As the rain dwindled and the sky lightened that afternoon, the only sound was the rain dripping heavily from the trees. People emerged, milling about the grassy field fronting the school. Packets of cookies had been passed around throughout the afternoon but did little to stave off our growing hunger as we realized we had arrived without provisions. A couple of our entourage scouted the local village in search of chickens or goats, but none were to be found. Nabanga had been plundered and picked over so many times the villagers had given up on livestock. What little they had, they hid.

Our growing anxiety was relieved when the two reporters from al-Jazeera came down the road tugging a large tan goat. It had been purchased by Machar, they said, for the extortionate price of seventy dollars. Straddling it, one slit its throat, and it soon crumpled to the ground. It was quickly strung up, skinned, and butchered while the smoke of a cooking fire filled the air. Someone obtained a large aluminum cauldron, and most of the meat went inside with water drawn from a nearby well and several handfuls of salt for flavor. What didn't make it into the pot was skewered and roasted. Viscera was tossed on the coals, and I hungrily chewed on tender hunks of liver and tough chunks of bony meat spiced with ash. The meat simmered for hours, turning into a frothy stew that we all ate with our fingers in the dark of night while dodging the drifting smoke. We gnawed the bones clean and tossed them into the bush. Nothing had ever tasted so good. Achingly weary, I crawled into my bag later that night and slept soundly on the concrete.

The sky lightened slowly the next morning, muted by a layer of unthreatening clouds that kept the sun at bay. I meandered down the road to the well, which spewed water from a clanky hand pump of welded pipe that had been set in a pad of concrete. Villagers took turns at the pump handle as the others filled plastic buckets and five-gallon jerry cans. One paused and waved me forward, allowing me a few moments to wet my head and torso, and then waved me away when I offered to pump for him.

Back at the camp, a bedraggled local soldier meandered oddly toward Brown and me as we hunkered down by the still-smoldering campfire. He stood before us unsteadily, grinning, nodding, and reeking of beer as he tried to light a cigarette. War had been good for this man. He wore relatively new jungle fatigues, partially laced black leather boots, and a tan cap with protruding earflaps that made him look clownish. We would have laughed had it not been for the AK-47 strapped over his shoulder. The match finally found the cigarette, and he puffed. The tobacco seemed to focus his thoughts, and we began a disjointed conversation that ended with his invitation to visit the local church.

Some distance past the well, the jungle revealed a large and low-slung thatch-roofed structure suspended by poles. We ducked inside, where our soldier friend demonstrated his skill on a homemade xylophone. It consisted of variously sized pieces of roughly hewn hardwood notched to sit on two large bamboo rails. He wailed on them mercilessly with sticks, the noise drawing a handful of villagers who were as perplexed at our arrival as at this soldier's drunken antics. Our concert was short-lived, as the villagers eventually gathered for a portrait, with the youngest boy, no more than eight years old, grasping an AK-47 as he posed.

Across from the camp, we paused to inspect a clinic, a building that had been locked up and secured but that revealed the remains of a few meager medical supplies. From a couple of huts nearby, a man wearing a black sport coat and rolled-up trousers shuffled toward us in rubber flip-flops and offered to sell us some Super Match cigarettes, packaged in red and featuring a soccer player. He too smelled of beer. The village, we learned, was known for honey production, harvested from wooden boxes made of sticks secured high in the trees. For the most part, they converted the honey into a locally brewed honey beer.

By midafternoon, many of the villagers were bellowing drunk, bargaining and bickering over cigarettes.

The local behavior disgusted much of the LRA delegation. One turned to me and, shaking his head, asked if I'd seen the movie *The Gods Must Be Crazy,* an amusing, insightful look at the clash of African and modern Western cultures, prompted when an empty Coke bottle falls from the sky. I had, I said, and with a wave of his arm, he laughed and said, "Well, this is it." The otherworldly sense of the place was only heightened when Green tuned his radio to the BBC's Africa news show sandwiched between other world news, which at the time was dominated by worries about the U.S. space shuttle being able to reenter earth's orbit safely. We wondered about our own reentry.

As the heat of the day rose and lethargy set in, the minutes and hours blended seamlessly. Emboldened by booze, more villagers stumbled toward the school, approaching whoever happened to be nearest for money. A couple of young boys introduced themselves as rappers, one handing me a notebook with song lyrics written in both English and Swahili. Brown and I looked them over and congratulated the lyricist, who called himself Bad Boy One, his partner being Bad Boy Two. Bad Boy One's eyes were bloodshot, and he shifted a bit uneasily as the odor of stale beer wafted toward us. He explained that the lyrics proclaimed his ability to perform sexually for hours on end. I asked him if he was feeling OK, and he said his bloodshot eyes were due to malaria. His buddy, Bad Boy Two, was equally "ill," he said, but not from malaria. He was suffering from gonorrhea, which he had contracted from the rain. Bad Boy One pulled out a cigarette and shrugged, saying it was his last one. I shrugged as well, so he asked me if I could give him money to buy more. "That way I'll remember you," he said. I apologized, saying I couldn't do that. If I didn't give him money, he said, he would be forced to steal. I said that was probably not a good thing to do. He looked at me, blinked his bloodshot eyes, and shook his head sadly. "God has denied me money today," he said, then turned and walked away.

Later that afternoon, a large plastic tub of corn flour arrived. It meant dinner, and the campfire was rekindled. The flour was emptied into the now clean cauldron, mixed with water, and slowly cooked until it was a lumpy paste that reminded me of grits. In Uganda it was called *posho* but was more widely known by the Swahili term *ugali*. Again, well after darkness had fallen, we dug into it hungrily with our hands, most of us having forsaken the affectations of civilization.

Despite our predicament, the barriers in our group refused to fall. The LRA delegates were friendly but unwilling to discuss their backgrounds or roles in this diplomatic jungle expedition. They shared a common secretiveness born of the branding of the LRA as a terrorist group by the United States. They were acutely aware of the brutality of authoritarian regimes, and their reticence to talk was their first line of defense. But they had all quickly assumed nicknames: Ambassador, Lawyer, America. America was a hulking Acholi who had landed in Los Angeles first, where he worked construction, then found work in Las Vegas, Nevada, where he and a couple of friends scavenged wooden shipping pallets and resold them, making several hundred dollars a day. America had been in charge of the *ugali* and put his weight into stirring the bulky contents of the cauldron. He admonished me to eat my fill. "This is Africa. Eat well. You don't know when you'll eat again."

A sense of familiarity settled into the school grounds the next day, along with the deepening realization that it would be a long wait. Martin Ojul, the leader of the delegation, spent an inordinate amount of time on one of several satellite phones the group possessed. Kony was on his way, he said, but had been delayed by the swollen rivers due to the recent rains. He had brought his sizable entourage, for reasons that became clear later, and the tedious crossings had been time-consuming. While Ojul talked on the phone, others cooked *mandazi*, dollops of deep-fried dough that looked like fritters and tasted like doughnuts. It was a multistaged affair, but once the oil reached the proper temperature, the *mandazis* floated in the bubbling oil till they were golden brown. We gobbled them quickly, washing them down with a tasty herbal tea.

Machar's cluster of huts was a diversion. He had been busy responding to yet another demand from Kony and Otti, one that could mean a breakthough in the increasingly tedious lead-up to the talks. Kony wanted Acholi elders and religious leaders brought into the talks, saying that they were the ones who held the keys to peace. If they insisted that Kony drop his so-called rebellion, then he would. But first, as was the custom, they needed to talk. The leaders Kony wanted were some of the same people with whom I had met: Archbishop Odama, the Acholi *rwot* David Acana, and Walter Ochora, then the district governor in Gulu. Kony's latest request meant another scramble and a logistical nightmare, but Machar agreed. We listened in as Machar cajoled some of these leaders into coming, after they complained they didn't have the time to meet with Kony in the jungle. But as he spoke, yet another opaque layer was peeling off this mystifying war. Had these same Acholi leaders, the ones who had been urging restraint, peace, and amnesty, also been quietly manipulating this war from behind their respective facades of governance, civility, and grace? Machar's willingness to arrange such a meeting confirmed his belief that the Acholi elders did play a role, perhaps a critical one. It was just enough of a twist to this unfolding drama for the news agency reporters to call in a story: "Kony Demands Meeting with Acholi Elders."

Moments later, Ojul strolled into Machar's hut and announced that Kony's advance guard had arrived. Otti would not meet with Machar until tomorrow, however, since he was suffering from malaria. Besides, Ojul said, the next day was the eleventh of July, and eleven was Otti's lucky number.

There were only five soldiers in the advance guard, and finally I was face-to-face with LRA elite fighters. They wore the rubber boots, brown fatigue pants, and camouflage jackets and sported short dread-locks. Their AK-47s were looped over their shoulders, and they rested their arms casually on the barrels crossing their bellies. They glanced furtively, looking much like the emotionless killers we knew they were, a notion they did not intend to dispel. They were of similar height and build and looked enough alike to be brothers, and perhaps they were—the trusted sons of Kony. They were also uneasy and out of their normal milieu, relaxing only slightly after we greeted one another and shook hands. They soon fell into a casual posture and spoke Acholi with the members of the delegation, who were intro-duced to them by a couple of LRA operatives who traveled between the bush, Juba, Nairobi, and Kampala. A couple of them leaned against a tree, clearly tired from their days of walking. Brown approached one, after taking numerous photographs, and offered to swap his glitter-ing wristwatch for the rebel fighter's leather wristband. The rebel con-sidered it for a moment, then shook his head, saying it was "not a good deal." The bracelet, of course, as well as the vial of holy oil that hung around his neck, were protective talismans. What good was a white man's watch in the jungle?

13

Jungle Rendezvous

RIEK MACHAR SAT IN his camp chair the next morning reading *From Violence to Blessing: How an Understanding of a Deep-Rooted Conflict Can Open Paths of Reconciliation,* a paperback filled with optimistic advice by Vern Neufeld Redekop. There was more than a little irony here. Machar had not only lived the title of this book several times over, he was now whacking his way through the jungle to find that overgrown path to reconciliation. The book title lingered in my mind as we loaded into the four-wheel-drives and fishtailed our way down the muddy, rutted roads. Were there blessings in the bloody violence that had been committed by the LRA? Or was this nothing but an appeal from the towers of academia? Machar gave no indication as to what he thought. He was too busy being the ringmaster in this three-ring circus. And there was much to be accounted for.

As I and the others waited to load the vehicles, nineteen-year-old Samson Jiptar stood nervously on the periphery of the camp. He had lost his father in an LRA raid on his nearby village about five months earlier. His father had been killed and his younger sister, Seba, fifteen, had been kidnapped, all for a couple of goats. Samson, distraught, had dropped out of school and had pleaded with Machar to help obtain his sister's release. Machar had made no promises.

We had gone only a few miles when we parked helter-skelter in the jungle, then hustled along a path through dense, thick growth to a clearing hacked out of the jungle by machetes. A dozen chairs had been carried to the site, and Machar settled into one. The sun was high and hot and the languid air was still as we waited in the jungle rendezvous for Vincent Otti. Fifteen minutes passed. Then thirty. Then forty-five. No sign of Otti.

After we had waited an hour in the leafy shade of towering trees, heavily armed soldiers came spilling along the path from the Congo, looking fierce as they fingered their weapons. They took up positions around one half of the camp, setting up a perimeter guard. Moments later, Otti appeared with his stooped physique, unassuming manner, and soft voice. It was hard to imagine he was deputy commander of this vicious rebel army.

Hands were shaken all around and Otti quickly sat down opposite Machar, uttering what Machar did not want to hear: Kony needed more time.

"I need to talk to [Kony] about the letter, about the importance of it," Otti said.

Machar's face fell. The peace talks had already been beset by delays, and Machar had hoped this trip could be completed quickly. It was Tuesday, and the talks were to start the next day in Juba. At the request of Uganda's top negotiator, a letter had been delivered weeks earlier to the LRA, asking that Kony upgrade the delegation to include commanders from among the LRA ranks. Machar had expected that this meeting would be with Kony and that the LRA's combatant negotiators would be presented so he could whisk them to Juba that afternoon.

"The world is running fast," Machar grumbled, suggesting that time was running out.

"You travel by plane," Otti replied. "We travel by foot these days."

Machar could only shake his head as Otti complained about the presence of the news media. Machar reminded him that the negotiations were to be more public than in the past. "You found that it helped."

"You're right," Otti conceded.

Considering that the Lord's Resistance Army was seen as an aimless, bloodthirsty militia led by a delusional psychopath, anything less sinister would probably be useful. But any image makeover was elusive. Only two weeks earlier, Kony had been splashed across the front page of the *London Times* in his first major public exposure in a decade. He had worn a blue short-sleeved shirt for the event, hatless, and had presented himself as a misunderstood mastermind. The *Times* called him Africa's most wanted man. Kony used the encounter to deny that his rebels kidnapped, killed, or mutilated people, insisting that it was all propaganda by the Ugandan government. It had long since become a pitiable refrain. Kony reiterated that he was fighting for the Ten Commandments, which were not his law but God's, he dutifully noted.

Otti's complaint about the news media reflected Kony's wariness of the press. A lot of pleading, cajoling, and scripting had gone into arranging that meeting for the *Times* story, and Kony had been convinced to do it with assurances that he'd get sympathetic treatment. He didn't. The journalist had alluded to himself as Henry Morton Stanley searching for Livingstone, then as an Evelyn Waugh–esque journalist fearlessly inserting his head into the jaws of death.

Machar abruptly called an end to the Otti encounter, saying he wanted a written reply to the request for an enhanced negotiating team. Another meeting was set for the next morning, 9:00 A.M. sharp. The dozen or so members of the recently formed LRA negotiating team were left with Otti. For most, it would be the first time they would meet Kony. They had a daunting task: convince Kony that negotiating was a give-and-take process, not an endless series of demands issued at the whim of a messianic warlord. Clearly, it was a mission impossible for people who had never confronted a man possessed with such a charismatic and sinister persona. We watched silently as they disappeared into the jungle guarded by Kony's home-grown killers.

Later, Machar looked irritated, fidgeting in his chair as he tried to paint this setback in bright colors. "It's a good sign," he said with a deep sigh, as if convincing himself.

But the reality was clear. Neither the LRA nor its novice negotiators were suited for the subtleties of ending twenty years of bloodshed involving two countries and multiple ethnicities. The LRA lived on the run and knew only how to fight and kill. The army was led by a man convinced he was a prophet. Machar understood this perhaps better than anyone else, since he too was heir to a family with heavenly connections and had lived a rebel's life for nearly as long. But Machar also was well grounded in the ways of *turuk,* or foreigners.

"It's a new challenge for them," he said to me, then looked over his glasses and wondered aloud, "Are they up to it?"

The next morning our diminished entourage rose at dawn. Again we piled into vehicles, and, with tires spinning and mud flying, we reached the rendezvous site in short order. Again we waited. After more than an hour in the stultifying jungle, one of the meeting facilitators who had remained with us shook his head sadly. Otti was not answering his phone. Machar had been calling Otti as well but with no luck.

Had Kony packed up and fled? Machar could only shrug. He then settled into his cane chair and produced yet another paperback: *A Brief History of Time: From the Big Bang to Black Holes* by Stephen

Hawking. Had we gone from a big bang to a cosmic black hole? Machar smiled as he read. The wait expanded and was only interrupted when journalist Matthew Green leaped up from the grass as a snake crawled under his legs. Though it was a small, nondescript creature, the soldiers quickly dispatched it, saying it was very poisonous. We were relieved.

After three hours of lounging in the grass, making endless small talk, and staring off into the mottled shadows of the towering canopy, a plastic tub of freshly cooked *ugali* arrived, prepared by Machar's rear guard, along with a bucket of boiled okra. We gratefully ate. Spirits revived, Machar voiced what we were all wondering: Would Kony show? Machar laughed, shook his head in dismay and barked out a headline: "Kony Chickens Out of Peace Talks." There were few chuckles.

Shortly after 1:00 P.M., the first of Otti's dreadlocked soldiers arrived, more heavily armed than the day before, some carrying machine guns, their torsos draped with ammunition belts. The fledgling negotiators filed along behind, taking up positions beside and behind Otti, looking exhausted and frustrated. There had been "a lot of discussion," Otti explained as he handed the written response to Machar.

Settling again in his chair, Otti reiterated the request that the Acholi leaders be brought to the jungle to meet with Kony. It was a request that Machar did not take to kindly since it constituted yet another major delay and would create yet another sideshow. Machar frowned. His mood soured further as Otti told him that although Kony was near, he would not show because of the few assembled press. Machar had not adequately warned Kony about the journalists, Otti said. Machar sighed and tapped his fingers on the arms of the cane chair. Machar was at the end of his rope. He then began a masterful, looping conversation in which he chided Otti for the militia's brutal, evasive, and mercurial behavior.

Machar badly wanted Otti at the negotiating table in Juba. Otti roughly equated in rank to Uganda's Minister Rugunda, and as the LRA's second-highest commander he would vastly enhance the clout and credibility of the peace team. Returning with Otti would have been a diplomatic coup for Machar, enhancing his reputation as the man who slogged though swamps and jungles to secure peace. But it was not to be.

"In Juba you will meet all of them," Machar said of the Acholi elders, whom he preferred to bring to Juba rather than all the way to Nabanga. But Otti steadfastly refused to come, saying, "The ICC indictments are still there," revealing both his and Kony's fear of capture and distrust of Machar.

"Patience of people doesn't last that long," Machar warned. "You can't expect someone to spend five days in the bush like this. You [shouldn't] take people for granted."

"You're not indicted with us," Otti replied.

Machar again shook his head. "We defied the world so you could come and say your viewpoints. It is best to talk peace directly with us."

He was in no hurry, Otti said, because reaching peace would be a long and drawn-out process. "Peace cannot come in one day. War cannot end in a day. It is not like playing ball. We fought for twenty years. We should take it step by step."

"Some of them are old people," Machar said of the Acholi elders Kony wanted to meet in the jungle. "They also have lives they fear to lose. I have a responsibility to protect their lives when they are in Sudan. Your people died at your hands. It is not a good excuse [to delay the talks]. I cannot tell you yes," that the elders would come to Nabanga, Machar said. Otti's insistence of meeting with Acholi elders before the peace talks continued raised a troubling thought for Machar, who now had his own doubts about the composition of the LRA peace team. "If Martin [Ojul] comes up with a peace agreement, will you honor it?" he asked Otti.

Otti nodded that the LRA would. "The time will come for people to go and sign. The time will come." But it would be up to Kony, not him, to ratify the agreement, Otti said. "He is the one to sign it, not me."

"You're making it go slow," Machar said of the process. "You're afraid to come out and talk to people. You're only ready for war. You find peace intimidating."

Otti dismissed Machar's concerns with a shake of his head. "We are ready for peace."

Machar hammered at Kony's reluctance to talk directly with him. Machar had taken a lot of risks to do what he was doing, and Otti and Kony clearly didn't understand that.

"Very few people trust you," Machar said bluntly. "You contribute to that because you isolate yourselves. You are now afraid to take the chance to show up. Even your leader is afraid to talk to the people."

Machar reminded Otti that war was possible if the talks failed. "We are reluctant to get into the war. We don't want it." But it was clear that war remained an option. "You made Sudan a battleground," he said bitterly.

Otti ignored Machar's complaint and repeated his request to see the Acholi leaders. "We want to . . . hear from them. They should come so we can settle."

Settle? Otti's comment had been made in the midst of this rolling banter but soon proved to be prophetic. Had some deal been made? I wondered. The word *settle* suggested that, and if a deal had been made and then broken, it clearly needed to be resolved.

"They are the fathers of this war," Otti said of the Acholi elders. "They should come and see their children." He waved his hand at the throng behind him. "We are their children." He paused to collect his thoughts as his voice rose in anger. "During the war, they almost rejected us," he said piercing the air with a finger. "[We] recruited their brothers to go to war. What Museveni was doing against the tribe was very bad."

With these few words, Otti had revealed the core of the LRA's angry and vicious war against its own tribe. In the months and years that followed Museveni's successful military coup in 1986, the LRA rebels had found ample reason to fight. It was initially to protect the Acholi people from what they feared would be another vicious reprisal like that conducted by Idi Amin. That the war had been conducted with the blessing of the loose alliance of Acholi clan chiefs was now an open fact.

Or was it? In his book *Living with Bad Surroundings: War and Existential Uncertainty in Acholiland, Northern Uganda*, Swedish anthropologist Sverker Finnstrom explored the claim of a war blessing presumably given to the LRA by the Acholi elders. Like most everything that surrounded this war, this apparent war blessing was mired in confusion. Finnstrom found that a blessing had been given— sort of—a fact the LRA had ignored. According to Acholi tradition, a blessing to conduct a war came from a consensus of clan elders who would identify an enemy and a valid reason for warfare. The leaders of the war party were blessed at an ancestral shrine and presented with sticks for making a fire, called *lapii*, a symbol of their authorization. They were also given branches of the *oboke olwedo* tree, a general blessing among the Acholi, which was further reinforced with *laa*, or spittle that the elders spewed upon their sons. This ceremony had apparently been performed for one of Kony's commanders in late 1986 or early 1987, when his Kony's army was still in its formative stages. But the commander had only been given the *oboke olwedo* tree branches, not the *lapii*, or fire sticks. The ceremony was incomplete and the LRA lacked the full sanction to conduct a war. Rwot David Acana, the current paramount chief of the Acholi, told Finnstrom that the war sanction had not come then because all the clan leaders could not be assembled. So it never happened fully. When questioned about this incomplete ceremony—a seemingly critical fact if it was used to justify twenty years of bloody war, one LRA commander reportedly quipped, "Our *lapii* is God."[1] In other words, God, and perhaps Kony himself, had completed the ceremony and they needed no more authority to fight.

If the Acholi war blessing had been given—even if it only was *assumed* by Kony and Otti to have been given—the reality was that it had been gradually ignored and withdrawn by the few elders who knew of it. The justification for the war was unknown by the vast majority of Acholi. Yet in the minds of Kony and his cohorts, the Acholi tribe, and in particular the elders, had betrayed them. This betrayal then justified the LRA's vicious behavior against its own tribe. By rejecting the LRA, the Acholi people themselves had become the enemy just as much as Museveni's hated National Resistance Army was the enemy. Any reluctance by the Acholi villagers to give food and aid, to join the rebel army, or to give up their sons and daughters to it was part of that betrayal. In the minds of Kony's fighters, therefore, the Acholi could justifiably be killed because they were complicit with the enemy of the true Acholi the LRA claimed to be defending.

That complicity included being herded into the internal refugee camps. The more brutal the LRA tactics were, the stronger the reminder to their Acholi tribesmen as to whose war the LRA was fighting. This perceived betrayal was a betrayal of everything Acholi: tradition, ceremony, a way of life, even their identity. Kony's claim to be a prophet who had been rejected by the Acholi only compounded the militia's perverse need to exact a swift and brutal punishment against its own tribe.

Kony would not relent from his demand to meet with the Acholi elders. Knowing little more would be gained from further talk, Machar sat back in his chair and motioned to the press; Otti had to answer a few questions.

"They are all good laws," Otti said when asked about his adherence to the Ten Commandments. "We should follow the law of God.

That is why we were fighting." The LRA had a legitimate political agenda, Otti claimed, but could not describe it. When asked why the LRA had agreed to peace talks, he was remarkably direct. "Peace talks come when the war becomes difficult." It was perhaps the first and only admission of a weakened LRA. Bereft of support from the Sudan government, effectively cut off from the Acholi in northern Uganda, and having retreated to a remote corner of the Congo with a massive UN force at its back, peace meant survival.

Again he was asked why the LRA continued to abduct people, and again he resorted to the stock denials. "We have only our children who have been born in the bush." The abductions, he said, were "a propaganda piece" by Museveni. "We don't abduct children."

With that, Otti slapped his thighs and stood, declaring an end to questions. Within minutes, Otti and the dozens of fighters who had accompanied him disappeared into the jungle.

Left in their wake were the LRA negotiators, who now included two combatants: Colonel Leonard Lubwa and Lieutenant Colonel Santo Alit. Later, I had time to talk privately with Lubwa, an educated and articulate man who had been with the LRA for well over a decade. Machar told me Lubwa had negotiated with the Congolese to allow the LRA to set up camp in Garamba Park, apparently with the agreement that they would not pillage and abduct.

Was the LRA committed to the peace talks?

"If we weren't serious, we wouldn't be here," Lubwa said with a huff.

How quickly could a peace deal be reached?

"It depends . . ." He explained that developing trust with the Ugandan government was critical. "We are only trying to defend the Ten Commandments," Lubwa asserted, but when I challenged him on that, saying the LRA routinely violated every commandment, he simply shrugged.

"The whole world had turned against the Ten Commandments to satisfy their desires," he said. "Those who are eager to propagate their ideologies . . . are at fault" for the situation in northern Uganda, he said, implying the dismal conditions in the north were due to Museveni's army, not the LRA.

The days of waiting and then of meetings in the jungle had been exhausting. Back at the camp, Machar complained that yet another chance to move the peace process forward had been lost.

"They have not grasped the initiative," he said of the LRA. He had been unable to lure Otti to Juba and was dissatisfied with the two additional negotiators. "They should have sent at least one [whom] the ICC has indicted. They lost that opportunity." Despite that, Machar was buoyed by the prospect that a meeting with the Acholi elders could break Kony's reluctance to participate in talks. "They have an agreement with their elders to fight the government," he said as he explained that he had made up his mind to arrange the meeting. "It is important to me. If the elders want, they can work out a mechanism to end the war. They are the key to the solution. It is these elders who asked for the fight against the government. [The LRA leaders] were instructed by their elders to fight the government. But then some of their people who instructed them . . . joined the government, abandoned them without deciding what to do." Kony had, in fact, been abandoned, Machar explained, if not by design, by neglect.

But Machar had his own country to worry about. More than a hundred thousand South Sudanese lived in Uganda's northwestern province of West Nile, having fled the factional fighting instigated in part by the LRA. "Our people will come back" once peace is secured, Machar told me. "They will come back to the areas destabilized by the LRA." This was driving his work as well as testing his patience, he said. "We want peace as human beings. We want development, be it timber, agriculture, oil. We want to catch up."

As we threw our bags atop the vehicles for the trip back, a convoy of seven hulking trucks loaded with supplies and foodstuffs groaned and sloshed down the road past Machar's army's outpost at Nabanga. I asked whom those supplies were for, and one of the soldiers quipped that the supplies were for the outpost. I laughed. It was enough for an army—Kony's army, which included well more than a thousand people counting fighters, women, and children. Machar kept them alive because it would keep Kony coming back.

———

In Maridi the next morning, we milled about the CARE center, nibbling on cookies and sipping tea, still numbed from the bouncing road. I had been puzzled by a very heated exchange the day before between Otti and Betty Achan Ogwaro, a member of the South Sudanese Legislative Assembly. Ogwaro, an ethnic Sudanese Acholi, had railed at Otti about the LRA's bloody attacks on Acholi villages in southern Sudan. She had made Otti squirm. As we stood in the muddy expanse of the parking lot, she explained that she was incensed that Kony and his fighters had attacked the Acholi clans in South Sudan. These were his fellow tribesmen, certainly, but had nothing to do with Kony's fight with the Ugandan government of Museveni. "They should have concentrated their fight on the military," she said. "It would have made a difference." Instead, innocent Acholi in South Sudan had died needlessly. The LRA had only incurred their enmity. "Death is painful," she had told Otti. "You are afraid to go to Juba to face the world. But you're not afraid to cut off the lips of innocent people."

She told me Otti had replied, "The cutting off of lips was not done by them." But she didn't believe him. Otti said he was fighting because the elders had "drummed the drums of war," he told her. "The war is theirs." Some former LRA fighters had joined the government and risen to positions of prominence. "It is how it became Acholis fighting Acholi," he had explained to her, but Ogwaro was dissatisfied. "Many people are not happy," she told me. "There is a misunderstanding that all Acholis are fighting this war."

We climbed up the ramp of a cargo plane shortly after it landed on the dirt strip at the edge of Maridi and lifted off the ground with most of Machar's soldiers sprawled on top of the collected luggage and equipment. An hour later we stumbled into the blinding sunshine of Juba, greeted by a gaggle of press expecting to see Otti. They were disappointed. Machar calmly dismissed the questions by saying that Otti's presence had never been a condition of the talks, only a wish on his part. But, he optimistically crowed, Otti "will join the peace talks later. The war has gone on for nearly ten years [in southern Sudan]. We will be patient."

Moments later, in the airport's VIP lounge, Olweny offered another answer. The LRA had the right to constitute the delegation the way it wanted. "We are ready to talk peace with the government of Uganda," he said, reading from notes he had scribbled in Maridi. The first issue on the table was agreeing to a cease-fire. When he was asked what the LRA would do if it didn't get a cease-fire, he looked up at me wearily. "We don't have a plan B. Our plan A is for peace. That is why we are here."

Brown and I hitched a ride in the back of the same pickup truck that I'd ridden in when I had first arrived in Juba two weeks earlier. Despite the dilapidated state of the airport and the potholed road to town, Juba now looked like the pinnacle of civilization. I was running out of cash, so we checked into another camp on the shady banks of the Nile River where we could save some money. It also had an excellent Internet connection by virtue of a satellite dish and a steady supply of electricity supplied by generators. We made it to the buffet line just before it closed, and I hungrily piled my plate with food. I had not eaten a decent meal in a week and went back for seconds. In the searing heat and humidity, I luxuriated in a long shower that washed away a week of sweat and dirt. Seated in a metal folding chair in the sweltering heat of the canvas tent that was the Internet café, I reconnected with the outside world.

Later that afternoon, I sat at one of the plastic tables in the open-air bar overlooking the placid Nile and distractedly peeled the label from a bottle of Nile Special beer. A rusted metal barge was stranded awkwardly on a small island about fifty yards from the bank. It typified what I feared would eventually happen to the talks as the world moved on at its slow but unrelenting pace. Machar had gone to extraordinary lengths to draw Kony out of the bush and would continue to do so. But Kony was not buying it, and I had the nagging suspicion that, despite Machar's noble intentions, catering to Kony's demands was a waste of time. My suspicions would quickly prove true.

The next day, as the twin-engine plane lifted off the runway in Juba and climbed into the low-hanging clouds, I was filled with relief and regret. Each time I climbed into an airplane and lifted off the ground, I felt that I was leaving a piece of my life behind, however small or large. But this time the feeling was overwhelming. The people I had left there were, of course, preoccupied with the events of the day. But it wasn't so much the press or international observers who were on my mind as it was those whose lives hung in the balance with the success or failure of these talks. They were trapped by circumstance of birth. They could pick up and leave, but go where? And eat what? Where would they sleep? It was not only those in South Sudan who had been traumatized, mutilated, and killed, but the nearly two million Acholis across northern Uganda. They now waited in the camps with one thing on their minds: When could they go home and not live in fear?

The talks began just like the faltering steps that had preceded them. As a horde of observers and the press gathered for this potentially auspicious event, the LRA launched a verbal attack. Rather than opening with conciliatory comments about peace, the LRA let the world know they were not at the peace table because they had been defeated.

"Our message to the Ugandan government is 'sitting down for peace does not mean the LRA are [sic] weak militarily.' No, we are not," Olweny said. "If Uganda believes they can settle this on the battlefield, they are in for a rude shock."[2]

The LRA's opening remarks were defensive, steeped in hatred and resentment, spoken out of desperation. Kony was running out of moves. His was a lost cause, something the LRA would never concede. Ironically, these were the noncombatants speaking, the Acholi diaspora already beyond the pale of this conflict. This oral onslaught had been their ambush on the government, an attack made in full public view. Slowly but surely, the credibility of the LRA delegation was beginning to crack. Word by word they undermined their ability to negotiate and sabotaged the legitimacy that they had hoped to represent, a legitimacy most were willing to grant them if only for the sake of peace. Nowhere had they stated what they wanted or expected to get out of the talks or, even more basic, how they expected to obtain it. They had turned the talks into another skirmish of the guerrilla war they had waged for decades.

Two days later, little had improved. On Sunday, both sides in the talks presented their positions. Uganda was typically adroit and concise. The government asked the LRA to:

Renounce and abandon terrorism

Cease hostilities

Dissolve itself and hand over all arms and ammunition

Assemble in agreed locations to be demobilized, disarmed, and documented

Accept amnesty for all combatants at the conclusion of the talks

Reintegrate into civilian life or into the Ugandan army

Return to school including vocational institutions, with assistance

Work with cultural and religious leaders to reconcile the combatants with the community

Uganda wanted all of this settled by September 12, fewer than thirty days. The government had adroitly sidestepped the nonsense and offered the LRA everything it could hope for. The LRA would be dissolved, and its fighters could walk away as free men. If they wanted schooling and training, they could have it. The government would help them resettle as farmers and cattle growers. The government would work for reconciliation. It was a skillful move because if the LRA negotiators refused, they would be perceived as unwilling, unreasonable, and uncooperative.

The LRA negotiators were being handed a gilded olive branch, but they didn't know it. Instead, they followed their opening-day threats with a fifteen-page litany of all that the government had done wrong in the north starting with the early days following Museveni's rise to power. It reiterated the abuse, arrest, and torture the Acholis had suffered, the rape and mutilation of the women. The Acholi had no choice but to pick up weapons and fight, they argued. The north had been deliberately pushed into poverty as Museveni's army stole as many as a million cows from the north. The north had been systematically victimized, and the internal refugee camps, the LRA concluded, were part of a concerted effort by Museveni's government to destroy the Acholi.

The LRA admitted, in a backhanded way, that it had committed atrocities but accused the Ugandan army of using Acholis in the camps as human shields and impersonating the LRA in order to commit crimes. The most outrageous example was the Barlonyo massacre.

Frustratingly, the LRA delegation did not outline what it wanted. Finally pressed, they came up with a list of demands. These included disbanding the refugee camps, compensation for the Acholis' stolen cattle, creation of a new national army with a proportional ethnic mix, which theoretically would include Acholi, a cease-fire, a power-sharing arrangement with the government, which would let the Acholi control the north, suspension of all land sales in the north, affirmative action for women, cessation of abusive language, economic restoration in the north.

Ten days after the talks had begun, they recessed for a "consultation" in the jungle at Nabanga. There had been virtually no progress toward a cease-fire, the first and most critical step. The break, however, allowed the more than one hundred people to make their way to Nabanga. For Kony, it was a public relations coup.

"I am an Acholi like you and . . . I am all for peace talks with Museveni," he said. "There have been wars in Sierra Leone, Congo, Sudan, and Liberia and all have been settled peacefully. Even other wars like this one can be settled peacefully. I am not a wizard who talks to spirits. I am a normal human being. . . ." Hoping to deflect the blame for the war that had been directed at him, he insisted, "It is not me who begun this war. I just offered to help those who were oppressed. . . . To you my elders, my brothers, my sisters, my fathers, and my mothers, now that you have come and seen for yourselves that I am not a monster with a tail and huge eyes, you have confirmed that I am a human being." Kony was kept abreast of the talks, and as he rambled it became clear that the LRA delegation was, in fact, reflecting the scrambled logic of its master. "Why is it that when talks begin, someone always comes up with an ultimatum that by this time, talks should have ended? Is that the way things must be? To my elders, we are your children. This war is like a game. I am giving an example of a cockfight where one might be stronger than the other, but they will keep chasing after one another in the compound the whole day."[3]

Like the fighting cock to which he had compared himself, Kony crowed that he did not need amnesty from the government he had fought. "They want to push me in a corner to surrender on their own terms. But you see my people here. They are very many. If I go, what will happen to them? And to you my brothers and sisters, you have heard a lot of things said about me. You have heard that the LRA is a small, disorganized group. I would like to tell you that LRA is a highly organized group. If we were not organized, you wouldn't see all these people here. . . . We are organized and we know what we are doing. I have my forces in Gulu, Pader, and Kitgum. I also have a lot of forces outside Uganda. We have graduates and elites in LRA. I want to ask you: Have you ever heard me making an appeal to treat my people? We have what it takes."[4]

Kony went on the offensive. "They are killing our people, but they blame it on LRA. I want to say that I don't kill my brothers. I don't kill my sisters. I don't kill my mothers and fathers. That is all propaganda, since it is the government of Uganda which controls all the media. Now that you have come here, let's find a solution and end this war."[5]

Kony appealed to the elders to pressure the government into agreeing to a ceasefire, saying it was critical. "We speak to government authorities as they shoot at us. We cannot have meaningful talks. We cannot trust the government of Uganda. Please make sure that you secure a cessation of hostilities so that we can talk in a good environment."[6]

When asked about the LRA's political agenda, his answer only confirmed what was obvious to most—there was none. "I would like to declare our political agenda. We are fighting for the Ten Commandments of God. If you look at the Ten Commandments of God, are they obeyed? They are violated everywhere. We are fighting because it's God who created us so we should fight for his rule. I am not fighting for the Constitution, which has been designed to give some people more time in power. I am fighting for the Ten Commandments. You elders of Acholi, you gave me the blessings to go and fight. Now why don't you give me the blessing to talk peace?"[7]

The much heralded meeting with Kony and the Acholi elders had little effect except to delay the talks. Machar again pressured Otti to join the delegation in Juba, and again he refused. When the negotiators finally returned to the bargaining table, it became clear why Kony had been so insistent on a lull in military action. He still had forces scattered across northern Uganda who were some of his most trusted and vicious fighters. He wanted to get them safely out of northern Uganda, across southern Sudan, and to his main force in the Congo. But the Ugandan army had struck. On August 12, less than a month after the talks had begun and before a cease-fire was signed, the Uganda army killed Raska Lukwiya, one of the five ICC-indicted LRA commanders. Lukwiya had been a key leader during the 2004 surge at the height of the LRA war and atrocities.

Two weeks later, on August 26, a formal Cessation of Hostilities agreement was signed. The agreement included the basics: hostilities would cease, and within three weeks the LRA soldiers would assemble at two locations, one in Eastern Equatoria and another in Western Equatoria, so that capitulation could begin. I began to think that maybe it would really happen, that somehow Kony and Otti could overcome their distrust and fear and step into a new reality for themselves and northern Uganda.

I sensed a deep longing in both of them to forgo the war and a despairing desire to return to northern Uganda and live as normal men. It surfaced in Kony's rambling address to the Acholi elders: "I was born in 1962 and I went to the bush at the age of twenty-three. I have not seen my brothers and sisters and age-mates since."[8]

Then forty-four years old by his own admission, Kony was homesick. Otti, who was probably twenty years older, was equally homesick. When I had sat within a few feet of Otti in the jungle clearing, I asked him what he and the LRA really wanted out of the peace talks. I asked the question to elicit some explanation of the LRA's political agenda.

Instead, he had looked at me and simply said, "To go home."

14

The View from Kilimanjaro

AT THE FOOT OF Mount Kilimanjaro, the town of Arusha in northern Tanzania serves as a comfortable base from which to ascend Africa's highest peak or roll across the expansive Serengeti grasslands to witness some of the world's most spectacular wildlife. I was fortunate enough to do both. The Tanzanian government long ago figured out that money could be made in wildlife tourism, so Arusha has a well-kept airport attended by safari vehicles that whisk visitors off to their adventures. The government also recognized that a vibrant tourism industry is impossible without political stability. Unlike most of its neighbors, Tanzania, formerly Tanganyika, has not had to struggle with genocides, civil wars, and marauding militias. This stability is perhaps why the United Nations established the International Criminal Tribunal for Rwanda in Arusha.

The Rwandan Tribunal was set in a complex of modest, multistory buildings where the world dispensed justice for those accused of masterminding the genocide of an estimated eight hundred thousand Tutsis during three months in 1994. Formally established in 1994, the tribunal saw its first trials begin in 1997. International justice is not cheap. For the 2006–2007 operating budget, the United Nations gave the tribunal $269,758,400 for salaries and associated expenses for some 1,042 people from eighty-five different countries who work in Arusha; Kigali, Rwanda; The Hague; and New York. By late 2007, after ten years of trials, twenty-eight people had been tried, six had appealed, three had been released, three had died, and five had been acquitted. Cases against another twenty-eight were ongoing, and six more awaited trial. Eighteen of the accused were still at large.[1]

Kony and the LRA were very much on the minds of the Rwanda prosecutors when I visited them in early August 2006. This group of lawyers was in the vanguard of international law and justice, and the court was setting precedents that would guide other courts and human rights cases around the world, including the International Criminal Court, which would try the Kony case. By establishing the Rwandan and other tribunals, the UN had gone beyond the notion of national sovereignty, which in most cases was crippled by corruption and political oppression, and asserted something more important: universal human rights.

———

A native of the small West African country of the Gambia, the tribunal's chief prosecutor, Hassan Bubacar Jallow, greeted me in his offices wearing traditional African garb. Tall and imposing, Jallow had a deliberate, thoughtful manner. He was appointed to his position in September 2003 and guided the prosecutor's office through some of its most difficult moments as it confronted unrepentant and combative Hutu purveyors of ethnic hatred.

The ramifications of the Rwandan genocide go far beyond those who died, Jallow said. "The whole community was a victim of the crimes." The physical losses were grotesque and severe, but the killing sent a psychological and spiritual shock wave throughout Rwanda, the region, and ultimately the world. The genocide, which the world refused to confront as it occurred, forced the international community to reconsider its responsibilities and obligations in the face of such horrific events. It also raised the question of what it means to be human. That one element in a compact society in mountainous Rwanda could turn on another with such ferocity and conviction was staggering. If anything, it reinforced the assertion that humans have hardly distanced themselves from the remorseless beasts with which we share the planet. This and other events such as the ethnically motivated massacres in the Balkans show that, despite the supposedly modifying influences of a civil society and religion, humankind remains quite capable of extreme savagery. If such acts are to stop, the prospect of punishment has to be presented.

Events as devastating as the Rwandan genocide have far-reaching implications, Jallow said. "They are not often purely local. What happens anywhere is everybody's concern." But concern is not enough. Despite the presence of an armed UN force that could have thwarted the Rwandan genocide, the decision to staunch the flow of blood was never made. International intervention, in the form of the Rwanda tribunal, came well after the crimes were committed. The killing only ended with swift and violent intervention by commander Paul Kagame, who led his Tutsi army from its bases in Uganda into his own country and restored order. Millions of Hutus then fled across the border into the Congo, where the killing has continued.

The UN cannot protect the rights of everyone everywhere, Jallow said. "We recognize we cannot do everything." The primary responsibility for orderly societies rests with national governments. But when these governments fail to protect basic human rights due to a lack of ability or lack of political will, the world must step in. Not only must the human rights violators be dealt with, but also the failing governments. "The international community is the last resort" but must act quickly, he said, if the level of violence is high and poses a threat. "If you don't intervene, you run the risk of creating more problems that have to be addressed. You can't have a viable peace when there is injustice. If local systems can't provide that justice, then we all have to work together as we did in Rwanda. We have to be our neighbor's keeper . . . if we believe that human rights exist."

The notion of universal human rights is not new. The U.S. Declaration of Independence states that humanity is "endowed by their Creator with certain unalienable Rights, that among these are Life, Liberty and the pursuit of Happiness." The idea of universal human rights was stated in the French Declaration of the Rights of Man and the Citizen in 1789, and again in the U.S. Bill of Rights in 1791. But it took more than 150 years for the idea to catch on worldwide. The Universal Declaration of Human Rights was adopted by the United Nations in 1948. More recent agreements on human rights are the European Convention of 1950, the International Covenant on Civil and Political Rights adopted by the UN in 1966, which went into force in 1976, and the African Charter on Human and People's Rights, adopted in 1981. Article 4 of the African Charter states that "Human beings are inviolable. Every human being shall be entitled to respect for his life and the integrity of his person. No one may be arbitrarily deprived of this right." Article 5 of the charter goes on: "Every individual shall have the right to the respect of the dignity inherent in a human being and to the recognition of his legal status. All forms of exploitation and degradation of man particularly slavery, slave trade, torture, cruel, inhuman or degrading punishment and treatment shall be prohibited."

Declaring rights is one thing; enforcing them is another. The emergence of international law that backs human rights perhaps began with the First Geneva Convention "for the Amelioration of the Condition of the Wounded and Sick in Armed Forces in the Field," which was first adopted in 1864 and revised nearly a hundred years later in 1949. It was soon followed by three more conventions regarding the sick and wounded at sea, prisoners of war, and finally protection of civilians in war. Three other protocols have subsequently been adopted, most pointedly Protocol II, which applies to civilian victims in noninternational conflicts. It includes a ban on the recruitment of child soldiers, defined as anyone under the age of fifteen, but also specifies that commanders are responsible for ensuring that their soldiers follow these rules. If they don't, commanders are responsible for the criminal acts of their soldiers.

This well-established principle clearly implicates Kony and his commanders. The Geneva conventions also state that anyone who ratifies them is responsible for their enforcement. It applies to "grave breaches" of the conventions, which accurately describe the work of the Lord's Resistance Army, and includes "willful killing; torture or inhuman treatment . . . willfully causing great suffering or serious injury to body or health; extensive destruction and appropriation of property not justified by military necessity . . . unlawful confinement of a protected civilian; the taking of hostages." Again, this places the burden to capture Kony on the shoulders of the Ugandan government, which signed the conventions in 1964, just two years after its independence and twenty-two years before the emergence of the LRA.

Barbara Mulvaney, an American attorney and senior member of the Rwandan tribunal prosecution team, said that it is often difficult to decide when, where, and to what extent the international community should intervene in humanitarian crises. But history has shown that "the sooner they're involved, the better." Too often human rights are violated by groups and governments unless or until someone or some country with clout feels that their interests are being impinged upon.

"If there's not some interest, who cares? If somebody actually cared about what was going on in northern Uganda," she said, the twenty-year war there would have ended. As the world's hyperpower, the United States has historically intervened in foreign countries under the nebulous mandate of protecting American interests. In the past that interest has been political and ideological, as in the Cold War, or economic, as in the case of protecting U.S. oil supplies.

Active military interventions to prevent humanitarian catastrophes have not been common. Other than Kosovo, most humanitarian interventions have been undertaken by the UN in Africa, such as the missions to the Democratic Republic of the Congo, Sierra Leone, and Liberia.

But reasons to intervene have broadened in recent years and are both personal and collective, Mulvaney argued. "On a personal level, you want to care because you're a human being." Collectively, we all want a more secure world. "For Americans to be secure, you can't have failed nations. You can't have hiding places," she said. To the assertion that the United States cannot police the world, she answers that if the UN can't or won't, then who else? Except for a handful of European countries, few have the means, might, or human rights records to justify such actions. Rather than waiting for a crisis to explode that requires a military response, Mulvaney advocates being "a little more creative about the solutions" for existing or looming crises. The decision by the international community to intervene can be made by answering one practical question, she said: "What kind of world do we want?"

One answer came with the creation of the International Criminal Court. Formed in 1998 at the direction of the UN Security Council, it became the world's first permanent court and was created by virtue of an international treaty called the Rome Statute. Previously, various tribunals were established to address specific situations: the International Criminal Tribunal for the former Yugoslavia, the International Criminal Tribunal for Rwanda, and the Special Court for Sierra Leone. The creation of this permanent court was resisted by many, especially the United States, which has refused to be a signatory to its creation, saying the court could be used as a political tool.

While this excuse is embarrassingly lame, U.S. foreign policy makers have cause for worry. Decisions such as invading Iraq to rid Saddam Hussein of nonexistent weapons of mass destruction could subject the United States to charges by the court, specifically for the crime of aggression. Also susceptible would be the questionable containment without charges of al-Qaeda suspects at Guantanamo, Cuba, treatment of prisoners at the Abu Ghraib prison in Iraq, and the widely publicized practice of extraordinary rendition. The United States has arrogantly refused to be subject to any other earthly power than itself. Regardless, 106 other countries are member states of the ICC. By maintaining its position, the United States has isolated itself and sabotaged its claim as the premier defender of human rights and liberty.

As an independent institution based in The Hague, Netherlands, the ICC has the power to investigate and conduct trials for genocide, crimes against humanity, war crimes, and, at some point, crimes of aggression. The Lord's Resistance Army was its first case. The war in northern Uganda was an appalling violation of human rights, the result of a concentrated and organized militia war waged across international boundaries. It was subject to charges under the ICC as well as the Geneva Conventions. After seventeen years of fighting, the LRA remained as powerful as ever, so President Museveni asked for help. In early December 2003, Museveni invited the ICC to investigate Kony and his army, and this request came none too soon. Within months, units of Kony's fighters committed one of their most gruesome massacres ever at the Barlonyo camp outside Lira. The ICC indictments against Kony and his top commanders were made public in October 2005, but as of spring 2008, nearly three years later, none had been arrested. Of the five, Raska Lukwiya was confirmed dead, having been killed by the Ugandan army, and the charges against him were dropped. In late 2007, deputy commander Vincent Otti was rumored to have been killed by Kony in a leadership dispute, but the death was not confirmed. Otti's death was a clear blow to the peace process because he had been one of the most vocal and approachable leaders in the LRA, and this, most said, led to his death. Otti was so active in the peace process that he was taking the LRA too far too quickly for Kony's liking.

The July 2006 talks in Juba, South Sudan, excited hopes that the agonizing war might end, but the talks also raised troubling issues that swirled around the LRA, the international court, and Uganda's amnesty program. Because the ICC lacked police power to make an arrest, this responsibility fell on the court's member countries. It also meant that as long as Kony moved between the Democratic Republic of the Congo and Sudan, he was likely to stay free of arrest because the Sudan government in Khartoum had not signed the accord creating the court. Sudan also resisted UN intervention in its western Darfur region. Khartoum's reluctance to cooperate further solidified when, in April 2007, the ICC issued indictments against two Sudanese leaders: Ahmad Harun, the minister of state for humanitarian affairs (which meant he regulated all humanitarian aid programs in Sudan), and Janjaweed leader Ali Kushayb, who were charged with a total of fifty-one counts of crimes against humanity and war crimes. Sudan took no action against either and denied they had done anything wrong. Clearly, Sudan would do nothing to facilitate Kony's capture.

The same could be said of South Sudan, the semiautonomous region that had not existed at the time of the signing of the Rome Statute. Vice president Machar's blunt talk with Kony and Otti in early 2006 left little doubt that South Sudan's army would attack the LRA if it didn't behave. But in his attempt to entice Otti to the Juba peace talks, Machar had assured Otti that he would be safe and bragged that other dubious characters lived freely in Juba, saying, "We have never handed them over." Criminal courts and trials were inventions of the Europeans, Machar said. Africans had other ways of dealing with things. "In Africa, people talk. They find the differences in themselves and resolve the problem. In Europe, they put people on trial. . . ."[2] In effect, Machar promised that Kony would not be bothered by South Sudan if a peace deal was signed.

The onus for Kony's arrest remained where it always had been, with Uganda. But it was increasingly doubtful Uganda would ever act. On the eve of the Uganda–LRA peace talks in Juba in July 2006, Museveni offered amnesty for Kony. But as quickly and suddenly as it had been offered, Kony had slammed the door on it, saying it amounted to surrender. While the offer appeared to be a dramatic reversal for Museveni, it was essentially a hollow gesture. Amnesty granted by Uganda did not preclude Uganda from turning him over to the ICC, and soon the ICC indictments became the critical issue of the Juba peace talks.

After a year and a half, the talks recessed in late November 2007 so that the rebel negotiators could conduct a series of so-called reconciliation consultations. In late November and early December 2007, Kony's negotiating team, led by Martin Ojul, went on a widely publicized tour of northern Uganda to meet with the victims of LRA atrocities. The team visited dozens of villages and camps, many of them sites of the rebels' vicious attacks on civilians, repeatedly asking people if they had forgiven Kony. In most cases, camp residents joyfully shouted that in fact they had, especially if it would bring a permanent peace to the north. The real purpose of the tour, however, was to whip up enthusiasm for the traditional reconciliation ceremony of *mato oput* and undermine the ICC indictments, because Kony equated a trial with his own death sentence, despite the fact that the court forbade capital punishment. In large part, the team's tour succeeded because it was able to convince people that reconciliation was a substitute for prosecution by the ICC. In fact, the two concepts and activities are totally separate and largely unrelated. Yet the team members repeatedly said the ICC was opposed to peace in the north and blamed it for blocking a peace deal. The statements went virtually unchallenged.

Saying that the ICC opposed peace was an absurdity, of course. Withdrawal of the ICC indictments against the LRA commanders would negate the reason the court had been created, regardless of what the rebels thought, and would destroy any credibility the court was struggling to achieve. It was like saying that the international tribunals for Yugoslavia, Rwanda, and Sierra Leone also opposed peace in those regions because they prosecuted war criminals. Likewise, saying that the ICC was an impediment to peace suggested that human rights did not exist in northern Uganda. It suggested that, as in the past, anyone was still free to take up arms at any time and kill with impunity. Yet the accusation that the ICC was blocking a peace deal was voiced across the north, both before and after the LRA peace team's reconciliation tour. The statements were widely accepted in northern Uganda, where everybody was so sick of war that they would do anything to end the violence, even if it meant "forgiving" Kony.

But the alternative that the LRA negotiators touted, the traditional *mato oput* reconciliation ceremony, was highly questionable. In the past it had been used to settle disputes between feuding families and clans for such things as stolen goats and cows, even fights, rapes, and murders. It was a useful tool to stop revenge, but it was absurd to suggest that this ceremony could effectively address twenty years of atrocities committed by an army that had killed and victimized tens of thousands and caused the displacement of two million people. While traditional Acholi *mato oput* ceremonies were perhaps important for the community's psychological healing, the ceremony provides neither punishment nor restitution on the scale that was needed. Public confessions of guilt, appeals for forgiveness, and vows to reform would not compensate for decades of death and mutilation. Traditional ceremonies generated no reason for things to change; rather they simply reinforced the status quo. Proponents of traditional justice admitted as much. Going after Kony, arresting him, and putting him on trial may remove him from the scene, some argued, but it would be a waste of time because it would not prevent another militia leader from arising. That would be true, certainly, if the *mato oput* ceremony alone was used with Kony, since it would send a signal that militias could murder and maim without fear of punishment.

The LRA's position never wavered. Speaking in April 2007 in Nairobi, Martin Ojul reiterated the rebel stance: "The common position of LRA is that the ICC arrest warrants should be dropped after the completion of Agenda Number 3 on Accountability and Reconciliation. Failure to do that shall mean the indicted LRA leaders shall not sign the peace agreement. . . ."[3] This threat to return to war was Kony's way of yet again intimidating the people of northern Uganda into appealing to the ICC to drop the charges. It was what Kony had done for twenty years: perpetuate his army's existence at the point of a gun. Now he told the north, *Forgive me or I'll kill you.* If nothing else, the LRA's insistence that the ICC indictments were an insurmountable obstacle to peace would give them a viable reason never to sign a peace deal. It was a sad reality as 2007 came to a close.

When I returned to northern Uganda in December 2007, I suspected that the widely reported forgiveness of Kony that was being proclaimed by the LRA was little more than a lie. My visits to the villages across the north, which a year and a half earlier had been impossible, proved my instincts to be right. The deeper into the bush I went, the more the resentment against the LRA intensified. At the Lataya camp north of Pader, it became clear that refugees had joined the forgiveness chorus because they feared reprisals from the LRA if they said anything different. And why not? They had been killed and mutilated for two decades by the LRA rebels who had already spawned a second generation of fighters. A peace deal had not been signed. Kony and his army were still alive and well and, although in the Congo, could come back with a vengeance.

When I asked David Ocaya, one of the camp leaders, what he thought about the peace talks, he shook his head disgustedly. "We don't think Kony is sincere," he said. "He only wants to survive," which was why the peace talks were taking so long. Like most others who followed the talks, he felt dismayed at the killing and disappearance of Vincent Otti. Ocaya suggested that Otti had pushed for peace because he was "a little wiser" than Kony and so was killed.

When I asked if he sincerely thought the *mato oput* ceremony was preferable to Kony facing the international court, he shrugged. "It is going to be difficult to arrest Kony," he said. If the peace talks fell apart, as many previous efforts had, "he might escalate the war again." As a result, most people "fear to say what the punishment should be." Given this reality, people in the Lataya camp saw *mato oput* as the easiest and fastest road to peace. If it required the ICC suspending the indictments, then so be it, he said, because they could be reactivated in the future and used as a deterrent. "If Kony fails to abide by the rules [of a peace agreement], then the ICC [indictments] should be put into effect."

But just a short distance from the camp, however, where Cisto Odongo and his friends were building new homes, a bolder attitude revealed itself. Odongo said he wasn't afraid of the rebels anymore because "they're all gone." As long as the LRA stayed at the peace table, he supported the *mato oput* process for the rank-and-file fighters. But the others needed to face the international court. "The top leaders should be arrested," Odongo said. "If they are allowed to only do *mato oput,* they can return to their old ways."

A couple days later, at the Pabbo camp north of Gulu, I encountered similar responses. The leader of one of the largest and oldest camps of the war, a place that had become a small city, Wilson Ajok explained that people in Pabbo had been in the epicenter of the rebel war for twenty years and would do anything for peace, even forgive Kony. It was a matter of expediency. They had suffered atrocities for too long, he said, to let this chance for peace slip away.

When I questioned that forgiveness, he insisted, "The forgiveness from the Acholi people is not forced. We would like the ICC to release the arrest warrants . . . so that Kony will come back here" and reconcile with the Acholi. "The ICC has become the barrier to peace talks for us."

But why was the ICC a barrier to peace, I asked, if putting Kony on trial might prevent similar armies and thousands of deaths in the future?

"If Kony was brought to Uganda and killed, it would do nothing," he said, suggesting that, unless the war was peacefully resolved, others would carry it on. "He must be with us and see what he has done . . . so we can begin a new life." Besides, he said, "If [Kony] is forgiven, there is no need to arrest him. There would be no need."

The underlying assumption of this newly found wellspring of forgiveness was that Kony was interested in peace, would sign a treaty, and would return to Acholiland to beg forgiveness. Did Ajok think Kony would do that?

He shook his head. "I don't believe it. Kony won't sign," he said of a peace agreement. "Kony is a very tough man."

So why all of this talk about forgiveness?

He simply shrugged. "If Kony refuses to sign the peace deal, then the ICC is free to execute its warrants."

I found this logic disturbing, but I realized finally that the effect of the LRA's reign of terror was vast and deep. If the people of the north had to feign forgiveness to cling to their lives, they would do it.

I went deeper into the bush. We drove our FWD some five miles along what was little more than a path through tall, six-foot grass and brush to a satellite of the Pabbo camp. It was obvious how the LRA had held sway here. Movement through the grass of large numbers of fighters could go undetected. We soon arrived at a collection of mud and thatch-roofed huts called the Pamin Lalwak, a semipermanent staging area for the eventual return of the residents to their original villages. The residents greeted our arrival with the usual flurry of activity as chairs and benches were arranged under a mango tree and elders chased away the swarm of children who converged around us. Jackson Oloya, thirty-eight, was the leader here, and he explained that, after twenty years of fighting, which had done nothing to bring peace, people across the north were willing to reconcile—if it meant the end of war. "They are calling for forgiveness because there is no other option," Oloya explained. Word had spread that if anyone didn't publicly support forgiveness and *mato oput*, "it may lead to the loss of your life," he said.

People had lived so long with the profound fear that countering the rebels in any way, now or in the future, meant certain death. Lurking in their consciousness was the suspicion that Kony would and could come back to exact his revenge.

Did Oloya think that a peace deal would soon be signed?

He shook his head. "Kony may not sign. He seems not to be interested in peace if he killed Otti."

So if Kony won't sign, I suggested, forgiving him is a useless gesture.

He agreed. In such a case, "then it is right to arrest him and have him face the law. Kony should face life in prison or hanging."

But shouldn't Kony face trial, regardless of traditional reconciliation ceremonies?

He readily agreed. "If he is left free, then others will plan to do the same thing. Others will be encouraged to do wrong things and go with it. Kony should be arrested," he concluded. Like many others, Oloya had suffered personal tragedies at the hands of the LRA. His brother and his son had been killed by rebels, he said, and he had taken his nephew, who had been blinded by exploding ordnance, into his family. "That kind of thing cannot be easily forgiven."

As we headed back to Gulu, I pored over my notes, trying to piece everything together. But the harder I looked, the less I found. Instead

I became angry at what I had heard, at the disconnected logic at work in the villages across the north. No one truly believed that Kony wanted peace, yet they were willing to forgive him, but only if it meant peace. If it didn't bring peace, then Kony should be arrested and brought to trial. But wasn't Kony guilty of crimes that had to be punished? When pushed, all would agree that he was. But yet he could be forgiven? They also agreed. So where did the basic concept of right versus wrong fit in here? Did they even exist here? What about human rights? The answers were nowhere to be found.

Before I left Gulu, I met once again with Yusef Adek, the elder member of the LRA's peace delegation to whom I'd spoken originally in the jungles along the Congo–Sudan border. In our meeting, the belligerent pride of the Acholi flared as never before. It was equal parts a disdain for outsiders, perhaps built upon years of oppression and marginalization, and a strong desire for recognition and respect. When I prodded Adek about the sincerity of Acholi's call for *mato oput* and rejection of the ICC justice, he became indignant.

"When others talk of arrest [of Kony] it is a declaration of war. He has guns," Adek said. "Let them [the ICC] not think of Kony, but of the people of the north. Those of us who have suffered most in this war want peace." As he continued, it seemed that, despite the atrocities, Kony was still considered a hero. "He has defeated the government of Uganda, Sudan, and the United Nations," Adek boasted. "Who is going to arrest Kony? He is a guerrilla." Just one of his LRA fighters equals fifty government soldiers, he said. "Let them come with their police and arrest Kony . . . if the ICC insists."

But just as quickly as Adek had angered, he softened his stance and insisted that a real peace deal was within reach, perhaps within a couple of months. "It is in our interest . . . that Kony sign," he said. Once that major hurdle is completed, he said, other things could happen to restore Acholi lands. Not only would general *mato oput* cere-monies be conducted across the north, but so would smaller, individ-ual ceremonies involving each rebel fighter and his victims, he said. Once forgiveness was bestowed and peace had taken hold, then Kony might face international justice, he said. "Let's see if Kony can sign [a peace deal]," Adek said. In such a case, then Kony might say, "'I can go face The Hague individually.'"

It was a shocking admission. Was he serious? Kony would volun-tarily face justice? I asked.

Adek nodded, as if to say *Why not?* But even if Kony didn't sur-render himself to the court, the path would be cleared for his arrest, Adek speculated, and he drew a parallel of Kony's situation to that of former Liberian president Charles Taylor, who at the time was on trial before the UN special tribunal in Sierra Leone. Taylor had been arrested while living in exile in Nigeria. "The same thing can happen to Kony," Adek said. "But for the time being, [Kony] still has the gun. Let us convince him to sign the peace agreement. He is a human being, like myself."

I felt good about the prospects for peace, finally, and Adek clearly believed it was possible. "The peace talks have reached a stage that can-not turn back now," he said. With this simple statement, he had helped clear up some of the failed logic that I had seen at work in the villages and, for the first time, had acknowledged that the ICC was a functioning entity that had influenced events and most likely would continue to do so. At the time, Adek and others in the peace delega-tion, along with more than a hundred other Acholi, were preparing once again to rendezvous with Kony in the jungle redoubt of Nabanga to discuss the next step forward.

But what, I could not help but ask, would happen if the peace talks failed?

Adek shook his head at the question, as if it were not possible. The only way they would fail, he said, would be if Ugandan president

Museveni sabotaged them. His eyes flared once again as he pointed a finger in warning. "If Museveni would spoil the peace talks, then Museveni will be the permanent enemy."

He looked at me for a long moment as he let the implications settled in my mind. I wondered, then, if peace would ever come to the north.

———

When I first landed in Uganda in August 2005, I had never heard of the Lord's Resistance Army. I had been warned that travel to the northern part of the country was dangerous, but it was not something I would have to worry about because I wouldn't need to go there. That warning had made me curious. The north was terra incognita, the unknown world.

Shortly after my first trip to the north, I was staggered by the fact that a war could have gone on for twenty years and claimed so many lives, many of them children's, and it wasn't general knowledge outside Uganda. I am, after all, a journalist. I follow the news because it is my job, but also because I like it. I like knowing about the world; it is my world as well as everyone else's. But few in the West had ever heard of this war or the rebel army that was conducting it.

And it wasn't just northern Uganda that was lost from the world's consciousness; it was also South Sudan and even Darfur. Is the world truly that deaf, dumb, and blind? I realized that I could not ignore this unique opportunity. But after more than a year of travel and work throughout Uganda, I still groped for answers. What had happened in the north and, more important, why?

But some things are clear. Underlying the twenty-year tragedy in northern Uganda is a remarkable lack of responsibility. Those directly and indirectly involved in the war and the peace talks acted as if doing nothing about the endless death and devastation of war was their preferred course of action. This appalling attitude permeated most of sub-Saharan Africa and was the main reason for the continent's endless cycle of violence. If you just waited long enough, as was the case with Uganda's Idi Amin, Zaire's Mobutu, and dozens of other dictators such as Zimbabwe's Robert Mugabe, the bad will eventually self-destruct and disappear. But in the process hundreds of thousands die needless, brutal deaths. No sooner does one bloodthirsty, rapacious killer rise to prominence only to disappear than several more surface.

The calls for the ICC to suspend its indictments against Joseph Kony and his commanders grew from the conviction that it would be much easier, if not effortless, to simply forgive and forget than to say no, never again. Better to sit back and hope it's a long time before another Kony comes along. The sad reality was that it was only a matter of when, not if.

Twenty years of atrocities had continued in northern Uganda because no one wanted to stop them. Denial fouled the fields and polluted the air of Uganda. Kony and Otti repeatedly denied that they or their commanders had committed any crimes, despite mountains of evidence and thousands upon thousands of victims. Instead, they blamed Museveni and then the Acholi people for having rejected their "prophet."

Likewise, the Acholi never acknowledged that the community itself bore responsibility for the existence of the LRA and shared guilt for the crimes committed by it.

The government of Uganda had never taken responsibility for the war in the north, first by not applying enough force to stop the LRA, and second by creating and maintaining inhumane living conditions in the camps with little or no security. Through calculated neglect, the government allowed Kony and his rebels to wage a bloody and inhumane war against his own people and then abused these same people it claimed to protect.

Finally, the international community stood by, clicking tongues, wagging fingers, and sighing deeply. And as it did, it sanctioned this deplorable disaster.

The purpose of the Rwandan tribunal in Arusha was to prevent such a tragedy from ever happening again. Yet a lesser form of murder and mayhem was taking place in neighboring Uganda and further north in Sudan even as the Rwandan trials were being conducted. "African countries must absorb the lessons of the Rwanda genocide in order to avoid a repetition of the ultimate crime on the continent," the tribunal proclaimed on its Web site. "Weak institutions in many African countries have given rise to a culture of impunity, especially under dictatorships that will do anything to cling to power." The declaration continued: "This [tribunal] is the first time high-ranking individuals have been called to account before an international court of law for massive violations of human rights in Africa. The Tribunal's work sends a strong message to Africa's leaders and warlords."[4]

Unfortunately, no one was listening.

Epilogue
Metamorphosis

FROM THE CLEAR SKIES over the northeastern Democratic Republic of the Congo, one sees verdant jungle, blotches of tall elephant grass, and an occasional muddy stream. As we descend, the town of Doruma appears as huts under the jungle canopy, marked by a ribbon of grit where we're to land our single-engine plane. We circle tightly over tin-roofed buildings that rise from an expanse of rain-washed dirt. It's the local Catholic missionary school, a defiant outpost of civilization on the edge of chaos. A crowd of thirty people clusters at the corner of the strip, alerted by a radio call from our pilot that visitors will be arriving and wanting interviews. We're here because the rebel Lord's Resistance Army, a relative newcomer to the nearby forests, struck Doruma on Good Friday 2008, looting the village and kidnapping a schoolteacher and three young women. The teacher escaped and is back in his Doruma classroom. No one knows what happened to the girls. The village chief greets us sporting a brown baseball cap. His right-hand man, the *chef des douanes,* or local customs official, wears an immaculately ironed blue shirt, dark blue trousers, and a black beret. There's not much business in Doruma for customs officials, I imagine, though we're about five miles from the border of South Sudan.

To get here, I have taken a twin-engine plane from Entebbe, Uganda, to Bunia, the major town in the Ituri region of the Province Orientale and the nexus of horrific ethnic bloodshed over the past decade. With the arrival of UN forces a few years earlier, Bunia has become a bastion of aid groups dishing out civility in this coveted gold and diamond region where massacres have been de rigueur since the late 1990s. I am with Congolese journalist Jacques Kahorha, who speaks French, English, and Swahili, the lingua franca of the region. We fly in a UN helicopter from Bunia to Dungu, the last major settlement and a UN base in this sparsely populated no-man's-land that extends northward to the border of South Sudan and the apocalyptic Central African Republic (CAR). The Garamba National Park sits just outside of Dungu. Joseph Kony has based his Lord's Resistance Army in the park's northern reaches for the past two and a half years after his late deputy commander, Vincent Otti, led an advanced force of LRA rebels here. In Garamaba, once a highly prized wild game park for Belgian colonialists, the LRA was supposed to peacefully coexist with its Congolese hosts and the wildlife. It has done anything but that.

Shortly after Otti's arrival, UN forces had a disastrous confrontation with the LRA rebels. In late January 2006, Guatemalan soldiers were caught in an intense firefight with LRA rebels in Garamba Park. At least fifteen of the rebels died, but eight of the Guatemalans were killed, and another five were wounded and evacuated to Bunia. "The unit which was conducting an operation in this area established contact with rebel elements at 6:00 A.M. There followed an exchange of fire lasting four hours, requiring the intervention of armed helicopters," according to a UN statement at the time.[1] Since then, the UN forces, referred to as MONUC, have simply monitored the region. But that may change, as they've completed a landing strip in Dungu capable of handling cargo planes and troop carriers.

The LRA's camp in the far north of Garamba Park is where the rebels have been lavished with foodstuffs, thanks to the largesse of the international community. Though some contend this constitutes aid to a terrorist group, the rationale is that the supplies thwarted the LRA's compulsion to raid, pillage, and plunder as peace talks progressed in Juba, South Sudan. For the most part the LRA behaved. Something changed in December 2007, and no one knows exactly why. The LRA began to raid local villages, having already driven some four hundred families from a village in the park, a Dungu community leader said. Since then the LRA has forced an estimated twenty thousand people from the region. Repeated confrontations with park officials were bloody as the LRA turned the northern half of the park into its own wild game slaughterhouse, wiping out rare white rhinos and decimating elephant herds.

Reports of occasional LRA attacks and abductions were suppressed as peace talks between the LRA and the Ugandan government limped through 2007, after a rocky start in July 2006. Then Kony's forces launched an extended raid in February and March 2008. The LRA unit of 100 or more fighters crossed into South Sudan, attacking the town of Yambio, then continued into the CAR where it attacked Obo, abducting an estimated 160 people. The unit returned through the Democratic Republic of the Congo, attacking villages, including Doruma. It covered about three hundred miles and netted hundreds of new captives and massive supplies.

A small fleet of motorcycles, the main mode of transportation other than foot, has been arranged in Doruma, and within moments we whiz down the dirt track to town, dodging puddles and stray chickens, to the École Primer Ndolomo. Here we find the abducted third-grade teacher, twenty-eight-year-old Raymond Rpiolebeyo, who has the lithe build of a teenager. In the short distance from the airport to the school our entourage has grown, and a dozen people crowd into the choking air of the small brick-and-tin-roofed office of the principal. Raymond arrives, wide-eyed and scared, and although we push everyone out of the office, he sits stiffly, suddenly confronted by strangers. I tell him to relax, we're not the LRA. He smiles weakly.

When the LRA struck Doruma, Raymond was riding his bicycle to his home village of Gurba, six miles away, intending to spend the Easter weekend with his family and friends. But heavily armed rebels stepped from the bush and grabbed him, tossing his bicycle aside. He made it to his village that day, but as a captive of the Lord's Resistance Army. After taking what they wanted, the rebels ordered Raymond to carry a heavy bag. Though he cursed his fate, he thanked God that he was alive: he was young and strong, and therefore useful. For the next eight days, he and the couple of hundred other abductees from South Sudan and the CAR walked from early morning to evening, carrying the rebels' cargo. They took long breaks in the heat of midday, always traveling in small units for tactical reasons: should they be attacked, only a small number would be lost. At night, he and other abductees slept in the sweltering heat under plastic tarps held in place by the bundles they carried. Each night, he lay awake drenched in his sweat. "We were not allowed to wash our clothes," he says with disgust. They ate the food they had taken, such as manioc, corn, and peanuts. He could think of nothing but freedom. "All along the road, I looked for an opportunity to escape," Raymond recalls. He was motivated by the certainty that he would be killed if the rebels decided he was no longer useful. "I was really afraid of dying," he says, and was "really angry at them" for having taken him. As if reading his mind, the rebels tried to sabotage his thoughts. "They told us that if any tried to escape, they would shoot them."

The threats did not deter Raymond.

Once at the rebel camp in Garamba, Raymond saw many other soldiers and was kept under armed guard. The rebels had settled in, he explains, and lived in mud-and-thatch-roofed huts, each about ten to twenty yards apart and each housing several soldiers or a "family" if the soldier had a "wife"—typically one of the hundreds of young girls the rebels routinely kidnap to carry loads, cook, and use as sex slaves. Raymond continued to sleep outside on the plastic sheeting. When he came down with a debilitating case of diarrhea, the soldiers kept him at a distance, but within sight. Medication didn't relieve his condition, so he began to lose weight. The rebels taunted him, saying that if he thought about escape, he would never be cured. They told him and the others to forget about ever returning home. But Raymond didn't accept that. "I kept silent," he says.

At the camp, the soldiers enjoyed some conveniences. Using a solar-powered battery system, they watched videos on a television, and he remembers a war movie but can't recall the name. During the day they listened to Congolese music. Though it is unlikely, Raymond believes that the LRA leader himself, Joseph Kony, led the raiding party. "It was at his house where the television was," he says. "I knew him during the trip" to Garamba. He notes that for security reasons, the leader moved in different parts of the raiding party, sometimes in the front, at other times in the middle or rear. In reality, Kony doesn't participate in such actions, preferring to remain in a command position protected by his guards. Yet, the soldiers told Raymond that the man was "chief number one." The leader "was quiet" and careful to ensure that the abductees were treated kindly, he says. "We was angry when the soldiers were bad to those [abducted]."

On the way to the camp, Raymond struck up an acquaintance with a man named Moise, another abductee who was from the Central African Republic and who wanted to escape as badly as he did. In the rare moments they were alone, they made a plan. Despite the obvious risks, they decided to chance freedom rather than remain with the rebels. A couple of days later, in the depth of the night, Moise crawled over sleeping soldiers clustered around Raymond, and in the dim light, Moise saw Raymond's rubber sandals beside his head. It was the agreed-upon signal whereby Moise could find Raymond. Moise tapped him on the head. Raymond slowly rose, careful not to make a sound, and the two quietly slipped into the dark foliage. They walked all that night, the next day, and the following night, he says, never stopping to rest, because they were being pursued. They eventually came to a small collection of huts near the town of Duru, at the western edge of Garamba Park. There the rebels turned back, fearing they would attract unwanted attention if they tried to recapture their escapees. Raymond's friend Moise left long ago, returning to Obo, and although Raymond is teaching again, he does not rest easy. "I'm still afraid," he confesses. "I'm scared because we were followed. The rebels know where I am."

Raymond's fear is not a random worry. Though no longer in northern Uganda, the Lord's Resistance Army is very much alive. As evidenced by raids like the one during which Raymond was captured, and from debriefings from LRA escapees and defectors, Kony has spent the last couple of years rebuilding his cultlike army. As many as two to three hundred new fighters were added to the LRA ranks in the first half of 2008 and were being trained. According to a UN expert who debriefed a defector, an LRA commander named Captain Rafael, Kony has been keen to blend "foreign" fighters into his force. By incorporating people from the region—South Sudan, the CAR, and the DRC—he integrates local language and knowledge into his organization, transforming his army into a viable and potentially destabilizing regional force. In addition to amassing a large cache of weapons, and letting it be known he's looking for more, Kony has increased his army to at least six hundred armed fighters, with another two hundred or so in training. An equal number of women and children round out the LRA.

What the LRA has become is clear, but to what end is unknown. A look at the region presents a couple of possibilities. To the east lies semiautonomous South Sudan, which, as of this writing, is wrestling with the Khartoum government over control of the largely untapped oil-rich Abyei region. The conflict has centered on the town of Abyei, situated on the border between north and South Sudan, and adjacent to the state of Southern Darfur. That area of Darfur has largely been in the control of the rebel Justice and Equality Movement (JEM).

The fact that the Khartoum government of President Omar al-Bashir has been collecting lucrative oil revenues from many foreign oil producers has not gone unnoticed by the JEM rebels. In October

2007, JEM rebels attacked an oil production facility in the Abyei region, kidnapping five oil workers: three Sudanese, an Iraqi, and an Egyptian. The rebels then issued an ultimatum to foreign oil firms, the Chinese in particular, to leave Sudan. The rebels accused China of being the main supplier of weapons to Sudan for use in Darfur— a charge the Chinese have denied. The five oil workers were seized in an attack on a facility run by the Greater Nile Petroleum Operating Company, a consortium involving China's CNPC, India's ONGC, Malaysia's Petronas, and Sudan's state-owned Sudapet. The oil field reportedly produces about half of the country's output of some five hundred thousand barrels of oil per day, much of which is exported to China.

Khartoum is desperate to protect its oil fields and its vital source of income and is prone to use proxy militias such as the Janjaweed in north Darfur to fight its battles. A well-armed and dedicated militia like the LRA could be highly useful to Khartoum, and its use of the LRA would be nothing new. Khartoum provided primary support for the LRA in its fight against Uganda in the years before and after 2000, and some suspect that its support has been renewed. And why not? The LRA could harass the JEM rebels in Southern Darfur, who use eastern Chad and northern Central African Republic as fallback positions. If the LRA were to attack JEM positions from the rear, it would create a second front for the Darfur rebels and damage JEM's effectiveness against Sudan's armed forces and the Janjaweed militia fighters in south Darfur.

A more likely scenario is that Khartoum intends to use the LRA against its former foe, South Sudan, in the fight over oil in Abyei. After waging one of Africa's bloodiest civil wars—a twenty-year conflict that took some two million lives—Khartoum and South Sudan signed a Comprehensive Peace Agreement in January 2005. It has been shaky at best. According to the agreement, a special commission was set up to determine who has rights to Abyei oil: Sudan or South Sudan.

After extensive study, the Abyei Border Commission decided Abyei belonged to the south.

President al-Bashir of Sudan dismissed that decision out of hand in late 2007. South Sudan withdrew from the unified government as a result, only to rejoin some months later. The two sides have asked for international arbitration on the issue. About the same time, Khartoum began arming Arab nomads known as the Misseriah, who seasonally graze their cattle around Abyei, along with elements of Sudan's northern army, and moving them toward Abyei. In May the town of Abyei was bombarded, forcing the South Sudan army to withdraw and Abyei's thirty thousand residents to flee.

Less than a month later and a couple hundred miles to the south, a unit of the LRA attacked the outpost of the South Sudan army at the border town of Nabanga. Ironically, Nabanga has been the meeting site for LRA negotiators and peace delegations from Uganda and the international community. In that early June attack, some twenty-five people reportedly were killed, about half of them South Sudanese soldiers. The LRA unit was said to consist of nearly one hundred soldiers, including a couple of Kony's commanders sought by the International Criminal Court. This attack on the Nabanga outpost has been largely unexplained but appears to be the opening salvo of what could be a second and diversionary front for the South Sudan army. If South Sudan is fighting the LRA in the south, it will have less military to commit to the Abyei in the north, which could significantly weaken South Sudan's ability to retake Abyei if the peace agreement ultimately collapses.

Back in the northern Congolese town of Dungu, however, such regional strategies for Joseph Kony and his Lord's Resistance Army mean little. The people of Dungu have more immediate concerns about the LRA. No one is more keenly aware of the LRA than Father Benoit Kinalegu. As head of the Dungu Diocese and the district's Peace and Justice Commission, Kinalegu receives a steady

flow of reports of LRA attacks in the region. Kinalegu is an imposing man, and with a baritone voice he readily recants the litany of
LRA abuses that began with the militia's arrival in the region in the
fall of 2005.

Over time, the LRA raids have become more frequent and brazen,
he says as we sit on the shaded porch of the diocese's complex of
offices and guest rooms. Less than a month earlier, a small unit of LRA
soldiers marched into the town of Kapili, some twenty-eight miles to
the north. The soldiers chased people out of their homes, then started
cooking food. "People were very angry that day. Some of them went
to the market to find machetes, saying this is not acceptable," he tells
me. But the local village chief confronted the displaced villagers and
convinced them that trying to chase armed fighters away with
machetes was madness. So they left the fighters alone and waited in
the bush. When the rebels left a couple of days later, they took seeds
and farming tools, which is disturbing, Kinalegu says, because it means
"they intend to settle down."

Kinalegu is convinced that the LRA has rearmed itself to become
a regional force. "We are afraid this can lead to war," he says, pulling
off his gold-rimmed glasses. "I think he is creating a mercenary force
that can be used against any government. They are not far from Sudan
where they trade for weapons." To prevent future bloodshed, he says,
"the most important thing is to cut off the supply of weapons." While
Kinalegu is keenly aware of the threat the LRA presents, he is equally
aware that there is no one to stop Kony. "Local people are really
afraid. Here in the DRC, it is empty."

The remoteness of the LRA camp in Garamba Park has allowed
Kony to remain blithely aloof and unaffected by the past two years of
peace talks with Uganda. Thoughts that he will sign a peace deal are
probably naïve and optimistic. For twenty years, Kony has known
nothing but war. He has been and continues to be a force that needs
to be reckoned with. Why would he give that up to be tried in The

Hague, and most likely die there? Yet, a peace deal was negotiated, and in early 2008 the successful conclusion to the peace talks seemed a fait accompli. A permanent cease-fire had been signed, and negotiators said peace was at hand.

But there were cracks in the facade.

In October 2007, word spread of a split in the LRA ranks. And shortly after, Kony killed his pro-peace deputy commander Vincent Otti, whom I had encountered in 2006. Some LRA commanders defected, turning themselves in to the UN forces in the Dungu area and eventually landing in Uganda. The defectors provided details of Otti's execution.

According to a top defector, Sunday Otto, Kony killed his long-time deputy Otti following a meeting with leaders of his Acholi tribe and the LRA negotiating team on the DRC–South Sudan border. "[Kony] told me that the LRA was divided and that most of the troops were more loyal to Otti than to him," Otto said. "He complained that his orders were no longer being followed. He had ordered his fighters to go and abduct but they refused because Otti had argued that this would spoil the talks. He had proposed to move to the Central African Republic, but Otti had refused," Otto continued. "'Who is the leader when I issue orders and people don't follow them but instead listen to Otti?' [Kony] wondered. [Kony] said he was very confident in what the spirit had told him, that he knew the [Uganda] government was planning to kill him and they were using the peace talks to have him arrested and killed. 'They deceive you and try to convince you to come out and then they kill you,' he said. 'Anybody who believes in peace talks will die. . . .'"[2]

On the morning of October 2, Kony ordered Otti arrested, taken to a spot not far from his camp, and executed. "[Otti] kept on begging and pleading: 'What crime have I committed? Are you really going to kill me? All along, I have been so good to you and the movement. Why can't you tell me what I did wrong? May God help you!'"[3]

Otto said that "Otti's seven wives were taken by force and distributed to the other commanders the same day. Of the four adult wives, one was given to Abudema, one to Odhiambo, one to Okuti, and one to Kony's brother, Major Olanya. The three underage girls were handed over to Kony."[4]

Otto revealed the frightening depths of Kony's paranoia and fear of the peace talks. When asked if he thought Kony would ever sign a peace deal, he said, "Signing from where? Otti was the one who persuaded [Kony] to go to Ri-Kwangba. He was also the one who pushed [Kony] to meet UN special envoy Joachim Chissano. At every assembly, Kony feared he would be killed. He would sit in every meeting with his pistol cocked."[5] Otti's body was left unburied for two days on Kony's orders, not only as an insult, but supposedly so that Kony could draw power from the event.

Details eventually emerged of what might have caused Otti to be executed. According to some sources, secret meetings took place in Mombasa, Kenya, involving high-ranking members of the Ugandan government. Money and promises of a house in Kenya or Uganda were reportedly passed to Otti via the LRA negotiators as enticements for Otti to defect and take a substantial number of soldiers with him. But Otti was killed before he could take his loyal soldiers out of the LRA. The death of Vincent Otti, of course, cast a dismal pall over the talks. Otti had been the prime mover of the talks, and his growing power threatened Kony. The persistent rumors of Otti's death were denied as the LRA peace team conducted a "reconciliation tour" of Uganda in November and December as they took a hiatus from the peace talks.

The tour was little more than an orchestrated public relations stunt that drummed up sentiment against the ICC indictments against Kony and his remaining two top commanders. The LRA peace team announced that Kony would sign a peace deal—if only the ICC would lift its indictments. The LRA was framing the situation in northern

Uganda as a choice between peace and justice. This was not the choice, of course, but it effectively shifted attention away from twenty years of atrocities, death, and displacement in northern Uganda and focused it on the ICC as an obstacle to peace. Uganda played along by agreeing to establish a special court in Kampala to try Kony. The apparent purpose was to negate the need to arrest Kony and put him on trial by the ICC in The Hague. There were serious problems with this. First, a war crimes court had never existed in Uganda, and the country had no laws against the crimes for which Kony had been charged: war crimes, crimes against humanity, sexual enslavement, forced recruitment of child soldiers, etc. And it was morally reprehensible for Uganda to tell the ICC that because Kony, who had fought the government for twenty years, didn't want to face the ICC, Uganda also didn't want Kony prosecuted, even though it had asked the court to do that in 2003.

With the coming of the new year, the fissures in the peace process were ominous. Shortly after the Juba talks resumed in early February 2008, they were recessed so that newly named LRA negotiator David Nyekorach Matsanga, who had replaced Martin Ojul, could meet with other new members of the team and supposedly with Kony himself. Matsanga was a Ugandan who had been living in England and maintained ties to Robert Mugabe, the president of Zimbabwe. Matsanga explained the changes in the LRA team by saying the others had been opportunists who were making money off the peace process. Crispus Ayena Odongo, a Kampala lawyer who has been acting as a legal adviser to the LRA, was replaced by Caleb Alaka, also a Kampala lawyer.

As the LRA had in the past, Matsanga presented the ICC charges as a stumbling block to peace. To resolve this, Matsanga led a small LRA delegation in early March to The Hague to ask that the charges against Kony be dropped. It was a bizarre move, of course. The ICC politely told Matsanga and Alaka that appropriate requests could be filed and would be duly considered. Unfortunately, the LRA's trip to The Hague was not seen for the diversion that it was. Even as the negotiators were traveling to the Netherlands, reports were surfacing that a large group of LRA fighters had entered South Sudan, apparently headed toward Yambio. The regional governor sounded an alarm, but no one was listening.

It became painfully apparent that Kony was not interested in signing the peace deal when on April 10, with some two hundred people waiting at Nabanga to witness the signing, Kony failed to show. Matsanga was apologetic, claiming that Kony balked because he wanted clarification on how the special Ugandan court would work. Matsanga then revealed that he had never really met with Kony and that Kony probably knew few details of the peace agreement. Rumors spread that Kony was demanding millions of dollars and a mansion in Kampala, and possibly a command position in the army, in exchange for signing the deal. The realization settled on everyone that Kony and his team had duped the entire international community. Matsanga beat a hasty retreat. He reportedly was detained briefly at the Juba airport as he boarded a flight out of the country with a wad of cash, his pay as head negotiator for the LRA for three months.

Kony then asked for yet another meeting with the Acholi elders and cultural leaders, and as before, his request was granted. A new date was set for the signing: May 12. An entourage of negotiators and the Acholi religious and cultural leaders returned to Nabanga. Again, Kony didn't show. This time, even the Acholis gave up in disgust.

The transformation in the LRA had taken place some five months earlier, according to Sister Seraphine Dika. As we sit in the Franciscan sisters' clean and orderly living quarters in Dungu, she tells me about the night of December 15, 2007, when she was working in the town of Duru, forty-five miles north. It was the LRA's turning point, she says. Sister Seraphine had worked with the Duru mission for two years, teaching practical skills such as sewing and helping at the Duru health center. It was about 8:00 P.M., she recalls, when six LRA soldiers burst into the residence. She and others quickly turned off the lights while some fled, running around the mission warning of the attack. One young boy began to ring the church bell in alarm. But it was too late. The soldiers moved from room to room, taking anything of value and demanding money, food, and medical supplies. Sister Seraphine was particularly devastated because she had been keeping about twelve thousand dollars—money she had collected from projects and donations to help buy supplies and renovate their modest clinic. The rebels stole it, then went throughout the hospital, taking what medications they wanted and destroying the rest while twenty other soldiers waited outside. Some locals were abducted to carry the loot. "We were all afraid."

Though the rebels did not kill anyone, they left a message, she explains, details of which ended up in one of Father Kinalegu's reports. The rebels made it clear that they were Kony's followers and claimed that since their arrival they had sought to live in peace with the Congolese. But they were angry that the Congolese government had conspired with the UN forces against the LRA. The government had installed MONUC in Dungu, and the UN had arbitrarily begun to arrest and detain LRA officers, even as the LRA was working to sign peace accords with Uganda, the rebels said. Because of this, they were now conducting reprisals against the local population and warned that they would continue to do so as long as the government allowed MONUC to remain in the region.[6]

It was an ominous warning, but ignored at the time, even though the LRA clearly was signaling the future. The rebels revealed their new stripes by again applying their trademark and twisted logic to past events. Instead of admitting that the LRA had suffered deep divisions and many desertions, the fighters blamed the UN for arbitrary arrests and detentions of its officers. Using the same justifications for their attacks on innocent civilians in northern Uganda—alleged complicity with the Ugandan government—the LRA was justifying attacks on Congolese civilians by accusing them of complicity with MONUC.

Sister Seraphine has no plans to return to Duru. "We're still afraid to go back," she says. "The LRA is still there. There is no government there at all. I can only go back there if the LRA is no longer there and the border is secure and forces are present in the village." She feels sorry for the people of Duru who face daily threats from Ugandan rebels. "People no longer go to the fields and no longer work. When the LRA comes, they all run." She and the others don't understand what the LRA wants. When the Ugandans arrived, they said they had no quarrel with the locals. "But now they've changed their speech," she says, and the LRA says "they'll fight up until the end."

That end is what worries Father Kinalegu.

When UN forces arrived in Dungu several years ago, they built a camp that now includes the heavy-duty airstrip. UN officials told me that the Congolese government plans to put one thousand soldiers in Dungu in the coming months. The purpose, of course, is to pressure Kony to behave or leave. "We don't care what means are used," Kinalegu tells me when we meet again the next day. "Local people want to see Kony out of the DRC."

But Kinalegu admits that putting the Congolese army in Dungu could have disastrous consequences if it means war with the LRA. If clashes with the LRA draw additional soldiers from Uganda and South Sudan, as has been suggested, the war becomes regional. In such a case, he says, locals must be given safe passage out. Just the presence of Congolese soldiers is itself a problem, Kinalegu says. They're notorious for abusing local populations, largely because they are poorly paid, if at all, and throughout eastern provinces of DRC have been accused of rape and theft. "We're afraid because of bad experiences we have had with the army. Cohabitation of people with the army has been very difficult. The rebels didn't live well with the people either, but we expect the army to chase the rebels." Perhaps, Kinalegu says with a shrug, UN troops can help control the notorious excesses of the Congolese. Regardless, the situation is dire. "We are victims of a war of which we do not know the origin."

At this writing, Kony is asking for the peace talks to resume, and his call typically comes amid confusion. Despite having quit and disparaged Kony, David Matsanga again has been named by Kony to lead the LRA peace delegation. This prompted the resignation of many in the LRA peace team. Speaking from Nairobi in early July 2008, Matsanga claimed that Kony will sign the peace agreement, but at the same time Kony wants more supplies for his army. As one person close to the situation has told me, Kony knows he can do whatever he wants as long as he continues to claim he wants peace. He has become a master at manipulation. When he fought in northern Uganda, he toyed with the Ugandan government. And now he has the international community dancing for him. The band plays on.

Afterword

Bring in the Drones

In early August 2012, U.S. Secretary of State Hillary Clinton was photographed holding a small drone that looked more like a model airplane than a weapon in the American military arsenal. The photo was taken while Clinton was at the U.S. Special Forces base in Entebbe, the Ugandan airport on the shores of Lake Victoria, where she discussed the small drones that she hoped would help track down Joseph Kony and his Lord's Resistance Army.

The photo gave me pause, not because of the subject matter, but because I never imagined that seven years after I had begun work on *First Kill Your Family*, Kony and the LRA would continue to wreak havoc in the heart of Africa. Kony and his men had been indicted by the International Criminal Court in 2005, had been the subject of two years of internationally sponsored peace talks, had been the focus of two missions by U.S. Special Forces advisers, and the topic of an Internet video viewed by a million people around the world. Yet, since abandoning northern Uganda in early 2006, Kony and the LRA were still terrorizing one of the most remote regions on earth, the no-man's-land where the Central African Republic, South Sudan, and Democratic Republic of the Congo (DRC) meet. During this time, a brief moment of hope that Kony's end might be near came in mid-December 2008 when the Ugandan army, with extensive help from U.S. Special Forces, attacked Kony's camp in northern DRC. The attack was botched and Kony escaped, sending his men on a rampage that killed nearly one thousand civilians in the region.

Like the earlier effort, the 2011–2012 infusion of U.S. military aid and Special Forces advisers to Uganda has had little effect. President

Barack Obama sent the U.S. soldiers there after signing The Lord's Resistance Army Disarmament and Northern Uganda Recovery Act of 2009, a bill that was the result of massive lobbying by humanitarian groups such as Enough, Resolve Uganda, Invisible Children, and others.

That Kony and his army continued to roam free should come as no surprise, however. Long before the disastrous December 2008 attack on Kony's camp, I suspected that Uganda had never truly wanted Kony and the LRA captured, despite the rhetoric to the contrary.

Now, four years since *First Kill Your Family* was published, I remain convinced that Kony is still more valuable alive than dead or in jail to Ugandan president Yoweri Museveni. Between 1986 and 2006, Kony waged a war largely against his own people, the Acholi tribe of northern Uganda. This played directly into Museveni's hands since the Acholi were his sworn enemies. Because Kony had turned on his own people, Museveni made only minimal efforts to stop Kony's atrocities.

Instead, Museveni turned to more lucrative pursuits and sent his army across the border into the mineral-rich mountains of eastern DRC. From 1996 until about 2003, Uganda successfully plundered their hapless neighbor either directly or through proxy militias. (Details of this are in my book, *Consuming the Congo* [Lawrence Hill Books, 2011].)

All the while, Museveni has collected money from the international community so that Uganda could keep fighting Kony, repeatedly promising that Kony's demise was just around the corner. Museveni continues to use this ploy with great success.

Not long after news stories appeared in April 2012 about how U.S. Special Forces were helping the Ugandans track Kony in the Central African Republic, a different story emerged. The Ugandan soldiers complained about how difficult and dangerous the hunt for Kony was. They grumbled of the heat, the flies, and the fact that two of their comrades had been attacked by crocodiles, and one had been killed. The

Ugandans said that when they reached the latest village attacked by Kony's men, the LRA fighters were long gone. The chase was useless.

Then came the stories that the Ugandans were running out of money and supplies, again, which was ironic. The United States had committed to spending $35 million in 2012 to find and fight Kony, according to news reports. Since 2008, the State Department had spent an additional $50 million to support Uganda's nonlethal efforts to capture Kony, such as securing helicopters to transport troops and supplies. Since 2008, U.S. officials estimated that about $500 million had been spent to help rebuild northern Uganda.

Where had the money gone? Since Kony is a source of revenue for the Ugandan leadership, Uganda has little interest in capturing Kony, despite the atrocities he continues to commit. Yes, Kony is Ugandan, but he has not been in the country since early 2006. Ugandans have understandably questioned why they need to carry the burden when Kony is in the Central African Republic and no longer a threat to them.

Although Kony is, in fact, Uganda's responsibility, there is little hope that Kony can be captured by the Ugandans or any of the other countries in the region, even with an air armada of U.S. minidrones. After twenty-five years of futile efforts by Uganda, it is clear that Kony can only be stopped by a combined international military mission— a mission that few, if any, countries inside or outside of the region are willing to undertake. The dilemma is unlikely to change, despite the untiring efforts of human rights groups and endless congressional resolutions calling for Kony's capture.

—Peter Eichstaedt
September 2012

Acknowledgments

First and foremost I must thank Duncan Furey for encouraging me to take on this project, and the many dedicated journalists at Uganda Radio Network who helped me. These include Sam Gummah, Rachel Mugarura, and Paul Kavuma. I owe a lot to the URN reporters who helped me find the stories that needed to be told: Joe Elunya in Soroti, Joe Wacha in Lira, David Rupiny in Arua, and Goodluck Musinguzi in Kabale. I was lucky enough to find guidance and inspiration from Father John Fraser, who led me to Father Joseph Russo and then to the Aboke girls. In Gulu I was fortunate to find Columbus Onoo, who works his own kind of magic. I want to thank journalist Matthew Brown, who befriended me in the bush. I owe a great deal to my editor, Susan Betz, and my agent, Michele Rubin, who believed deeply in this book from the beginning. And finally I want to thank my wife, Dina, who has helped me in ways words fail to describe.

Notes

Prologue: Richard's Story

1. Berkeley-Tulane Initiative on Vulnerable Populations. *Abducted: The Lord's Resistance Army and Forced Conscription in Northern Uganda,* June 2007.

1 Faded Luster of the Pearl

1. Churchill, Winston. *My African Journey,* New York: W. W. Norton & Co., 1991, 118.
2. U.S. Central Intelligence Agency World Fact Book, October 2007.
3. Warrant of arrest for Joseph Kony issued on July 8, 2005, as amended on September 27, 2005—27.09.2005 ICC-02/04–01/05–53; warrant of arrest for Vincent Otti—September 7, 2005—ICC-02/04–01/05–54; warrant of arrest for Raska Lukwiya—September 7, 2005—ICC-02/04–01/05–55; warrant of arrest for Okot Odhiambo—September 7, 2005—ICC-02/04–01/05–56; warrant of arrest for Dominic Ongwen—September 7, 2005—ICC-02/04–01/05–57.
4. Behrend, Heike. *Alice Lakwena and the Holy Spirits: War in Northern Uganda, 1986-97,* Athens, OH: Ohio University Press and Oxford, England: James Currey Ltd, 1999, 2004, 17.
5. Ibid., 24, 25.
6. Ibid., 25, 26.
7. Ibid., 57–62.

8. Finnstrom, Sverker. *Living with Bad Surroundings: War and Existential Uncertainty in Acholiland, Northern Uganda,* Uppsala, Sweden: Uppsala University Press, December 2003, 282.

9. Behrend, 179–84.

3   Anatomy of an Attack

1. United Nations Security Council Resolution 1663, March 24, 2006.

2. Darfur Peace and Accountability Act of 2005 (S.1462/H.R 3127), Senate Resolution 336 of 2006, and the Northern Uganda Crisis Response Act (S. 2264) of 2004.

3. Civil Society Organizations for Peace in Northern Uganda. Counting the Cost: Twenty Years of War in Northern Uganda, Gulu and Kampala, Uganda, March 2006.

4   God, Grace, and the Aboke Girls

1. Bureau of Democracy, Human Rights and Labor, U.S. Department of State. International Religious Freedom Report, 2003.

5   Witch Doctors, Rattles, and Unholy Ghosts

1. Behrend, Heike. *Alice Lakwena and the Holy Spirits: War in Northern Uganda, 1986–97,* Athens, OH: Ohio University Press and Oxford, England: James Currey Ltd, 1999, 2004, 98.

2. Ibid., 57.

3. Ibid., 56–62.

4. Ibid., 60.

5. Testimony of George Abedo, Uganda Supreme Court, Thursday, April 20, in Kizza Besigye trial, as transcribed in the *Daily Monitor* (Kampala), online edition, April 21, 2006.

6. Ibid.

6   A Game of Blood and Spiritualism

1. Nyakairu, Frank. "From Captivity to Slavery," *Daily Monitor* (Kampala), March 31, 2006.
2. Ibid.
3. Ibid.
4. Nyakairu, Frank. "Gov't Fires Ex-LRA Bosses from Gulu Captives' Farm," *Daily Monitor* (Kampala), April 13, 2006, posted to the Web April 12, 2006.

8   Degrees of Darkness

1. Museveni, President Yoweri. "The Truth About Kony's LRA," remarks of May 4, 2006, transcribed in *Sunday New Vision,* May 7, 2006.
2. Ibid.
3. Usinfo.state.gov/ei/Archive/2006/Apr/27–769770.html.
4. Kalinaki, Daniel K. "Tinye Exposes 10,000 Ghosts," *Daily Monitor* (Kampala), February 4, 2004.
5. Egadu, Samuel O. "3,000 Ghost Soldiers on Payroll—Muheesi," *Daily Monitor* (Kampala), May 19, 2007.

9   Back to the Land

1. Author unspecified. "I collected the pieces of my husband's skull," *New Vision* (Kampala), Thursday, April 20, 2006.
2. Ibid.

10   The Call for Peace

1. Blair, David. "Man Who Harboured bin Laden Is Lodestar for Terrorists," *The Telegraph* (UK), January 30, 2006.
2. Ibid.

3. Museveni, President Yoweri. "The Truth About Kony's LRA," remarks of May 4, 2006, transcribed in *Sunday New Vision* (Kampala), May 7, 2006.

11   Armed Conflict Is a Health Risk

1. Video recording of April 2006 meetings with Joseph Kony, Vincent Otti, and others, Nabanga, South Sudan, videographer unknown.
2. *Sudan's Comprehensive Peace Agreement: The Long Road Ahead,* Africa Report No. 106, March 31, 0206, International Crisis Group, Brussels, Belgium.

12   In Search of Joseph Kony

1. Video recording of April and May 2006 meetings with Joseph Kony, Vincent Otti, and others, Nabanga, South Sudan, videographer unknown.
2. Behrend, Heike. *Alice Lakwena and the Holy Spirits: War in Northern Uganda, 1986–97,* Athens, OH: Ohio University Press and Oxford, England: James Currey Ltd, 1999, 2004, 85, 86.
3. Scroggins, Deborah. *Emma's War,* New York: Vintage Books, Random House, 2004.
4. Ibid.
5. Ibid.

13   Jungle Rendezvous

1. Finnstrom, Sverker. *Living with Bad Surroundings: War and Existential Uncertainty in Acholiland, Northern Uganda,* Uppsala, Sweden: Uppsala University Press, December 2003, 283.
2. "Ugandan Rebels Talk Tough as Delayed Peace Talks Open," Agence France Presse, July 15, 2006.

3. Nyakairu, Frank, and Gyezaho, Emmanuel. "Uganda: Kony Talks—'We Are Fighting for 10 Commandments,'" *Daily Monitor* (Kampala), August 2, 2006.

4. Ibid.

5. Ibid.

6. Ibid.

7. Ibid.

8. Ibid.

14 The View from Kilimanjaro

1. Overview, status of cases, International Criminal Tribunal for Rwanda, www.ictr.org, November 25, 2007.

2. Video recording of April and May 2006 meetings with Joseph Kony, Vincent Otti, and others, Nabanga, South Sudan, videographer unknown.

3. "Uganda Rebels Urge UN to Drop ICC Arrest Warrants," Xinhua News Agency, April 19, 2007.

4. International Criminal Tribunal for Rwanda, www.ictr.org, November 25, 2007.

Epilogue

1. "Peacekeepers Killed in DR Congo," *BBC News*, January 23, 2006, http://news.bbc.co.uk/2/hi/africa/4639610.stm.

2. Author unspecified. "How Vincent Otti Was Killed," *Sunday New Vision* (Kampala), December 9, 2007.

3. Ibid.

4. Ibid.

5. Ibid.

6. Kinalegu, Abbe Benoit. "Mission d'Evaluation de la Situation: Pillage Dans la Paroise Mater Die Duru du 15 Dec. 2007," 18 Dec. 2007, p. 2.

Index